DATE DUE

AG 5'99			
MR 28 02			

DEMCO 38-296

The fictional representation of the family has long been regarded as a Dickensian speciality. But while nineteenth-century reviewers praised Dickens as the pre-eminent novelist of the family, any close examination of his novels reveals a remarkable disjunction between his image as the quintessential celebrant of the hearth, and his interest in fractured families. Catherine Waters offers an explanation of this discrepancy through an examination of Dickens's representation of the family in relation to nineteenth-century constructions of class and gender. Drawing upon feminist and new historicist methodologies, and focussing upon the normalising function of middle-class domestic ideology, Waters concludes that Dickens's novels record a shift in notions of the family away from an earlier stress upon the importance of lineage and blood towards a new ideal of domesticity assumed to be the natural form of the family.

DICKENS AND THE POLITICS
OF THE FAMILY

DICKENS AND THE
POLITICS OF THE FAMILY

CATHERINE WATERS

University of New England
New South Wales

CAMBRIDGE
UNIVERSITY PRESS

OF THE UNIVERSITY PRESS OF CAMBRIDGE
gton Street, Cambridge CB2 1RP

NIVERSITY PRESS
The Edinburgh Building, Cambridge CB2 2RU, United Kingdom
40 West 20th Street, New York, NY 10011–4211, USA
10 Stamford Road, Oakleigh, Melbourne 3166, Australia

First published 1997

Printed in the United Kingdom at the University Press, Cambridge

Typeset in Monotype Baskerville

A catalogue record for this book is available from the British Library

Library of Congress cataloguing in publication data
Waters, Catherine
Dickens and the politics of the family / Catherine Waters.
p. cm.
Includes bibliographical references and index.
ISBN 0 521 57355 6 (hardback)
1. Dickens, Charles, 1812–1870 – Political and social views.
2. Family in literature. 3. Politics and literature – England –
History – 19th century. 4. Political fiction, English – History and
criticism. 5. Domestic fiction, English – History and criticism.
1. Title.
PR4592. F36W38 1997
823′.8--dc20 96-44933 CIP

ISBN 0 521 57355 6 hardback

For Mary and Ron

Contents

Acknowledgments

This book owes much to the assistance and encouragement of family, friends and colleagues. It began as a PhD dissertation under the supervision of Margaret Harris, for whose inspiration and guidance I remain grateful. For giving generously of their time to read and comment on parts of the manuscript, I thank Fred D'Agostino, Robert Dingley and Alison Hoddinott. I gratefully acknowledge the support of the University of New England for granting me a semester of study leave to work on this project. I also acknowledge the support of the University of Leicester for awarding me an Honorary Visiting Fellowship there in 1994, and I thank the Director of the Victorian Studies Research Centre, Joanne Shattock, for her help and advice. Finally, I owe special thanks to my parents for their unfailing encouragement and emotional support.

Note on the texts

The World's Classics Edition for
  Christmas Books, Ruth Glancy (ed.), 1988
  David Copperfield, Nina Burgis (ed.), 1983
  Dombey and Son, Alan Horsman (ed.), 1982
  Great Expectations, Margaret Cardwell (ed.), 1994
  Little Dorrit, Harvey Peter Sucksmith (ed.), 1982
  Martin Chuzzlewit, Margaret Cardwell (ed.), 1984
  The Mystery of Edwin Drood, Margaret Cardwell (ed.), 1982
  Nicholas Nickleby, Paul Schlicke (ed.), 1990
  Oliver Twist, Kathleen Tillotson (ed.), 1982
  Our Mutual Friend, Michael Cotsell (ed.), 1989
  The Pickwick Papers, James Kinsley (ed.), 1988
  A Tale of Two Cities, Andrew Sanders (ed.), 1988

The New Oxford Illustrated Edition for
  Barnaby Rudge: A Tale of the Riots of 'Eighty, 1954
  Sketches by Boz: Illustrative of Every-Day Life and Every-Day People, 1957

The Norton Critical Edition for
  Bleak House, George Ford and Sylvère Monod (eds.), 1977

The Everyman's Library Edition for
  Christmas Stories, 1910

CHAPTER I

Introduction: the making and breaking of the family

Writing from Paris in 1856, where he was attempting to assuage his chronic restlessness with travel, Dickens confided his marital unhappiness in a letter to John Forster. The comment is thoroughly characteristic in its perverse animation of the inanimate: 'I find that the skeleton in my domestic closet is becoming a pretty big one.'[1] At the time when Dickens made this allusion to the dreadful secret lurking within his home, he could hardly have anticipated the public scandal that would attend his separation from Catherine two years later. As his friend Percy Fitzgerald wrote afterwards, 'Who . . . could have conceived or prophesied that in the year of grace 1858 the whole fabric should have begun to totter . . . Who could have fancied that . . . so disturbing a revelation of his domestic life should have been abruptly placed before the astonished public?'[2]

The growth of speculation and innuendo concerning the break-up of his marriage prompted Dickens to attempt a public repudiation of these increasingly prurient narratives. On 12 June 1858, habitual readers of *Household Words* were amazed to find a proclamation on the front page announcing the editor's separation from his wife, and attempting to controvert rumours about the differences which had occasioned it. Dickens addressed himself to the public under the heading 'PERSONAL':

Some domestic trouble of mine, of long-standing, on which I will make no further remark than that it claims to be respected, as being of a sacredly private nature, has lately been brought to an arrangement, which involves no anger or ill-will of any kind, and the whole origin, progress, and surrounding circumstances of which have been, throughout, within the knowledge of my children. It is amicably composed, and its details have now but to be forgotten by those concerned in it . . .

By some means, arising out of wickedness, or out of folly, or out of inconceivable wild chance, or out of all three, this trouble has been made the occasion of misrepresentations, most grossly false, most monstrous, and most cruel – involving, not only me, but innocent persons dear to my heart, and innocent persons of whom I have no knowledge, if indeed, they have any existence – and so widely spread, that I doubt if one reader in a thousand will peruse these lines, by whom some touch of the breath of these slanders will not have passed, like an unwholesome air.[3]

The simile of pollution recalls the imagery of disease spread by noxious winds, so prevalent in *Bleak House*, and indicates the strength and vehemence of Dickens's indignation. But according to Fitzgerald, the belief that all his readers had heard of some slander concerning his domestic trouble was a 'delusion' on Dickens's part: 'People were all but bewildered and almost stunned, so unexpected was the revelation. Everyone was for the most part in supreme ignorance of what the document could possibly refer to.'[4] As a result, Dickens's declared wish in writing this document to 'circulate the Truth' was overshadowed by the titillating revelation made to otherwise uninformed people that the man held to be (in the words of one contemporary reviewer) 'so peculiarly a writer of home life, a delineator of household gods',[5] was embroiled in a domestic scandal.

This episode has traditionally been a focus for discussion in biographical studies of Dickens, where it is commonly interpreted as a climax in the sequence of events leading up to the end of his marriage. Edgar Johnson describes Dickens's publication of his 'PERSONAL' statement as 'the maddest step he had yet made in his unhappy and hysterical state';[6] Norman and Jeanne Mackenzie conclude that 'Dickens had lost control of himself, and in his fury and anxiety he continued to draw unwelcome attention to his domestic scandal';[7] and Fred Kaplan observes that Dickens 'felt frantic with being attacked by forces that he could not control, as if he were under siege or being held hostage to ignorance and maliciousness'.[8]

These twentieth-century efforts to explain Dickens's behaviour follow the accounts of his contemporaries. According to Forster, Dickens was moved to take this measure because it had become impossible for him to continue his public readings with his name 'so aspersed'.[9] Edmund Yates attributed his action to 'a certain bias in the direction of theatrical ostentation' and to the prominence he gave 'in his thoughts to the link which bound him to the public'.[10] What all of these commentaries upon this most notorious episode share is a concern to explain the traits of character supposedly driving Dickens's extraordinary behaviour, a concern to establish the 'truth' of the circumstances involved, and, at least in the accounts produced by modern biographers, to note the ironic gap apparently opened up between Dickens the novelist and Dickens the husband and father. Such accounts assume a distinction between narratives of 'truth' and fiction, and between private and public identities.

However, read in the light of recent theories concerning the political implications of textual representation, the controversy surrounding Dickens's marriage break-up yields more than just information about the psychology of the novelist, or evidence of an ironic discrepancy between his fiction and his lived experience. As a scandalous revelation of a family skeleton published in the press of the day, the episode participated in the growing phenomenon of 'sensationalism' that was already being denounced by conservative critics for indulging the lower appetites of human nature. An exploration of the ideological investments disclosed in this episode will demonstrate the approach that informs my analysis of the politics of the family in Dickens's fiction; for it is the disciplinary function of the family that may help us to understand the strangeness of Dickens's response to the rumours about his marriage break-up.

The basic story of Dickens's separation from his wife is well known. After a period of growing dissatisfaction and 'restlessness', Dickens's differences with Catherine came to a head in May 1858. The final break is alleged to have been caused by the mis-delivery to Catherine of a gift intended for Ellen Ternan. Dickens left the house during the disturbance which followed, and after negotiations lasting some two or three weeks his wife was induced to agree to a legal separation. After the formalities were completed Dickens wrote his address for *Household Words*, arranging for its publication in other newspapers and journals as well.

Both Forster and Lemon advised Dickens against the publication of his 'PERSONAL' statement. As Edmund Yates observed, 'the mistake which it will be generally held Dickens made was that which is usually known as "washing dirty linen in public"'.[11] This comment neatly identifies the problem with which he was confronted in choosing to mount a press campaign in his own defence: Dickens's statement relied upon a simultaneous construction and deconstruction of a distinction between public and private life. The contradiction is implicit in the 'PERSONAL' heading given to his public announcement, and it emerges in the form of the statement itself, which draws its rhetorical power from an emphasis upon respect for the very boundary it transgresses.

The controversy surrounding Dickens's marriage break-up illustrates the fundamental division of the world into 'public' and 'private' spheres that came to constitute the dominant definition of 'reality' in Victorian middle-class culture. The model of a binary opposition between the sexes was used to ground the division between these supposedly 'separate spheres', shaping and legitimising this social arrangement according to sexual differences that were apparently fixed and immutable. Crucial to the maintenance of these divisions was the worship of the family – that nucleus of English society. However, the representation of the family ironically threatened the division between these two domains, betraying fundamental contradictions and instabilities within the ideologies of sexual difference and separate spheres. These discontinuities, and the political effects they enable, become evident in an examination of the controversy surrounding the end of Dickens's marriage and of the representation of the family in his fiction.

After some preliminary remarks concerning his 'relations with the Public', Dickens opens his 'PERSONAL' statement with a declaration that lays emphasis upon the 'sacredly private nature' of his 'domestic trouble'. The privacy of this 'trouble' is rhetorically inscribed in the euphemism and circumlocution employed to designate it. Dickens's concluding denunciation of the allegedly 'false' reports insinuates its object with conspicuous reticence in a reference to 'all the lately whispered rumours touching the trouble at which I have glanced'.[12] The reliance upon reserve, upon refraining from disclosure, creates the illusion of an inviolable private sphere that the very existence of this public statement would seem to contradict.

This extraordinary public exposure of a family affair is prefaced by an admission of the singularity of the step taken:

For the first time in my life, and I believe for the last, I now deviate from the principle I have so long observed, by presenting myself in my own Journal in my own private character, and entreating all my brethren (as they deem that they have reason to think well of me, and to know that I am a man who has ever been unaffectedly true to our common calling), to lend their aid to the dissemination of my present words.[13]

Dickens's assertion of a distinction between his personal and public identities is reiterated in the penultimate paragraph of his statement:

Those who know me and my nature, need no assurance under my hand that such calumnies are irreconcilable with me, as they are, in their frantic incoherence, with one another. But, there is a great multitude who know me through my writings, and who do not know me otherwise; and I cannot bear that one of them should be left in doubt, or hazard of doubt, through my poorly shrinking from taking the unusual means to which I now resort, of circulating the Truth.[14]

The contrast between direct and indirect forms of acquaintance used to justify his resort to these 'unusual means' is implicitly embedded in another opposition between 'Truth' and fiction: the 'I' whose voice is heard in this 'PERSONAL' statement must be distinguished from the narrator of his novels in order to establish the authenticity of his declaration. However, it is the very process of articulation, of putting oneself into words, that compromises the self it would seek to justify. Dickens's claim of self-presence implicitly rests upon the newspaper convention of the 'Personal Column'; but these notices were themselves highly codified appeals, as Sherlock Holmes was to demonstrate in his use of them later on in the century. The opposition between 'Truth' and fiction is destabilised by the rhetoric displayed in Dickens's public performance. The hyperbolic style is created by an extraordinary preponderance of superlatives, emotive expressions and exclamatory protestations. As the Mackenzies observe, 'This [is] strong stuff, more fitting for a sensational novel than a quasi-legal document';[15] and this comment about the mixing of generic categories highlights the way in which the oppositions upon which Dickens relies here – between fiction and truth, public and private identity – are made problematic by the very form of their expression.

While Dickens had hoped to keep his marriage break-up a private affair, with Forster acting on his behalf and Lemon acting for Catherine, talk about his relationship with Ellen Ternan began to spread; and by mid-May 1858, comment was abroad that the separation had occurred because he had fallen in love with another woman. This allegation was soon supplanted by the more scandalous accusation that the marriage was breaking up because he was having an incestuous affair with his sister-in-law, Georgina Hogarth, who had elected to stay with Dickens and his children following the departure of Catherine. This juicy gossip about Dickens's supposed intrigue with his sister-in-law was relayed to Thackeray on his way into the Garrick Club. 'No . . . no such thing', said he, in an effort to counteract the 'other much worse story'; '– it's with an actress'.[16] As Kaplan notes, 'Dickens must have been hard put to determine whether he should focus on denying incest with Georgina, adultery with Ellen, or both.'[17]

The variation in the degree of damage attributed to these two stories (by Thackeray and others) derives from assumptions associated with the doctrine of separate spheres. The first rumour, the allegation of Dickens's affair with an actress, though sufficiently injurious in itself, refers to a transgression that is explicable in terms of the sexual double standard. According to the dominant middle-class code of sexual mores, unregulated sexual activity was to be condoned in men as a sign of masculinity, but deplored in women as a sign of deviant behaviour, a loss of femininity.[18] As W. R. Greg argued in his plan to solve the problem of prostitution by exporting 'redundant women' to the colonies, the regulation of sexuality in men and women must be organised according to the 'natural' difference between active male sexuality and passive female sexuality.[19] Indeed, in the very year preceding the end of Dickens's marriage, Parliament had enshrined the sexual double standard in the new Divorce Act, when it agreed to allow wives to divorce their husbands for adultery only when it was aggravated by cruelty, bigamy, wilful desertion for four years or incest. Parliament was much more ready to tolerate male than female philandering, for as Cranworth, the Lord Chancellor, had argued in support of his divorce bill in 1854, 'it would be too harsh to bring the law to bear against a husband who was "a little profligate"'.[20] This argument is another formulation of that binary organisation of sex which grounded the doctrine of separate spheres; thus, according to this view, Dickens's adultery must be accepted as inevitable and natural.

According to Peter Ackroyd, at some point in May 1858 Mrs Hogarth actually threatened Dickens with action in the new Divorce Court.[21] If this is so, it would help to explain his intense hostility towards his mother-in-law and strengthen the grounds for his charge that Mrs Hogarth was responsible for repeating what he referred to, in a letter to his lawyer, as 'these smashing slanders' concerning his relationship with Georgina.[22] For the implication of a threatened divorce suit was that Dickens had committed incest with Georgina, thereby providing Catherine with the grounds for action under the new law. Forster wrote an urgent letter to Dickens's solicitor, Frederick Ouvry, seeking clarification of the new Act, and Georgina was examined by a doctor. The Hogarths apparently dropped the threat of court action, but the speculation did not cease. When Dickens published his disclaimer on 12 June, the *Court Circular* reported:

The story in circulation is that his wife has left his roof – according to the mildest form of narrative, 'on account of incompatibility of temper' – according to the worst form, 'on account of that talented gentleman's preference of his wife's sister to herself, a preference which has assumed a very definite and tangible shape'...[23]

and later, in October, when he was in the middle of his first reading tour, Dickens received a letter from a well-wisher in Glasgow who reported having heard that Dickens 'was the outcry of London' and that his 'sister in law had three children by him'.[24]

This second rumour concerning Dickens's alleged incestuous relationship with Georgina reflects the controversy which surrounded the question of marriage with a deceased wife's sister in the nineteenth century. A bill on this issue was introduced into Parliament in 1842, proposing the exemption of a wife's sister from the list of fixed degrees of consanguinity and affinity within which marriage was prohibited. It was repeatedly debated and defeated as a perennial legislative problem, and, in addition to issues surrounding the preservation of property, contention over the bill throughout the Victorian period was closely related to a growing concern over the defence of 'family purity'.[25] Even as late as 1907, the year in which it was finally passed, Lord Shaftesbury was able to argue: 'It is the sanctity of home life, and the peace and purity of the English home, which are threatened by the Bill.'[26] Dickens's supposed liaison with his sister-in-law thus challenged the ideology of the family in a much more radical way than an alleged affair with any other woman could do.

Infuriated by these rumours, Dickens refused to proceed with the settlement arrangements for Catherine until Mrs Hogarth and her youngest daughter, Helen, agreed to disavow the allegations about Ellen and Georgina which he believed they had spread. On 25 May 1858 he composed a long 'letter' outlining his position which he gave to the manager of his public readings, Arthur Smith, instructing him to show it 'to any one who wishes to do me right, or to any one who may have been misled into doing me wrong'.[27] When the Hogarths reluctantly agreed to sign a statement drawn up by Ouvry declaring their disbelief in the rumours, this disclaimer was attached to the letter given to Smith and privately circulated. The deed of separation was finally signed. Two months elapsed, and then just when the publicity surrounding Dickens's 'PERSONAL' statement was beginning to die out, this earlier letter, written in May 'as a private and personal communication',[28] found its way into the New York *Tribune* on 16 August, from which it was soon copied into the English newspapers. Beginning with an account of the incompatibility and lack of understanding held to plague his relationship with Catherine, Dickens went on in this document to declare his gratitude to Georgina for assuming the

responsibilities of a mother towards his children: 'Mrs Dickens and I have
lived unhappily together for many years', he wrote, and

Nothing has, on many occasions, stood between us and a separation but Mrs
Dickens's sister, Georgina Hogarth. From the age of fifteen, she has devoted herself to our house and our children. She has been their playmate, nurse, instruc-
tress, friend, protectress, adviser and companion. In the manly consideration
toward Mrs Dickens which I owe to my wife, I will merely remark of her that the
peculiarity of her character has thrown all the children on some one else.[29]

He goes on to defend an unidentified 'young lady' whose name, he claims,
has been besmirched by 'Two wicked persons who should have spoken
very differently of me' (undoubtedly Mrs Hogarth and her daughter
Helen). 'Upon my soul and honour', he says, 'there is not upon this earth a
more virtuous and spotless creature than that young lady. I know her to be
innocent and pure, and as good as my own dear daughters.'

It was in a letter to Angela Burdett Coutts of 9 May 1858 that Dickens
first began his attack on Catherine for her alleged failure as a mother:

We must put a wider space between us now, than can be found in one house. If
the children loved her, or ever had loved her, this severance would have been a
far easier thing than it is. But she has never attached one of them to herself, never
played with them in their infancy, never attracted their confidence as they have
grown older, never presented herself before them in the aspect of a mother. I
have seen them fall off from her in a natural – not unnatural – progress
of estrangement, and at this moment I believe that Mary and Katey (whose dis-
positions are of the gentlest and most affectionate conceivable) harden into stone
figures of girls when they can be got to go near her, and have their hearts shut up
in her presence as if they were closed by some horrid spring.[30]

Michael Slater asks why Dickens should suddenly begin calling Catherine
a bad mother so insistently in May 1858, and concludes: 'It was not
gratuitous cruelty, I believe, but something that Dickens *had* to get himself
to believe so that he could the more freely pity himself in the image of his
own children, a psychological trick that he had shown himself perfectly
understanding of when he had created Dombey.'[31] This psychological
explanation is persuasive; but it is also important to consider the ideological implications of Dickens's change of tack. To Forster, Dickens had complained for some time about Catherine's temperament, attributing his
own 'wayward and unsettled feeling' to the 'tenure on which one holds an
imaginative life'.[32] But the public credibility of this excuse can be gauged

from Elizabeth Barrett Browning's sceptical comment in a letter to a friend, 'Incompatibility of temper after twenty-three years of married life! – What a plea!'[33] By charging Catherine with incompetence in rearing her children and running the household, Dickens deployed the doctrine of separate spheres to justify his own infraction. If Catherine had failed as a mother and as a wife, then Dickens could hardly be held responsible for breaking up the family, since it was upon her superintendence of the domestic sphere that the sanctity of the home depended. The ideological value of this appeal to the middle-class ideal of womanhood is strengthened by his attribution of all those womanly virtues, supposedly missing in Catherine, to Georgina: she is held to embody the self-sacrificial devotion, the moral influence and dutifulness expected of the Victorian Angel in the House.

Significantly, Georgina is only referred to as 'Mrs Dickens's sister' or as the 'aunt' of the children throughout this document. Dickens never names the relation in which she stands to himself. This rhetorical manipulation of family relationships to deflect criticism of his own position is also apparent in his veiled comment upon the accusations levelled against Ellen. In proclaiming that she is 'as good as my own dear daughters' Dickens not only asserts his belief in her virtue; more importantly, he also suggests that the relationship he enjoys with this 'young lady', for whom he has such a 'great attachment and regard', is that which would be shared by a father and daughter. (The irony of this strategy is apparent, of course, to readers aware of the extent to which father–daughter relationships are so frequently charged with erotic feeling in his fiction.) As if to offer a final proof of his innocence, in the last paragraph Dickens positions himself amongst his children, claiming his own share of the candour and artlessness they are all held to evince: 'All is open and plain among us, as though we were brothers and sisters.'

Dickens was reportedly 'shocked and distressed' by the appearance of this document in the newspapers. He asked Ouvry to inform Catherine that though 'painfully necessary at the time when it was forced from me, as a private repudiation of monstrous scandals ... it was never meant to appear in print'.[34] He always referred to the document thereafter as the 'violated letter' – a name which reaffirms the distinction between 'public' and 'private' that was made so problematic in his earlier 'PERSONAL' statement. But, as a number of commentators have remarked, it is not really clear who had violated it.[35] The vagueness of the instructions given to Smith suggests the possibility that Dickens may have intended the letter to be made public without his being seen to sanction its appearance:

a version of having one's cake and eating it, that makes his peculiar investment in the distinction between public and private life even more equivocal. In the episode of the 'Violated Letter', Dickens attempts to evade the
ideological instability that beset his 'PERSONAL' statement. His entry
into public discourse in *Household Words* had already collapsed the very
division of spheres that he tried to support in defending the privacy of his
'domestic trouble'. However, by functioning as the mark of a shameful
transgression, Dickens's 'Violated Letter' simultaneously seeks to re-
constitute the domain of privacy through its admission of a breach.

The appearance of Dickens's 'Violated Letter' provoked severe comment in the English press. *John Bull* observed, 'Qui s'excuse, s'accuse', and
added that Dickens had 'committed a grave mistake in telling his readers
how little, after all, he thinks of the marriage tie'.[36] The *Liverpool Mercury*
declared: 'we consider this practice outrageously impertinent as regards
the public, and so wantonly cruel as regards the private persons whose
names are thus forced into a gratuitous and painful notoriety, that we feel
called upon to mark it with indignant reprobation'.[37] These comments
echoed the criticisms made earlier in the year about the publication of
Dickens's 'PERSONAL' statement. *Reynolds's Newspaper* had reprinted
Dickens's address in full, accompanying it with some editorial comments:

The names of a female relative and of a professional young lady, have both been,
of late, so freely and intimately associated with that of Mr Dickens, as to excite
suspicion and surprise in the minds of those who had hitherto looked upon the
popular novelist as a very Joseph in all that regards morality, chastity, and
decorum ... No journalist had heretofore any right to interfere with Mr Dickens
in his domestic concerns; but, as he now thrusts them before the public, the case is
altered ... Let Mr Dickens remember that the odious – and we might almost add
unnatural – profligacy of which he has been accused, would brand him with life-
long infamy.[38]

However, it is not simply the revelation of domestic disorder that this commentator objects to. It is the manner in which this disclosure has been
made to the public:

Mr Dickens has been ill-advised. He should either have left the 'calumnies' to die
a natural death, or have explained them away in a style less ambiguous and stilted
than that he has adopted in the ... letter.[39]

He has told too much, or else too little; and, what with (wordy) incontinence on
the one hand, and ill-considered reticence on the other, he is in danger of having
divers most ugly interpretations put upon his explanation.[40]

Together with the other protests levelled against Dickens's publication of his private affairs, Reynolds's objections to his statement echo the criticisms of sensational journalism that were being expressed in the latter half of this decade. In June 1856, for example, the *Saturday Review* published a rebuke of the English press for its 'long accounts of crime and criminals, [written] professedly with the object of denouncing the hypocrisy of society . . . but really for the sake of pandering to that prurient curiosity about wickedness which is one of the lowest appetites of human nature'.[41] A similar tendency to awaken the 'prurient feelings' of readers is detected by Reynolds in his comments upon Dickens's 'PERSONAL' statement. But the sensationalism surrounding his marriage break-up is not confined to the use of tantalising narrative techniques and scandalous subject-matter. The episode reveals Dickens's impossible attempt to sustain a highly tenuous distinction between his public and private life – an instability that Victorian sensationalism exploited.

Subsequent commentators have focussed upon the apparent divergence between fiction and reality exposed by the whole episode of Dickens's marital break-up. Forster explained Dickens's behaviour throughout according to the requirements of his imaginative genius:

Not his genius only, but his whole nature, was too exclusively made up of sympathy for, and with, the real in its most intense form, to be sufficiently provided against failure in the realities around him. There was for him no 'city of the mind' against outward ills, for inner consolation and shelter. It was in and from the actual he still stretched forward to find the freedom and satisfactions of an ideal, and by his very attempts to escape the world he was driven back into the thick of it.[42]

Writing in 1970, Margaret Lane perceives a disparity between Dickens's passionate desire for the domestic ideal in his fiction and the painful reality of his experience:

Delight in the pleasures of home, in food and drink and children's games, even in such practical details as the choice of wall-paper or the pattern of a shower-curtain, is expressed with an intensity of feeling far beyond the normal. And yet, in spite of all, the marriage, the home, the children, the festivities, all after twenty years are flung violently away, as though the discrepancy between what he had and what he *meant* to have, the lack of that 'one happiness I have missed in life, and one friend and companion I never made,' had become finally unbearable.[43]

However, the controversy surrounding the end of Dickens's marriage reveals more than just an ironic contrast between the sanctification of the hearth in his fiction and journalism, and the disharmony of his own family life. Dickens's ambiguous publication of his private affairs, the rumours spread about his behaviour, and the arguments he used to justify the separation, all show evidence of the ways in which the ideologies of sexual difference and separate spheres were simultaneously constructed and contested in the controversy surrounding the break-up of his marriage. Rather than juxtaposing Dickens's fiction with his lived experience to discern an ironic contrast between the two, we can see here a continuity in the ideological functions served by the representations of the family involved in each case. The identification of such a continuity entails examination of the family's function as a *construct* in Dickens's writing and a consideration of the way in which the production of this construct is inescapably political.

'FAMILIAR IN THEIR MOUTHS AS *HOUSEHOLD WORDS*'

Analysis of the family and of its relationship to wider social forms has occupied an important place in feminist and Marxist scholarship, and much study has been devoted to the history of its development.[44] Most historical accounts have been influenced by a sociological tradition extending back to the developmental model of the family produced by the nineteenth-century French demographer, Frederic Le Play.[45] For example, Talcott Parsons and his followers have pursued a functionalist account, arguing that the nuclear family has developed in response to the structure and values of modern industrial society, its role being to socialise children appropriately, and to provide the emotional environment that would protect and sustain the (male) worker from the damage inflicted by the alienating world of work. Marxist accounts of the family have also tended to explain its development as an effect of external factors in their argument for the emergence of its nuclear form as a result of the relations of production that obtain under capitalism (Engels, for example, analysing the history of changing family forms in terms of the development of individual private property). Whatever the explanation for its development, the middle-class family in the nineteenth century was primarily nuclear in structure.[46] However, my study is not concerned with family structure so much as familial ideology, which is equally subject to historical change. It is the ideology of family life, as distinct from families themselves, that I am concerned to analyse in Dickens's fiction.

Definition of the 'family' remains problematic, as our present concept involves the conflation of two elements that were quite separate in earlier periods: kinship and co-residence. Jean-Louis Flandrin provides a history of changing definitions of the word derived from older English and French dictionaries. According to Flandrin, 'In former times, the word "family" more often referred to a set of kinsfolk who did not live together, while it also designated an assemblage of co-residents who were not necessarily linked by ties of blood or marriage.'[47] Not until the nineteenth century, argues Flandrin, were the elements of co-residence and kinship united in the concept of the family. Raymond Williams made a similar study of the social history of the word 'family' from its first appearance in English in the late fourteenth and early fifteenth centuries (originally from Latin *familia* 'household' and *famulus* 'servant').[48] From its earliest use to describe a household, 'family' was extended in the fifteenth century to refer to a 'house', in the sense of a particular lineage or kin-group descending from a common ancestor. In the Authorised Version of the Bible (1611) 'family' is used to describe a large kin-group, often equivalent to a 'tribe'. Williams notes a long line of influence from aristocratic use of the term 'family' in the sense of lineage, observing that 'Class distinction was expressed as late as the nineteenth century (and residually beyond it) in phrases like "a person of no family", where the large kin-group is evidently in question but in the specialized sense of traceable lineage.'[49] However, between the seventeenth and the nineteenth centuries there was a specialisation of the term to describe a small kin-group sharing the same household, and the eventual dominance of this definition can be related to the rise of what is now called the 'bourgeois family' and to the distinction made between 'work' and 'family'. Williams quotes an early nineteenth-century definition by James Mill – 'the group which consists of a Father, Mother and Children is called a Family' – but observes: 'the fact that the conscious definition is necessary is in itself significant'.[50] Clearly, the overlap of the varying senses of lineage, household, large kin-group and small kin-group in the definition of 'family' does not disappear with the advent of the nineteenth century; and this ambiguity is evident in Dickens's fiction, where the shifts in the meanings given to the notion of the family are implicated in the construction of class and gender differences.

Further evidence of the fluidity which characterises the conception of the family in the Victorian period may be found in the 1851 Census Report. The family was taken to be the basic 'social unit' in the census, consisting of 'a head and of dependent members, living together in the same dwelling'.[51] However, actual living arrangements varied widely, and

the difficulty of accommodating these within the definitions proposed by
the Registrar-General's office points to a revealing gap between ideology
and social practice. The inadequacy of the categories employed from the
beginning of the census in 1801 emerged in the confusion experienced by
enumerators, who were required by the Registrar-General's definitions to
count those boarding in another man's house as part of his family, but to
count lodgers as single families. As a result of the confusion, in the Act for
taking the census of 1851 a distinction was drawn between 'occupiers' and
'families', thus narrowing the definition of the latter to match more
accurately the reported 'type of the family': namely, 'the community in a
house, consisting of the husband, wife, children and servants; but the most
common of all particular cases is that of a husband, wife, and children'.[52]
The nineteenth-century specialisation of the term 'family' to describe the
small kin-group occupying a single house, identified as the 'type' in the
1851 Census Report, is evidence of the hegemonic definition of the family
established by the middle classes.[53] The formation of a shared notion of
family life – as 'naturally' based on close kinship, with a male breadwinner
necessarily venturing forth into the alienating realm of commerce and
industry in order to support the haven of privacy superintended by his self-
sacrificing wife – helped to create a coherent and distinct class identity and
to mark clear ideological boundaries that distinguished the middle classes
from those social and economic groups above and below them.

   While the Report of the 1851 Census recognises the possible inclusion of
'servants, relatives, visitors, and persons constantly or accidentally in the
house' within the family headed by the 'occupier' of the house, it also
expresses the demand for privacy that characterised the middle-class
ideology of the family. By the early nineteenth century it was no longer
socially or economically desirable for middle-class families to live on
premises which combined workplace with living space. They were increasingly living, or desiring to live, in homes which were separated from work,
away from the pressures of business and the presence of apprentices and
employees. The house became both the setting and the symbol for the
middle-class family. According to the Census Report, 'The possession of
an entire house is, it is true, strongly desired by every Englishman; for it
throws a sharp, well-defined circle round his family and hearth – the
shrine of his sorrows, joys, and meditations. This feeling, as it is natural, is
universal.'[54] The 'naturalness' and 'universality' of this feeling are somewhat belied by the Registrar-General's admission that the towns and cities
of the two northernmost English counties and of Scotland are built in
the continental style, 'and the families of the middle classes, as well as of

the poor, live in large flats, which constitute separate tenements within the same party walls'.[55] What is important to note for the purposes of examining familial ideology in the nineteenth century, however, is the function of a normative conception of the middle-class family and home in shaping the expectations of the census-takers.

The fictional representation of the family has long been regarded as a Dickensian speciality. As a reviewer of *David Copperfield* in *Fraser's Magazine* remarked, 'There is not a fireside in the kingdom where the cunning fellow has not contrived to secure a corner for himself as one of the dearest, and, by this time, one of the oldest friends of the family.'[56] He attributes Dickens's widespread popularity 'above all' to the novelist's 'deep reverence for the household sanctities, his enthusiastic worship of the household gods'. Margaret Oliphant praised Dickens, in an 1855 review for *Blackwood's*, as the pre-eminent novelist of the middle-class family:

The middle class in itself is a realm of infinite gradations ... But nowhere does the household hearth burn brighter – nowhere is the family love so warm – the natural bonds so strong; and this is the ground which Mr Dickens occupies *par excellence* – the field of his triumphs, from which he may defy all his rivals without fear.[57]

Similarly, an obituary article in the *Saturday Review* noted Dickens's 'unvarying respect for the sanctity of home and the goodness of women',[58] while another commentator remarked that 'his sympathy with the affections of the hearth and the home knows no bounds'.[59] However, as a number of readers have been quick to discern, Dickens's reputation as the purveyor of cosy domestic bliss would seem to be at odds with the relatively small number of happy and harmonious families depicted in his fiction. Any close examination of his novels reveals a remarkable disjunction between his image as the quintessential celebrant of the hearth, and his fictional interest in fractured families. While some critics have noticed this curious discrepancy – Margaret Lane, for example, noted in 1970 that 'an attentive reading of the novels, or indeed of almost anything that Dickens wrote, letters included, discovers a wry observation of domestic life in general and of connubial happiness in particular, a long way removed from the coy relish of the celebrated domestic set-pieces'[60] – few have attempted to explain it. My study of the politics of the family in Dickens's fiction offers an explanation of this puzzling gap between Dickens's reputation and the evidence of his novels by examining the disciplinary functions served by his representation of the family in the context of nineteenth-century culture.

While Dickens's preoccupation with the family has long been recognised in critical commentary on his work, it is surprising that the complexity and ambivalence evident in his representations of the family have not, until recently, been the subject of a book-length study. Anny Sadrin's penetrating analysis of the oedipal conflict between fathers and sons shown in Dickens's plots of inheritance addresses a crucial aspect of the family in its investigation of the tensions inherent in parent–child relationships.[61] But my study focusses instead upon the function of the family as an imaginary construct in Dickens's fiction – a construct that was produced through historically specific representations of class and gender. While critical discussion of Dickens's interest in the family has hitherto drawn upon psychoanalytic models to illuminate recurrent features of his work – his preoccupation with the relations between fathers and daughters and his tendency to orphan his heroes, for example – I concentrate on the ideology of the family. The increased emotional importance assumed by the institution of the family in the nineteenth century is a commonplace in cultural studies of the period, and I examine Dickens's participation in this process by considering the various ways in which his novels help to formulate definitions of normality and deviance with respect to the family. I draw upon feminist and new historicist methodologies to explore the function of domestic ideology in the formation of middle-class cultural authority.[62]

Dickens's fictional interest in fractured families needs to be studied in the context of the discourses which helped to formulate normative definitions of the family in the nineteenth century. One of the most crucial sources for the dissemination of domestic ideology in the period was the so-called 'family magazine'. As Joanne Shattock and Michael Wolff have pointed out, 'the press, in all its manifestations, became during the Victorian period the context within which people lived and worked and thought, and from which they derived their ... sense of the outside world',[63] and the overwhelmingly popular family magazines provided a wide range of readers from the middle and working classes with a common fund of images, information, attitudes and values associated with the celebration of home and family life. They provided the cultural milieu from which the serial novel emerged, and, in turn, the original part-issues of Dickens's novels often contained advertisements for various journals devoted to the family.

The *Waterloo Directory of Victorian Periodicals* lists approximately forty entries using the term 'family' in their title. The 'family magazines' included cheap periodicals, like the *Family Herald* (1842–1939) and the *London Journal* (1845–1912), penny weeklies which dominated the mass market in the 1840s and 1850s,[64] as well as more 'genteel' publications with a middle-class audience and smaller circulation, such as Dickens's *Household Words* (1850–9), which was a twopenny weekly. While the *Family Herald* and *London Journal* enjoyed a combined sale of at least 750,000 per week by the mid-1850s, *Household Words* began at 100,000, but settled back to an average sale of 40,000 during its best years.[65] Other family-oriented magazines included *Eliza Cook's Journal* (1849–54), a weekly costing one and a half pence which sold 50–60,000 in its first year, the *Family Friend* (1849–1921), a fortnightly which boasted 50,000 subscribers, and the *Family Economist* (1848–60), a penny monthly. In keeping with the institution of anonymous journalism, most of the writing published in these periodicals was unsigned – a practice that lent support to the protection of that privacy so crucial to the ideology of domesticity. As one commentator in *Blackwood's* remarked in 1859,

if the anonymous is abolished, and we are permitted to speak each in his own name and each in his own character, then gradually it must come to this – not only that privacy will be invaded, not only that retirement will be a jest, solitude an impossibility, and home the shadow of a dream, but public life will be outraged.[66]

The family magazines owed their popularity to their effort to cater for every income and taste. The motto of the *Family Herald* was 'Interesting to all – offensive to none', and the editor boasted in a reply to one of his correspondents, 'The *Family Herald* is so very cheap (and yet so very good), that it is already domesticated in many thousand families, and is experiencing a welcome in every nook in the empire.'[67] The *Magazine of Domestic Economy* (1836–44) outlined its aim to use 'language as is intelligible to all, and can be offensive to none', as well as its endeavour 'to render the work accessible to even the humblest families, by the lowness of its price'.[68] The form of the miscellany enabled the family magazines to cater for a range of readers differentiated by class, gender, generation and locality. Typically, they incorporate a mix of fictional tales, poetry, informational articles, advice about gardening, household matters, recipes, puzzles or riddles, and so on. But despite the heterogeneity of the subjects dealt with, and the varied styles of their treatment, these journals are framed by a common ideology of family consumption. *Johnstone's Penny Fireside Journal* (1843–5), for example, advertises its aim 'to render the whole a pleasing and profitable companion for the domestic fireside',[69] and the *Family Friend* makes a similarly self-reflexive gesture in boasting that its patrons 'will find us in FACT, as in NAME, *The Family Friend*'.[70] An advertisement for the *Family Friend*, appearing in the first number of *Little Dorrit*, quotes the praise received from a reviewer in the *Bradford Observer*: 'It is the very thing we want after the curtains are drawn and the candles are lit, for a long pleasant evening.'[71] Eliza Cook begins the first issue of her journal with 'A Word to My Readers' in which she casts herself as hostess at a 'plain feast' held in the hope, she says, that 'I shall have a host of friends at my board, whose kind words and cheerful encouragement will keep me in a proud and honourable position at the head of the table'.[72] The presentation of didactic or factual material in these journals is frequently 'softened' or domesticated by the mediation of a familial figure: for example, 'Aunt Peggy's Letters to her Niece' are used to discuss the proper duties of husbands and wives in the *Family Herald*,[73] while the *Family Friend* employs 'Grandfather Whitehead' to explore scientific subjects and 'Aunt Mary' to discuss history. The illustrations appearing on the title-page to the bound volumes of some of these journals depict the scene of their own reading, or the domestic ideal celebrated in their pages. The title-page to volume 1 of the *Family Friend*, for example, is surmounted by a large crown, beneath which a domestic group is shown gathered around a grandfatherly figure, complete with skull-cap and rug over his knees, who reads to his family. Vignettes of women doing needlework or painting appear at either side of the title, while at the bottom of the page a mother in medieval dress reads to her daughter. The title-page to the first volume of the *Family Economist* includes a poem celebrating the 'cottage homes of England', together with an illustration showing the interior of such a cottage, where mother and daughter sew by the hearth, a younger son plays with his toys, and baby sleeps in its cradle. The father can be seen working in the garden through the open window. While explicitly 'devoted to the moral, physical, and domestic improvement of the industrious classes', the *Family Economist* illustrates the way in which the middle-class domestic ideal was represented as the form of the family that was natural for everyone in the popular periodicals of the 1840s and 1850s.

The ideology of domesticity that underpins the purpose and form of the family magazines is also evident in their contents. Women are defined as domestic creatures, responsible for creating and maintaining the home, and rearing their children; men are associated with the public sphere, the world of industry and business. Through the female maintenance of the home as a haven or 'temple of the hearth',[74] social stability could be ensured, for the family home constituted the very nucleus and foundation of the state. As an advocate of 'Home Power' in *Eliza Cook's Journal* declared, 'It is really the Home which governs the world, for it is there that those principles of conduct and action are imbibed which men afterwards carry with them into active life,' and woman 'is the chief director of this home power'.[75] Or as another commentator in the *Magazine of Domestic Economy* explained,

It is equally true, that as the treatment which woman receives is the index of the degree of civilisation, so the manner in which woman conducts herself is the index of the moral state. This moral state is the foundation of all domestic happiness, as well as of all prosperity and greatness, whether public or private; and therefore it is that the proper conduct of woman, viewed as one upon whom domestic duties more immediately and completely devolve, is the most important subject to which attention can be directed.[76]

Hence the existence of this journal and the importance of the separation of spheres to which it is dedicated. Women are charged with the moral guardianship of society here, because it is their special duty to preserve the home as a 'place of happiness . . . which alone can make compensation for all the troubles, and toils, and struggles, with which men of all classes must meet in public life, and business, and occupation of any description'.[77] Proper maintenance of the home by a successful domestic economist is held to be an essential requirement in the formation of male subjectivity, for without a home, the Englishman's identity is incomplete: 'the business world, the social world, the public world, are all extrinsic of the man himself; and be his merits what they may, he is "*among* the people of these worlds, not *of* them"'. As the sphere assigned to woman, whose reproductive labour is held to be coextensive with her female nature, the home provides the antidote to the alienating effects of the marketplace. And in order to preserve the non-alienation and self-consistency characteristic of woman's nature and role, it is essential to observe that 'the grand division of labour' must be

the division into the public and professional labour of man, and the home and domestic labour of woman; and every tendency that there is to jumble together, and confound in their operations, these two distinct sets of functionaries, is a falling backwards towards a less civilised and less efficient condition of society.[78]

The idealisation of the home in the family magazines entailed a new definition of female subjectivity that was not determined by social position or economic value, but by the embodiment of domestic virtue. Woman's domestic responsibilities were understood to be an extension of her natural attributes, thus making the family and female identity part of one cultural formation. The *Ladies Cabinet* of 1844 defined the ideal woman as a successful 'Domestic Economist':

Enter the humblest dwelling under the prudent management of a discreet and rightly educated female, and observe the simplicity and good taste which pervade it. The wise mistress has nothing gaudy in her dress or furniture, for she is superior to the silly ambition of surpassing her neighbours in show. Her own best ornaments are cheerfulness and contentment; her highest displays, those of comfort and a comely gladness; her house is the abode and token of neatness and thrift; of good order and cleanliness; which makes it, and its various divisions, look better than they really are.[79]

The virtues of the home-making woman are implicitly contrasted here with the qualities of those women whose wealth is manifested in a pre-occupation with ornamentation and display of social position. Frugality, neatness and cheerfulness are the qualities which make the domestic woman 'superior' to those who feel obliged to parade the signs of status in the manner of aristocratic women. This woman is valued for the domestic virtues she embodies, rather than for her family name or social connections, and her representation helps to define the middle-class idea of the family in opposition to the values and practices held to characterise other social groups.

The hegemonic function of home-worship in family periodicals of the 1840s and 1850s is evident in the frequency with which the domestic ideal is held to transcend differences of class, gender or generation, uniting readers in the veneration of a common object. Noting with reference to the definition of 'home' that 'the word and the reality know no difference of station', for example, the *Magazine of Domestic Economy* assumes a unifying function in its conception of the family as a microcosm of the nation, and in the claim that 'if men are without that principle of attraction and union in society, *which is attainable only by the proper feeling and possession of home*, all the Solons and Lycurguses that ever lived might legislate in vain for the promotion of their greatness and happiness in communities and nations'.[80] A commentator upon cheap reading in *Eliza Cook's Journal* discloses the hegemonic influence of family periodical writing which provides a common background and shared experiences for readers otherwise differentiated by a range of social factors:

The province of the literary philanthropist is clear – to circulate widely, under every shape, elements of truth; to strengthen the bands of society by instruction, and to cement national union by social and domestic recreation. The love of families engendered by this potent, but quiet influence, extends and evolves itself into patriotism, and a correct sense of social and political freedom, grounded on the only safe basis – discipline of mind.[81]

However, even though the family magazines dedicated themselves to the propagation of home values, the spread of domestic ideology in their pages was never complete or unmixed. Not all the discourses which found their way into these miscellanies upheld the dominant values of the middle-class family. For example, the 'Answers to Correspondents' columns, which became such a popular feature in penny publications like the *Family Herald*, could play a rather ambiguous role in relation to support of the family ethos proclaimed elsewhere in the journal. First, it is clear from the replies printed that the actual circumstances of the paper's correspondents are much more diverse than the domestic ideal presented for emulation in its pages would suggest. For example, letters are received from readers who are not part of a family circle. One dubbed 'Censor', who evidently complains about the column of riddles, is told by the editor of the *Family Herald*,

We will not designate our correspondent by the name which he anticipates; but perhaps we may be indulged the privilege of suspecting that he is a bachelor too long unyoked, who has forgotten his boyish feelings, or who has never known what it was to sit round a table with his brothers and sisters exercising his ingenuity in the solution of puzzles.[82]

Secondly, despite the anonymity of the letter-writers, the correspondence itself frequently transgresses the boundary between public and private life. In an 1858 article on 'the universal public of the penny-novel journals' published in *Household Words*, Wilkie Collins describes the 'Answers to Correspondents' in terms which suggest the subversive potential of this material:

There is no earthly subject that it is possible to discuss, no private affair that it is possible to conceive, which the amazing Unknown Public will not confide to the Editor in the form of a question, and which the still more amazing editor will not set himself seriously and resolutely to answer. Hidden under cover of initials, or Christian names, or conventional signatures, such as Subscriber, Constant Reader, and so forth, the editor's correspondents seem, many of them, to judge by the published answers to their questions, utterly impervious to the senses of ridicule or shame. Young girls beset by perplexities which are usually supposed to be reserved for a mother's or an elder sister's ear only, consult the editor. Married women, who have committed little frailties consult the editor ... Now he is a father, now a mother ...[83]

Not only does the editor become a recipient of confidences more properly shared between family members, but his cryptic manner of replying to these disclosures often has a titillating effect. The reader of these public replies to private requests is made to feel like a voyeur or eavesdropper. Many replies, for example, deal with intrigues of love, such as the one to 'Fanny Evans', who is told that she 'should address her dear Henry through the penny-post, or a special messenger, say a carrier-pigeon, or a turtle-dove. We must not encourage dear-ing too much in our vehicle'; or the reply to 'A. M. L. T.': 'Better adapted for a private post-paid communication to the lady herself, as the public would not understand it sufficiently to appreciate it.'[84] Another rather tantalising response is made to a correspondent identified as 'G. Allcorn', who had presumably sent in a manuscript of poetry: 'Somewhat too luscious for modern modesty. Our correspondent has been following the old poets too closely. These wrote for men, but poets now write for boys and girls as well as adults, and it has been found necessary to clip the wings of Pegasus. They are spirited pieces, however.'[85]

The kind of speculation encouraged by the editor's intriguing replies to his correspondents is akin to the techniques of sensational journalism and fiction – that genre of writing decried by conservative reviewers as an assault upon the family. Such speculation was precisely what drew the objections of those who protested against Dickens's 'sensational' publication of his private affairs in 1858. While the serial publication of Wilkie Collins's *The Woman in White* (from 26 November 1859 to 25 August 1860) is generally held to mark the starting-point for sensational fiction, stories of a thrilling kind had been published in cheap family papers like the *London Journal* from the early 1850s. With the removal of the newspaper stamp tax in 1855 and subsequent explosion in the growth of popular penny newspapers the publication of crime stories, which fed the appetite for sensationalism, increased. Journalism played a crucial role in the genesis of the sensation novel by exposing hitherto 'unknown' areas of aberrant behaviour and illicit experience, and thereby stretched readers' conceptions of the real and the probable. What was sensational about Victorian sensationalism was not only its predilection for salacious subjects like bigamy and adultery, but its dependence upon narrative strategies designed to tantalise the reader by a reluctance to divulge family secrets. As one commentator in *Temple Bar* explained:

It is on our domestic hearths that we are taught to look for the incredible. A mystery sleeps in our cradles; fearful errors lurk in our nuptial couches; fiends sit down with us at table; our innocent-looking garden walks hold the secret of treacherous murders; and our servants take £20 a year from us for the sake of having us at their mercy.[86]

Criticisms of the press reportage of criminal trials were voiced with increasing frequency throughout the 1850s, and reveal the paradoxical way in which sensational journalism depends upon domestic ideology in order to generate its distinctive effects. For example, in the 1856 article on 'Our Civilisation' quoted earlier, the *Saturday Review* criticised the suggestion 'that the orderly surface of society is but an external covering, and that it serves only as a cloak for bruises, wounds, and putrefying sores'.[87] However, the reviewer's objection is not so much to the *fact* that 'external decorum frequently covers the most awful abysses of wickedness' as it is to the appropriation of sphere ideology involved in its publication: 'we deem it a libel on society to publish long accounts of the villany [*sic*] *as something distinctive of, and peculiar to, the decorum*'.[88] The subversiveness of this kind of journalism thus stems not so much from its representation of deviance, as from its exploitation of domesticity to enable a narrative strategy of sensational disclosure, an exposure of the private to public gaze that is predicated upon the existence of the very boundary it subverts. Similarly, sensation fiction depends upon Victorian domestic ideology, with its insistence upon the inviolability of the home, as the very condition of its narrative logic. Despite the overt conservatism of the genre, in which bigamy and other vices are finally punished as part of an eventual validation of marriage and the family, the leverage provided by the obsession with privacy remains a fundamental source of subversive energy in sensation fiction.

The sensation novelists identified Dickens as their model, and a number of the writers associated with the development of sensational journalism and fiction, such as George Augustus Sala and Wilkie Collins, served their apprenticeship under Dickens on *Household Words*. As John Sutherland has pointed out, '*Household Words* can be seen as a nursery of investigative journalism and a cradle of sensation fiction – stories with the immediacy of the day's newspaper headlines.'[89] Ironically, *Household Words* was a family journal for middle-class readers intended in part to replace the villainous fare of crime and sensation found in cheap periodicals with more wholesome writing. Like other family periodicals, it was a miscellany that cast itself as the friend and companion of its fireside readers. In the 'Preliminary Word' heading the first number, Dickens expresses the hope that his journal will be allowed into the sanctuary of the family home:

We have considered what an ambition it is to be admitted into many homes with affection and confidence; to be regarded as a friend by children and old people; to be thought of in affliction and in happiness; to people the sick room with airy shapes 'that give delight and hurt not', and to be associated with the harmless laughter and the gentle tears of many hearths. We know the great responsibility of such a privilege; its vast reward; the pictures that it conjures up in hours of solitary labour, of a multitude moved by one sympathy . . .[90]

The reference to the 'multitude moved by one sympathy' captures the hegemonic function of the family in Dickens's writing. The role of *House-hold Words* as a family friend was projected in the personal attitude shown in its pages. An intimacy of tone linking the journal with its readers was suggested in the direct addresses and personal appeals: for example, one storyteller assures us, 'This is no fiction, reader, no exaggerated picture',[91] while another writer asks, 'What will the reader think of the following out-fit for a traveller by stage-coach in the reign of Charles the Second?'[92] However, in spite of its overt dedication to the cosy values of the middle-class family, the discourse of domesticity in *Household Words* was not unmixed. While Dickens's choice of title for his journal signalled the family orientation that he meant to characterise its pages – 'We aspire to live in the Household affections, and to be numbered among the Household thoughts, of our readers'[93] – the title later became fuel for a satiric 'impromptu' in *Reynolds's Newspaper* when his marriage break-up with Catherine was publicised in *Household Words*:

> With tongue and pen, none can like Dickens judge;
> But now, in vain, in virtue's cause he pleads:
> Henceforth the public will his virtues judge
> Not by his 'Household Words', but household deeds.[94]

Ironically, as we have seen, Dickens's family journal became a key site in the controversy surrounding his marriage break-up, and its closure was brought about by the refusal of his publishers, Bradbury and Evans, to print in *Punch* his explanation for the parting from Catherine.

THE POLITICS OF THE FAMILY

Despite the idealisation of the family as a sanctuary guarded by a domestic angel in the pages of journals like *Household Words*, the challenge to the traditional image of Victorian women as passive and dependent creatures begun by feminist social historians such as Patricia Branca, Leonore Davidoff and Catherine Hall, and the revisionist accounts of Victorian sexual mores by Michael Mason in recent years, have indicated the extent to which attitudes and beliefs may depart from social realities.[95] As the bitter failure of Dickens's marriage shows, the family was often in fact a source of tension and discord. However, my study is about the discursive formation of the family in Dickens's fiction, rather than the historical realism (or otherwise) of his representations. My methodology owes much to recent work within Victorian studies which has adopted a post-structuralist orientation to history and focussed upon the power of repre-sentation to materialise ways of being – to produce subjectivity. By insisting upon the 'reality' of words, these analyses challenge the divisions between productive and reproductive domains inherited in the project of the human sciences as differences with a history that were established in the gendered formation of the disciplines. The work of Michel Foucault in challenging traditional models of historical causality has significantly influenced this new focus upon the relations between power and knowl-edge, and the role of discourse in the formation of historically specific subjectivities. His focus on the 'capillary' forms of power, produced at the level of the local and everyday through a range of texts, institutions and social practices, has turned literary criticism in the direction of cultural studies, encouraging critical approaches to nineteenth-century writing which test generic and disciplinary distinctions by attending to the symbolic productivity of discourse.

Foucault's view of the family as a site where the deployment of sexuality brings the manifold relationships of force into play, and his conception of power as a grid running unevenly through social formations, rather than as a centralised social structure or institution, have both influenced Jacques Donzelot's analysis of the family. In *The Policing of Families*,[96] Donzelot goes beyond earlier Marxist and functionalist accounts to explore the disciplinary function of the family in the formation of the modern, liberal state. In the same way that Foucault considers power as a productive network, Donzelot argues that 'policing' must not be 'under-stood in the limiting, repressive sense we give the term today, but accord-ing to a much broader meaning that encompassed all the methods for developing the quality of the population and the strength of the nation'.[97] Donzelot regards the family and its historical transformations as a positive solution to the problems posed by a liberal definition of the state: that is, how to reconcile individual rights and freedoms with the interests of the state, and how to justify the necessary construction of public services and facilities without compromising the idea of self-autonomy.

Under the *ancien régime*, Donzelot argues, the interests of families and of the state were each served by the establishment of convents, foundling hospitals and brothels, which brought harmony to the family by absorbing its undesirables (rebellious adolescents, illegitimate children, women of ill repute) and consolidated the force of the state by providing the bases for a policy of conservation and utilisation of individuals, and for a series of corrective interventions in family life. However, in the nineteenth century, the formation of power relations between the family and the state took on a new shape. A transition from a government *of* families to a government *through* the family was effected by a technique of normalisation. For example, Donzelot identifies a host of bills passed in England and France from the 1840s to the end of the nineteenth century – decreeing standards for the protection of children, laws on child labour, housing, supervision of wet nurses, and compulsory education – as a normalisation of the adult–child relationship which no doubt improved the plight of many children, but which also permitted a form of state intervention in those families unable to ensure their autonomy through the observance of state norms. According to Donzelot,

The placing of the family outside the sociopolitical field, and the possibility of anchoring mechanisms of social integration in the family, are not the result of a chance meeting between the capitalist imperative of maintaining private property and a structure dedicated to producing subjection by means of the Oedipus complex or what have you, but the strategic outcome of a series of interventions that wield family authority more than they rest on it. In this sense, the modern family is not so much an institution as a *mechanism*.[98]

While Donzelot does not refer to his work, it is clear that this analysis is indebted to Foucault's account of the exercise of disciplinary power in the nineteenth century. His history of the family as a mechanism of social control accords with Foucault's attention to the power of the 'norm' in the creation of a subject ideally suited to inhabit a modern disciplinary society. As developed by Donzelot and Foucault, the theoretical model of the family as a disciplinary mechanism underlies my analysis of the way in which Dickens's fiction is implicated in the formation of the Victorian middle-class family. However, Donzelot's and Foucault's studies neglect the issue of gender, and Foucault is notorious for his relative silence upon the question of political resistance. The analytic possibilities opened up by their theoretical approach therefore remain limited when situating Dickens's representation of the family within nineteenth-century ideological constructions of class and gender. Involved as they are in the formation of these categories of difference, his fictions test the hegemonic discourse of the middle-class family even as they seek to affirm it.

The conceptualisation of the family for which Dickens was celebrated in his own day is the ideal of domesticity depicted in set-pieces like the description of the Cratchits' Christmas dinner. To be sure, more often than not his fiction delineates families made memorable by their grotesque failure to exemplify the domestic ideal. However, this ideal is almost everywhere implied as the standard against which the families portrayed in the novels are evaluated, and herein lies the explanation for the paradox involved in the apparent disjunction between Dickens's reputation as the celebrant of domestic bliss and his fictional interest in fractured families. What condemns Mrs Joe in *Great Expectations*, for instance, is her failure to embody the maternal ideal that goes with the worship of the hearth. What condemns Mr Dombey is largely his failure to distinguish between family and firm – to separate private and public life as required by the ideal of domesticity. What makes David Copperfield's eventual choice of Agnes as his proper partner in marriage function as a sign of his maturation and moral development is the ideal of domesticity that underwrites this choice. These representations of the family illustrate the normalising function of middle-class domestic ideology in Dickens's fiction. His novels record a historical shift in notions of the family away from an earlier stress upon the importance of lineage and blood towards a new ideal of domesticity assumed to be the natural form of the family. I am concerned to analyse the ways in which his deployment of competing conceptualisations of the family are symbolically productive in the formation of middle-class cultural authority. Although I discuss a selection of Dickens's novels in chronological order, it should be clear from the omissions – *David Copperfield*, *Bleak House* and *Hard Times* most notably – that no comprehensive survey of the representation of the family in his fiction is offered here. Rather, my concern is to analyse a range of texts which engage with the ideology of the family in various ways in order to show how Dickens's fictions work as enabling representations in the Victorian social economy.

CHAPTER 2

Fractured families in the early novels
Oliver Twist and *Dombey and Son*

Readers of Dickens commonly note significant differences of design, structure and social vision when comparing his earlier and later novels. An increasing complexity is evident in the works produced during his middle years, and *Dombey and Son* is often discussed as the novel which most clearly exhibits this transition in Dickens's artistic practice. Its position as the harbinger of the later novels is largely determined by the function of the railways as an ambiguous symbol of bourgeois industrial progress in the book: a symbolic function that looks forward to the role played by more complex unifying images, such as the Court of Chancery or the Circumlocution Office, in the later novels. What generates the complexity and darker social vision of the later fiction is Dickens's attempt to offer a symbolically coherent account of a divided society whose problems are now shown to be *systemic*. It is hardly surprising, then, to find that the later novels, from *Bleak House* onwards, offer more complex renditions of the politics of the family.

However, it is nevertheless true that Dickens's interest in the family is pervasive in all his writing. The prevalence of fractured families, and the relegation of idealised 'happy families' to the margins of the narrative, are features evident in the early, as in the later, novels. Some of the more complex ideological functions performed by the figure of the family in the later works are shown in the early fiction too. For example, Dickens's continuing interest in the relationship between public and private life, between the market and the home, contributes to the symptomatic role of the family in his early novels. The economic woes suffered by the fathers in *Nicholas Nickleby* and *Dombey and Son* look forward to the function of the family in mediating the critique of industrialism and the economy in later works, like *Little Dorrit* and *Our Mutual Friend*. The representation of decaying homes and appalling families, such as the Squeers, the Chuzzlewits or the Murdstones, or of parodic families, such as the band of thieves who inhabit Fagin's den, is part of the normalisation of domesticity that can be seen throughout Dickens's writing. Similarly, while the female ideal embodied in heroines such as Esther Summerson, Little Dorrit or Lucie Manette is foreshadowed in the depiction of Rose Maylie, Florence Dombey and Agnes Wickfield, all of whom exemplify the virtues of the domestic woman, this middle-class ideal is reinforced by the depiction of 'other' women – fallen women, absent or inadequate mothers – whose negative example contributes to the normalisation of domesticity in the fiction. Figures of deviance are frequently used to signify a familial norm that eventually provides a resolution to the narrative. This norm encodes certain class and gender assumptions that display the novel's political investment in the family.

Just as Dickens's later novels belie the generalisations often made about his idealisation of the happy Victorian family, his early fiction shows a remarkable preoccupation with fractured families. One parent, at least, is usually missing, creating an opportunity in the fiction for the formation of a variety of atypical familial relationships, together with a host of social, emotional and moral problems for the hero or heroine to solve. Clearly, the figure of the orphan has always held strong imaginative potential for novelists, but it may have been a particular source of fascination for the Victorians because of its utility in representing their anxious relation to the past. The desire to recover a fixed origin is evident in the dominance of developmental narratives in varying discourses throughout the nineteenth century,[1] for, as Nina Auerbach points out, 'Industrialism, religious conflict, and scientific discoveries had orphaned the Victorian age of its sense of its own past.'[2] The orphan's lack of a family becomes a way of exploring ontological anxiety in the Victorian age. Whatever the larger cultural significance of fictional interest in the orphan, however, Dickens's abiding concern with this figure is inseparable from his representation of the family, and amongst his earlier novels *Oliver Twist* shows the significance of the orphan for the ideological work of the family quite clearly.

OLIVER TWIST

Oliver Twist draws upon the foundling tales and picaresque narratives of the eighteenth century to tell the story of the orphan's progress from poverty and anonymity to the revelation of his pedigree and the recovery of his inheritance. It is a novel about the hero's retrieval of lost family origins, about the discovery of his identity and social position through the recovery of his birthright. From the very beginning of the book, Oliver's face and speech display his patrimony, however much the circumstantial evidence of his clothes or his companions might seem to mark him as a pauper or criminal. As a number of critics have pointed out, Oliver's impeccable English accent is a sign both of his innate goodness and of his birth. The incorruptibility of his language is an index to his true moral and social position. Michal Peled Ginsburg's study of the speech patterns of the characters in *Oliver Twist* has uncovered the ideological function of the use of unmarked and marked language in the novel, and points out that because unmarked language is monolithic and context-free, it appears as the norm and establishes the middle-class world-view as 'given' in the narrative.[3] Despite having been born and bred in a workhouse, Oliver shares the language of the Brownlows and the Maylies rather than the corrupted speech of his early associates, Mr Bumble, Noah Claypole or Fagin, thus indicating the world to which he truly belongs.

Similarly, Oliver's face is a sign of his true moral and social status, not only because it is a 'living copy' (72) of his mother's, but because it reveals his native goodness. Mr Brownlow's recurrent awareness of 'something in that boy's face . . . that touches and interests me' (63) is a thinly veiled clue to Oliver's patrimony, based as it is upon the unrecognised resemblance to the portrait of his mother which hangs in Mrs Bedwin's room. While Mr Brownlow is led to recall 'a vast amphitheatre of faces over which a dusky curtain had hung for many years' when he first encounters Oliver, he is unable to trace the resemblance. But his exercise in imaginative recollection acknowledges the irresistible power of nature to reveal its truth in the human face: what the narrator describes as 'the beaming of the soul through its mask of clay' (63). So Oliver's face involuntarily expresses his innocence, as Mr Brownlow discovers when questioning him about the pickpocketing incident at the bookseller's. Despite the appearance of falsehood in Oliver's report of his real name, the narrator notes, 'the old gentleman looked somewhat sternly in Oliver's face. It was impossible to doubt him; there was truth in every one of its thin and sharpened lineaments' (72). The embodiment of truth in Oliver's face works to naturalise his real social position by linking the evidence of his hidden family origin to his native innocence in the one rhetorical figure. His innate goodness shows through the same medium that discloses his inheritance. None of the painful social experiences of life in the workhouse or in Fagin's den has been able to cover over the evidence of nature written in his face: Oliver belongs to the world of Mr Brownlow, both by virtue of his goodness and by virtue of his birth.

Dickens uses the rhetoric of 'nature' in *Oliver Twist* to show, as he announced in the novel's preface, 'the principle of Good surviving through every adverse circumstance, and triumphing at last' (xxv). This argument involves a critique of nineteenth-century political and economic theories concerning socially determined development.[4] However, critical discussion of the novel has not duly considered the significance of Dickens's rhetorical appeals to nature for his representation of the family. While pastoral writing is used to clean away social stains of various kinds in the novel by removing the victim to an asocial realm where class and gender determinants are supposedly transcended (as in Oliver's rural retreat with the Maylies), such writing unobtrusively reintroduces the social through the figure of the family that is invoked in the process.

Mr Brownlow's rejection of social evidence as an index to Oliver's character appeals to a rhetoric of nature that unites and affirms the orphan's true moral and social position. This rhetorical strategy links the material fact of blood-relatedness to the evidence of Oliver's essential innocence in a mutually authorising relationship which subsumes the class differences involved in the process. It is highly significant for the politics of the family in this novel that his innate goodness and his genealogy are indisputably written in his face, for the appeal to nature involved in their reading draws on a conception of the family that is based on aristocratic premises to legitimate middle-class origins.

As a narrative about the recovery of origins, the novel draws upon an aristocratic conception of the family as a lineage. This is the form of family that defines itself in terms of blood-relatedness. Together with his native innocence, Oliver's patrimony is embodied in his face and voice in such a way that genealogy and moral being serve to naturalise his true social position. The social stigma of his illegitimacy is erased by the pastoral argument as Oliver's identity and social position are secured through the discovery of family origin. The hero's pedigree, like his natural innocence it seems, can never be entirely covered over by the narratives of social experience, and its revelation enables him to recover the inheritance of which he has been fraudulently deprived by his half-brother, Monks. Not surprisingly, his legitimacy is found by invoking a notion of the aristocratic family; but what he recovers by these means is a position that embraces the domestic ideal. An aristocratic conception of the family is used to establish Oliver's place in the world of middle-class respectability. His story provides a fable of identity for the newly risen middle classes, a myth of origins that could serve to strengthen their precarious sense of social legitimacy.

However, despite the importance of genealogy in securing Oliver's personal and social identity, the family that is reconstituted at the end of the book contains only one relationship that is based on blood. Oliver discovers that Rose Maylie is his aunt, but rejects this relationship and insists upon regarding Rose as a quasi-sister: '"Not aunt," cried Oliver, throwing his arms about her neck: "I'll never call her aunt – sister, my own dear sister, that something taught my heart to love so dearly from the first! Rose, dear, darling Rose!"' (337). Mr Brownlow adopts Oliver as his son, and removes with him and Mrs Bedwin, who, like Mrs Maylie, has acted as a surrogate mother to Oliver throughout, to within a mile of the parsonage-house where Rose and Harry Maylie live. In the narrator's words, he 'thus linked together a little society, whose condition approached as nearly to one of perfect happiness as can ever be known in this changing world' (348). The emphasis upon surrogate familial relationships and the cosy harmony of this 'little society' indicate that the family has been reconstituted according to the middle-class ideal of domesticity. In this way, *Oliver Twist* shows evidence of the competing definitions of the family available in Victorian culture, and some of the political effects that appeals to these definitions enable. One might say that Oliver's story provides the site where two competing conceptions of the family are brought into play as part of a larger struggle for cultural hegemony in the Victorian period.

This ideological struggle is also evident in the representation of state institutions and the criminal underworld in the novel. The figure of the family is used to establish a continuum between these two worlds, and to offer an alternative middle-class world of privacy where natural character may flourish. Apparently displacing the family from the central position it was supposed to assume in Victorian society, the novel centres instead upon marginal figures such as the orphan, pauper and criminal, and the alien world they inhabit. These outcasts form parodic images of the family, establishing a model of deviance that contributes to the normative effect of familial ideology in the novel, while yet remaining as evidence of the underlying failure of the family. After all, the very existence of these outcasts reveals a truth that is ignored by the hegemonic myth of 'hearth and home'. Moreover, it is Oliver's illegitimacy which causes his initial plight and subsequent misadventures, and which is responsible for bringing such respectable members of the middle classes as Mr Brownlow into contact with the London underworld.

When Oliver Twist loses his mother at birth, the parish authorities decide that he should be

'farmed,' or, in other words, that he should be dispatched to a branch-workhouse some three miles off, where twenty or thirty other juvenile offenders against the poor-laws, rolled about the floor all day, without the inconvenience of too much food or too much clothing, under the parental superintendence of an elderly female, who received the culprits at and for the consideration of sevenpence-halfpenny per small head per week. (3)

The hypocrisy of the elderly female's maternal pretensions (she is significantly named Mrs Mann) is clearly signalled in her expertise as an 'experimental philosopher' and her obsequious behaviour towards Mr Bumble. What is most important here, however, is the way in which the workhouse, the prison and the family are linked together. These three institutions form a nexus in which the conflation of supposedly incongruous figures becomes the source of Dickens's satire. But their conjunction also suggests a symbolic link between the workhouse and the prison that is developed throughout the narrative as part of Dickens's critique of the New Poor Law.

At nine years of age, Oliver is led away from this 'wretched home' (7) by Mr Bumble and deposited again in the workhouse proper. Like Mrs Mann, the workhouse authorities invoke the model of the family to disguise their exploitation and tyranny. When Oliver is being prepared for his proposed apprenticeship to Mr Gamfield, the chimneysweep, Mr Bumble explains, 'The kind and blessed gentlemen which is so many parents to you, Oliver, when you have none of your own: are a-going to 'prentice you: and to set you up in life, and make a man of you' (17). Similarly, at the beginning of chapter IV, the narrator ironically endorses the board's paternalistic image of itself in drawing an analogy between family traditions and workhouse practices:

In great families: when an advantageous place cannot be obtained, either in possession, reversion, remainder, or expectancy, for the young man who is growing up: it is a very general custom to send him to sea. The board, in imitation of so wise and salutary an example, took counsel together on the expediency of shipping off Oliver Twist, in some small trading vessel bound to a good unhealthy port; which suggested itself as the very best thing that could possibly be done with him. (20)

Such disguise of institutional abuse with the rhetoric of familial ideology is not uncommon in Dickens's fiction, and another notable instance occurs in his next published novel, where Mr Squeers announces that the pupils at Dotheboys Hall 'are all under the same parental and affectionate treatment. Mrs Squeers and myself are a mother and a father to every one of 'em' (55).

The readiness of the workhouse authorities to exploit the figure of the family by projecting an image of themselves as surrogate parents links them to the criminals depicted later in *Oliver Twist*. For Nancy and Sikes employ similar self-serving tactics to control Oliver, and Fagin's gang is managed by equally grotesque appeals to the ideology of the family. Nancy's stratagem in posing as Oliver's sister successfully exploits middle-class beliefs about sisterly affection and filial duty in order to recapture him. Dressed in a clean white apron and straw bonnet, and carrying a little covered basket in one hand and a door-key in the other, Nancy is suitably attired to make her appeal to the bystanders who witness Oliver's re-capture: 'Make him come home, there's good people, or he'll kill his dear mother and father, and break my heart!' (93). Oliver is overpowered by the ideological force of the family as much as the physical force of Sikes and Nancy here. Later, when Sikes embarks upon the robbery at Chertsey with Oliver, he disguises their mission by posing as a father travelling with his son.

Fagin's den offers perhaps the most notable parody of the middle-class family in the novel, and much of the suggestion of menace which charac-terises the underworld derives from his grotesque rhetorical appeals to the ideology of domesticity. Oliver is introduced into Fagin's family by the Artful Dodger in chapter VIII. In Cruikshank's memorable illustration of the scene, Fagin is poised over the fire with a toasting-fork in his hand, and the narrator describes his 'matted red hair' and grinning countenance as he turns around to express his hope for having the honour of Oliver's 'intimate acquaintance' (50). On the one hand, this scene establishes Fagin's association with the devil;[5] but on the other, it represents a parody of domesticity. Fagin is shown presiding over the hearth – that sacred symbol of Victorian family life – cooking the evening meal, and sur-rounded by an assortment of household utensils and a crowd of hungry boys. Again, in chapter XVIII, a similarly homely scene is described when Fagin draws Oliver to sit beside him at the hearth, and leads the conversa-tion 'to the topics most calculated to interest his hearers' (115). Fagin's home appears to offer the comfort and cosiness held to be provided by the Victorian middle-class family circle. The function of the den as a refuge for thieves serves to literalise the figurative construction of the home as a haven or shelter in middle-class ideology.

The underworld parody of the family is also apparent in Fagin's assumption of paternal authority over the boys in his charge. He controls the cash gained from fencing the stolen goods they bring in, and the 'stern morality' he displays in reproving any failure to bring home spoil is a grotesque imitation of parental discipline: 'Whenever the Dodger or Charley Bates came home at night, empty-handed, he would expatiate with great vehemence on the misery of idle and lazy habits; and would enforce upon them the necessity of an active life, by sending them supper-less to bed' (58). When Oliver is recaptured by Nancy and Sikes, Fagin reads Oliver 'a long lecture on the crying sin of ingratitude' and lays 'great stress on the fact of his having taken Oliver in, and cherished him, when, without his timely aid, he might have perished with hunger' (109). The Artful Dodger also espouses the virtues of Fagin's family, admonishing Oliver, 'You've been brought up bad . . . Fagin will make something of you, though, or you'll be the first he ever had that turned out unprofitable' (113). Fagin is characterised throughout as the 'preceptor' (75) of the young thieves, and he is quick to exploit the didactic potential of any occasion – such as the dispatching of Nancy to recapture Oliver, when Fagin turns to his boys 'shaking his head gravely, as if in mute admonition to them to follow the bright example they had just beheld' (79).

Remarkably, Fagin combines his exercise of paternal discipline with the maternal duties of the home-maker. He is the one who cooks meals, arranges accommodation, educates his 'pupils' and 'plays' with them. When Sikes demands a cash advance from him in chapter xxxix, Fagin resembles a housewife in straitened circumstances, as he protests 'with many solemn asseverations that that would only leave him eighteen-pence to keep house with' (247). Like the motherly Mrs Bedwin, who amuses Oliver with 'a great many stories' (82) about the adventures of her children, Fagin tells his 'family' 'stories of robberies he had committed in his younger days: mixed up with so much that was droll and curious, that Oliver could not help laughing heartily, and showing that he was amused in spite of all his better feelings' (115). This tendency to combine aspects of the maternal and paternal roles defined by the middle-class ideology of the family contributes to the suggestions of sexual perversion involved in Fagin's portrayal. As a grotesque embodiment of mixed gender positions, Fagin emerges as a sinister figure whose 'care' of his boys is shaded by obscure hints of paedophilia. In his 'relish' of Oliver's 'pale face and trembling limbs' (110) in chapter xviii, Fagin exhibits the sort of combined sexual titillation and sadism shown by Mr Creakle, the schoolmaster, in *David Copperfield*, who takes a particular delight in caning 'chubby boys'.

In contrast to the parodic family formed by the criminal underworld, the novel sets out an alternative realm of middle-class domesticity that is located in the homes of Mr Brownlow and Mrs Maylie. Significantly, the opposition is highlighted by the pairing of Nancy and Rose as foils in the narrative. In *Oliver Twist*, as in the later novels, the representation of female identity is an integral part of the ideology of the family, since the ideal middle-class home is largely defined by the domestic woman at its centre. Clearly, Rose Maylie exemplifies the virtues of the domestic angel:

The very intelligence that shone in her deep blue eyes, and was stamped upon her noble head, seemed scarcely of her age, or of the world; and yet the changing expression of sweetness and good humour; the thousand lights that played about the face, and left no shadow there; above all, the smile; the cheerful, happy smile; were made for Home; and fireside peace and happiness. (181)

The evidence of Rose's domestic virtue, which apparently transcends the presumption of her illegitimate birth, is part of Dickens's argument about natural innocence and the rejection of social and legal legitimacy as an index to character. But it is also a crucial factor in establishing the boundary between the underworld, and the world of middle-class respectability in the novel. The separation is observed by Nancy, who is described at the beginning of chapter XL as having 'shrunk' from Rose 'as though she could scarcely bear the presence of her with whom she had sought this interview' (254), and as if to mark an invisible barrier between them. Rose's virtue manifests itself in the impulse to rescue the fallen Nancy, and it suffuses the pastoral retreat where Oliver becomes 'completely domesticated with the old lady and her niece' (203). He now spends his days learning to read and write, walking with Mrs Maylie and Rose, listening to Rose read or play the piano, collecting groundsel for her birds, or plundering the hedges to gather wild flowers for a nosegay to present to her. Dickens invokes Wordsworthian ideas about the restorative powers of nature and imagination to describe Oliver's rebirth 'into a new state of being' (201).

Oliver's pastoral retreat is not entirely safe from underworld intrusions – as the attempted robbery makes clear. At the end of chapter XXXIV, he is terrified by the apparition of Fagin and Monks observing him through the open window while he is half-asleep. But the inviolability of his new home is preserved in other ways which serve to affirm the sanctity of the middle-class family. For example, the whole process of bringing the culprits to justice in the novel is characterised by the exclusion of the police from the real work of detection and the substitution of an 'amateur' investigation that is carried out by Mr Losberne and Mr Brownlow.[6] *Oliver Twist*'s distrust of state institutions, which are shown to be implicated in the maintenance of a delinquent milieu, is extended to the police who, as public

officers, are held to be part of this process. The workhouse, with its brutal-
ising conditions, provides the breeding-ground for the members of Fagin's
gang. Similarly, Mr Fang, the magistrate, assists in the criminalisation of
the offenders brought before him, imposing a delinquent character upon
Oliver that is contravened by the innocence written in his face. The
famous Bow Street Runners, called in by Mrs Maylie's butler, Giles, to
investigate the robbery, relied heavily upon informers for their
effectiveness at detection. Dickens recalled that they 'kept company with
thieves and the like', and formed 'a very slack institution' whose head-
quarters were 'a public-house of more than doubtful reputation'.[7] Significantly, the Bow Street officers Blathers and Duff share the idiom of the
criminals, announcing that the robbery 'warn't a put-up thing' (191), to the
complete incomprehension of Mr Losberne and Mrs Maylie, who require
a translation of the thieves' cant. Given this association of Blathers and
Duff with the underworld, it is hardly surprising that the privacy of the
middle-class family in the novel is secured by the exclusion of the police.

Rose's first reaction to the discovery of Oliver is to propose a private
plan of rescue that assumes the moral foundation of the middle-class
family:

think that he may never have known a mother's love, or the comfort of a home;
that ill-usage and blows, or the want of bread, may have driven him to herd with
men who have forced him to guilt. Aunt, dear aunt, for mercy's sake, think of this,
before you let them drag this sick child to a prison, which in any case must be the
grave of all his chances of amendment. (184)

However, Giles and Brittles have already sent for the police, and the intru-
siveness of the Bow Street officers is immediately apparent on their
arrival: Blathers is described as 'a portly man in a great-coat, who walked
in without saying anything more, and wiped his shoes on the mat, as coolly
as if he lived there' (188). Mr Losberne advises Rose and Mrs Maylie not to
co-operate with them, because he is certain that Oliver's real story will
not be believed and will only attract unwelcome publicity. He works to
baffle the investigation by intimidating the servants into confusing their
testimony. He then rewards Blathers and Duff with a couple of guineas,
and they subsequently return to town 'with divided opinions on the subject
of their expedition' (196). His intervention substitutes Rose's 'benevolent
plan of rescuing [Oliver] from misery' (191), with its affirmation of
domestic ideology, for the regulatory mechanisms of the state.

Similarly, when the diabolical role of Monks is disclosed by Nancy,

Mr Brownlow determines that 'he is to be dealt with by us, and not by the law' (265), not only in order to protect their informant, but because, he says, 'there must be circumstances in Oliver's little history which it would be painful to drag before the public eye' (295). Accordingly, Mr Brownlow arranges for Monks to be 'kidnapped in the street' (313) by some men whom he has indemnified, and brought to his own house where a ritual of questioning and confession is carried out in which the coward is 'over-whelmed by these accumulated charges' (318) of his guilt. The private 'trial' of Monks concludes in chapter LI, with the full disclosure of Oliver's genealogy and the restoration of his patrimony. By dealing with Monks privately, Mr Brownlow seems to avoid police intrusion into the family's affairs, and to maintain the ideological boundary separating the under-world from the world of middle-class respectability.

While Monks is prosecuted in private, Sikes and Fagin are brought to justice in a very public fashion in the break-up of the underworld which follows the murder of Nancy. However, as a number of critics have noted, Sikes's death is remarkable for representing a public execution that is not carried out by the state but by the criminal himself, thus continuing the pattern in which the narrative seeks to dispense with state intervention. Sikes is goaded and eventually driven to his death by the haunting eyes of the woman he murdered when he is brought to bay on a rooftop by an 'infuriated throng' of 'hundreds'. Nancy's death galvanises the populace into action to apprehend the murderer, providing the only moment in the novel when the disparate inhabitants of the teeming city are united by a single purpose. With the subsequent state execution of Fagin as well, the underworld characters are purged from the novel, and the way is paved for the reconstitution of the family, and Oliver's enjoyment of his natural inheritance.

DOMBEY AND SON

The plot of the hero's reclamation of his birthright so memorably portrayed in *Oliver Twist* recurs in other early novels, for instance, in *Nicholas Nickleby* and *Martin Chuzzlewit*. In each of these, however, the restoration of hereditary status is combined with a plot of moral causality, as the hero's adventures enable him to learn from his experience. *Martin Chuzzlewit* explores the fortunes of the Chuzzlewit family in general, and of young Martin in particular, as part of a study of selfishness. The original title of the novel in its serial form indicates the nature of its focus:

The Life and Adventures of Martin Chuzzlewit, His Relations, Friends and Enemies. Comprising All his Wills and his Ways: with an Historical Record of what he did, and what he didn't: showing, moreover, who inherited the Family Plate, Who came in for Silver Spoons, and Who for the Wooden Ladles. The whole forming a complete key to the House of Chuzzlewit.[8]

The emphasis upon inheritance here foreshadows its key role in the plot, as the fortune of Martin's grandfather provides a motivation for the greed and self-interest shown by various family members. The reference to the 'Silver Spoons' and 'Wooden Ladles' echoes the story told in the introductory chapter about the gravy-spoon that one of the 'ancient' Chuzzlewits parted with to his 'uncle'.[9] This satirical chapter 'Concerning the Pedigree of the Chuzzlewit Family' serves to establish the Paradise Lost motif that pervades the novel, as it traces the dubious genealogy of the Chuzzlewits who 'undoubtedly descended in a direct line from Adam and Eve' (1). Like the parodic genealogies used by Thackeray to expose the social vanity of his characters, it also highlights the poor moral inheritance of the Chuzzlewits, whose family vices of selfishness and pride are the main study of the narrative. The satire upon genealogy, and the final restoration of hereditary status as a reward for Young Martin's moral reform, are evidence of Dickens's early interest in the relationship between family and the formation of identity. But the episodic structure of the narrative means that the representation of the family lacks the complexity that is such a compelling feature of the later novels. While sharing the satiric spirit with which *Martin Chuzzlewit* mocks the pretensions of tracing a pedigree, in its greater elaboration of design and planning *Dombey and Son* marks the beginning of Dickens's engagement with the family as a complex cultural construct that is an integral part of his wider moral and social analysis.

Feminist analyses of *Dombey and Son* have generally read the novel as a critique of the binary oppositions fundamental to patriarchal society.[10] In an important early essay published in 1976, Nina Auerbach argued that *Dombey and Son* is Dickens's 'most thorough exploration of his own and his contemporaries' doctrine of the "two spheres", with each sex moving in a solitary orbit inaccessible to the other one'.[11] According to Auerbach, the novel explores the problems associated with the cultural abyss which separates the male and female spheres. However, a focus on the representation of the family in the novel indicates that the thematic patterns of the narrative are more complicated than such an account of its dualistic structure suggests. The novel is about the consequences of a *failure* to separate these two spheres according to the dictates of middle-class domestic ideology, as is apparent from a consideration of the class-specific definitions of the family deployed in it. Above all, in the relationship between Mr Dombey and his daughter, the novel documents the consequences of a failure to understand the crucial role of the domestic woman in symbolically resolving some of the anxieties associated with the rapid growth of industrial capitalism. In exploring the role of the family as it mediates between the market and the domestic sphere in a narrative which interweaves multiple plot strands, the novel clearly provides a more complex account of the politics of the family than *Oliver Twist* does.

Dombey and Son is the product of a decade which saw an explosion of competitive energy in capitalist expansion. It was the era of the 'railway mania', when 8,652 miles of new line were authorised and thousands invested money in railway shares, only to be ruined by their losses when the bubble burst in 1845. This rash of speculation was encouraged by the selective granting of limited liability to railway projects through the legalisation of joint-stock companies. As Lord Hobart later explained,

By the grant of limited liability to a particular class of undertakings, all the capital which, owing to the state of the general law of partnership, was in vain seeking associative employment, would naturally be attracted to these undertakings; and as the amount of capital in this condition was out of all proportion to the dimensions of the channel which was opened for its reception, the result was an extravagant appreciation of railway shares, and a great consequent loss to the country.[12]

Endeavours to remove all forms of restraint on commercial association led to a gradual deregulation of company law throughout the first half of the century, and a mounting call for the introduction of limited liability, with the Companies Act of 1844 allowing the registration of joint-stock companies so that they could sue and be sued in a single name. Alongside the unleashing of speculative activity in the railways, the free trade movement was growing in impetus, with Sir Robert Peel acting to reduce import duties in the early 1840s. The repeal of the Corn Laws in 1846 was the most significant triumph of the free trade campaign, and dealt a decisive blow to the mercantilist system. Not surprisingly, the same arguments put forward for the removal of protectionist trade policies drove the call for limited liability, as the *Westminster Review* challenged Parliament in 1856: 'Let it consent to deal with free partnership as Sir Robert Peel dealt with free-trade, not by devising restrictions, and conditions, and limitations, and saving clauses, but by scattering all to the winds.'[13]

This context of economic ferment makes its presence felt in *Dombey and Son* through the description of the railroad and the entrepreneurial activities of Mr Carker. Clearly, the novel emerges from a period of urgent transformation in economic life, with the old mercantilist system giving way to the speculative ventures of industrial entrepreneurs and the triumph of free trade. This movement is underscored in the novel by the implicit contrast drawn between the forms of commercial association represented by the family firm of Dombey and Son and by the railways. As a common partnership, the House of Dombey and Son is bound by the principle of unlimited liability. This principle was being increasingly eroded throughout the 1840s by the granting of *ad hoc* exemptions to meet the needs of the moment – as demonstrated in the commercial provisions made for railway projects – and by the general call for freedom of commercial association. Dickens's novel registers this shift in economic relations in its portrayal of the House of Dombey and Son and Mr Dombey's financial undoing at the hands of his ruthlessly ambitious manager. In the process, the novel explores the connections between family relationships and the cash nexus, offering a critique of the effect of the economic calculus on the home.

The family is obviously an important topic in the novel, and the ambivalence of its treatment has been noted. Robert Clark, for example, comments on Dickens's affirmation of the family as 'an ideally nonviolent, noneconomic zone of felicitous relationship' in the portrait of the Toodles, while this affirmation is 'completely at variance with the recognition not only that Dombey's household is not like this, but that Dombey's household is the more general case'.[14] However, the normative effect of such representations of deviance in the novel also needs to be considered, together with the specific class and gender determinants involved. The family is usually regarded as a unitary institution that is turned into yet another site of exploitation under the impact of the business ethic in existing discussions of it in the novel, and most commentators tend to focus on the psychodynamics of the relationship between Mr Dombey and his daughter. Undoubtedly, a number of psychoanalytic studies of the novel have yielded important insights into the anxieties and reversals evident in the representation of the father–daughter relation.[15] But much remains to be said about the family as it is implicated in the workings of ideology in the novel. A more discriminating analysis of the varying family models drawn upon in the narrative sheds new light on Dickens's representation of economic change. The defeat of Mr Dombey's dynastic ambitions may be correlated with the demise of mercantilism and the triumph of a form of family that values domestic affection rather than the pride of lineage. Analysis of *Dombey and Son* can be extended and complicated by observing the competing definitions of family at work in the narrative.

The novel's opening immediately establishes the identification of family and firm that is the source of Mr Dombey's extraordinary pride. In the first three paragraphs of chapter I, the father and son are referred to solely by means of their designation in the firm's name:

Dombey sat in the corner of the darkened room in the great arm-chair by the bedside, and Son lay tucked up warm in a little basket bedstead, carefully disposed on a low settee immediately in front of the fire and close to it, as if his constitution were analogous to that of a muffin, and it was essential to toast him brown while he was very new. (1)

The House of Dombey and Son is described in dynastic terms, Mr Dombey having 'risen, as his father had before him, in the course of life and death, from Son to Dombey' (2). The new Son is to be christened Paul, after his father, and his grandfather before him, thus emphasising the correspondence between the firm's descent through the male line, and the patrilineal arrangements of an aristocratic family. Indeed, Mr Dombey's marriage was originally motivated, it seems, by the importance he placed upon 'the perpetuation of family firms', and, rather than looking forward to the birth of a son, his wife was to be encouraged by the 'hope of giving birth to a new partner in such a house'. This identification of family and firm is continued in the disparaging reference to Florence: 'But what was a girl to Dombey and Son! In the capital of the House's name and dignity, such a child was merely a piece of base coin that couldn't be invested – a bad Boy – nothing more' (2). The complete devaluation of the daughter indicates both her disqualification by gender as a business partner, and her subordination within a family defined by the practices of patrimonialism and patrilineality.

Paul's delivery is supervised by Doctor Parker Peps, 'one of the Court Physicians, and a man of immense reputation for assisting at the increase of great families' (3). The aristocratic pretensions signalled by his hire are continued in the effusions of Mrs Chick, who repeatedly flatters her brother's preoccupation with descent through the male line by asserting that the baby is 'quite a Dombey!' (5). Not surprisingly, 'Florence', says Mrs Chick to her friend Miss Tox later, 'will never, never, never, be a

Dombey . . . not if she lives to be a thousand years old' (41). It is only at the end of the novel, when the dynastic model of the family has been abandoned, and the domestic ideal has been restored in the union of Florence and Walter, that Dombey and Son turns out to be a daughter after all (707).

Mr Dombey's mutual identification of his family and firm betrays the ambivalence of his position, as he is torn between his adherence to the principles of competitive individualism associated with the growth of capitalism in the novel, and his commitment to maintaining the hierarchical social arrangements of an earlier economic order. When he is compelled to hire a wet-nurse for his son, he insists upon renaming Polly Toodle as 'Richards', and regarding her care for his son as 'a mere matter of bargain and sale, hiring and letting' (14). His overweening pride and jealous regard for Paul make his dependence upon the services of Polly – 'a hired serving-woman' (13) – a 'sore humiliation' to him. His desire to make her employment as nurse purely 'a question of wages' is a manifestation of the cash-nexus thinking that the novel associates with industrial capitalism. By asserting the contractual nature of the bond between Polly and baby Paul, Mr Dombey commodifies the nourishment she provides, and applies the economic calculus of the market within his own home.

However, this manifestation of Mr Dombey's commitment to the hard-nosed business ethic, which would seem to characterise him as an exemplary capitalist entrepreneur, is combined with evidence of his adherence to an older model of economic enterprise that helps to suggest his impending demise as a businessman. Mr Dombey's identification with his firm expresses a principle of personal responsibility for his enterprise that is based upon aristocratic premises. Partnerships were left as the central form of economic enterprise in the wake of the Bubble Act of 1720, which prohibited the formation of all unincorporated companies. Requiring no formal contract, partnership was simply a relationship between people who were 'intimately known to one another and usually working together'.[16] 'Much like a family member', explain Davidoff and Hall, 'every partner could act as an agent for the other but was also liable for all debts.'[17] The essence of the relationship was its personal nature, with potential investors in the company judging its viability on the basis of the reputation of individual partners. Credit was extended to a business according to the perceived trustworthiness of those who had 'lent their names' to it. Both the principle of unlimited liability, and the emphasis given to the personal character of the partners in evaluating an enterprise, are the product of an earlier, feudal economy, where ownership of landed property provided not only the greatest source of wealth, but a claim to honour and social identity through the combination of such substantial possessions as land and blood. The solidity of land provided the basis for a concept of 'personality' as grounded in real property, and a concomitant distrust of those involved with the abstractions of credit.

The form of enterprise organisation which emerged with the shift to liquid capital continued to rely upon this kind of anchorage in the form of personal responsibility. The partnership, as an economic enterprise, grew directly from the family household, and tied the entrepreneur and his family very closely to the fortunes of the business. Before the introduction of limited liability in the 1850s, business was founded upon the principle that each man would be responsible for the debts of his enterprise 'to the last shilling and the last acre', in the much-quoted words of the Chancellor, Lord Eldon. Unlimited liability yoked moral and economic responsibilities together to form a model of undivided identity, and a concept of the family, that were based upon aristocratic premises. But this policy severely restricted the raising of investment capital, and eventually led to the mid-century implementation of limited liability, whereby the investor and his dependants would be liable for the debts of an enterprise only to the extent of his original investment. As Andrew H. Miller has argued, the Joint Stock Companies Act of 1856 distinguished sharply between public and private spheres by separating economic and ethical identities, and limiting liability to the former.[18]

This development of increasingly impersonal forms of enterprise organisation is explored more fully in *Little Dorrit* (as I will show in chapter 4), which was published in the midst of the controversy in 1855–7; but some of the issues involved in the shift away from unlimited liability are raised in the close relationship between the family and firm in *Dombey and Son*. As an enterprise founded upon the principle of personal responsibility, Dombey and Son exemplifies the form of business described by Davidoff and Hall in which 'the personality of the entrepreneur, or partners *was* the firm'.[19] It is this constitutive relationship which strengthens the morally symbolic connection suggested in the narrative between the break-up of Mr Dombey's family and the failure of his firm, and which enables the fall of the House to function as a threat to his identity. In the event, it proves to be a fortunate fall, paving the way for his moral regeneration. Indeed, an important part of Mr Dombey's redemption is established through his insistence upon paying all creditors 'to the last farthing of his means' (684).

But the novel also insists upon the damaging effects of Mr Dombey's failure to separate his family from his firm. The title given to chapter III – 'In Which Mr Dombey, as a Man and as a Father, is Seen at the Head of the Home-Department' – continues the identification of family and firm begun in chapter I, and the early chapters go on to display the destructive effects that result from regarding familial ties in economic terms. Mr Dombey's inability to think of baby Paul in terms other than as the Son of the firm is repeatedly indicated: 'If there were a warm place in his frosty heart, his son occupied it; if its very hard surface could receive the impression of any image, the image of that son was there; though not so much as an infant, or as a boy, but as a grown man – the "Son" of the Firm' (76). Completely enmeshed in mercantile values, Mr Dombey's influence spreads everywhere as the language of business pervades the narrative of Paul's upbringing. The question of Paul's godparents is discussed in terms of the firm's independence from any extraneous human claims or ties – 'Paul and myself will be able, when the time comes, to hold our own – the House, in other words, will be able to hold its own, and maintain its own, and hand down its own of itself, and without any such common-place aids' (39), says Mr Dombey – and it is finally settled when Miss Tox is 'chosen and appointed to office' (40). Indeed, the marriage motive underlying Miss Tox's interest in the family is hinted at in commercial terms by the narrator's ironic reference to 'the nature of that lady's faltering investment in the Dombey Firm' (74).

The aristocratic model used to characterise Mr Dombey's firm as a dynasty is reinforced by the portrayal of his manager. Rather than demonstrating the thrusting energy of capitalist competition, Mr Dombey emerges as a curiously passive businessman who leaves all the aggressive work to his confidential agent, Mr Carker. Mr Dombey is a merchant prince, a 'pecuniary Duke of York' (7), who enjoys the wealth of possession rather than the risk of the commercial game itself. At his offices in the City, 'two degrees of descent' are interposed between Mr Dombey and 'the common world': 'Mr Carker, as Grand Vizier, inhabited the room that was nearest to the Sultan. Mr Morfin, as an officer of inferior state, inhabited the room that was nearest to the clerks' (143). Characterised as a sovereign of commerce, Mr Dombey's inherited position as Head of the Firm is contrasted with the voracious business activity of his manager, who works to establish himself through the exercise of his native wit and powers of surveillance. Mr Carker affects the demeanour of a feudal retainer in order to flatter his employer with a constant show of deference:

His manner towards Mr Dombey was deeply conceived and perfectly expressed. He was familiar with him, in the very extremity of his sense of the distance between them. 'Mr Dombey, to a man in your position from a man in mine, there is no show of subservience compatible with the transaction of business between us, that I should think sufficient.' (144)

He is variously described throughout the novel as Mr Dombey's 'faithful friend and servant' (306), a 'mere dependant of Mr Dombey's' (440), and as his 'confidential agent' (474). Mr Dombey is referred to as Carker's 'icy patron' (320), who is 'apt to assert his chieftainship' (328) over his manager and to treat him with 'condescension and patronage' (497). Mr Carker feigns gratitude for the regard bestowed upon him by his great employer, but his obsequiousness is all too apparent in the excess of his humility: after purchasing 'a few poor rarities of flowers for Mrs Dombey' in chapter xxxi for example, he humbly explains to his patron, 'A man in my position, and so distinguished to be invited here, is proud to offer some homage in acknowledgment of his vassalage' (371).

Far from exemplifying the impersonal business relation between employer and employee associated with the development of industrial capitalism, the relation between Mr Dombey and his manager draws upon an earlier model of personal service associated with the aristocratic household, where loyal retainers, as well as kin, might be considered part of the family. The peculiarly personal nature of their relationship is demonstrated most remarkably in Mr Dombey's eventual 'employment' of Carker as a go-between to demand Edith's submission to her husband's imperious will (the quotation marks indicate that the concept of employment assumes a distinction between public and private life that is put into question by Mr Dombey's action). The insult offered to his wife by this mode of proceeding depends upon Carker's nominal status as Dombey's 'paid servant' (525); but what permits the very suggestion of this scheme is the ambiguously familial character of the relation between patron and retainer. When Mr Carker disingenuously observes to Mr Dombey that 'my defined and recognised connexion with your affairs is merely of a business character', he prompts his employer to the grand acknowledgment that he is more than a paid employee:

'Carker,' said Mr Dombey, 'I am sensible that you do not limit your –'
'Service,' suggested his smiling entertainer.
'No; I prefer to say your regard,' observed Mr Dombey; very sensible, as he said so, that he was paying him a handsome and flattering compliment, 'to our mere business relations.' (496)

The personal service exacted from his manager by Mr Dombey according to the model of aristocratic patronage not only serves to demonstrate his overweening pride, but also links him to an earlier feudal economy and helps to suggest his demise as a merchant prince in an era of entrepreneurial capitalism. Throughout the 1840s, the proponents of free trade were increasingly brought into conflict with the older mercantile monopolies in their push for the removal of protectionism. Dickens himself supported the repeal of the Corn Laws in the *Daily News*, the newspaper he launched in January 1846. The National Anti-Corn Law League, he wrote,

is not a creation of certain wealthy and discontented manufacturers; it is a symptom of the condition of society; a decisive symptom, indicating transition; and the legislative note of that transition will be the abolition of the Corn Laws. The wheels have revolved; the hands point to the hour, and the clock must strike.[20]

As Suvendrini Perera has pointed out, the East India Company – that classic monopolist enterprise whose House is located 'just round the corner' (27) from the offices of Dombey and Son – would be dismantled in 1858, signifying 'the movement of capital from its overtly expansionist mercantile phase to the free trade strategies of triumphant industrialism'.[21]

The calls made by political economists for the abandonment of a system they saw as hostile to the freedom of enterprise were based upon a rejection of paternalism. Much of the argument against the restriction upon forms of commercial association resulting from the principle of unlimited liability revolved around the liberal objection to state intervention. The *Westminster Review* responded to the claim that government should direct the middle and working classes in the investment of their savings: 'They are grown men and not children, and self-government, not paternal government, is what they require – freedom of action, not maternal leading-strings.'[22] Much of Mr Dombey's greatness stems from his capacity to patronise his subordinates and show a lordly beneficence when his favour is sought by them: he condescends to reward Miss Tox by allowing her to become Paul's godmother, and when Walter Gay seeks a loan to release his uncle from debt, Mr Dombey permits Paul 'to begin to be Dombey and Son' (112) by lending the money to Walter. The patronage and paternalism that characterise Mr Dombey's behaviour eventually lead to his financial undoing at the hands of his manager, who has 'treasured up, at interest, for years' (646) every proud word and look from his patron. The description of the fall of the old mercantile firm of Dombey and Son can be read, then, as a contribution to the debates over free trade and commercial liability, with their association of protectionism and paternalism.

However, this pattern of economic transformation in the novel is interrupted by the remarkable anomaly of the business owned by the Ships' Instrument-maker. Introduced in the same chapter which details the location of Dombey and Son at the hub of mercantile activity, the Wooden Midshipman is described as an antiquated business that has been left behind in the wake of rapid economic change. Its owner, Uncle Sol, laments his own obsolescence:

'When that uniform was worn,' [he tells Walter] pointing out towards the little Midshipman, 'then indeed, fortunes were to be made, and were made. But competition, competition – new invention, new invention – alteration, alteration – the world's gone past me ... Tradesmen are not the same as they used to be, apprentices are not the same, business is not the same, business commodities are not the same. Seven-eighths of my stock is old-fashioned. I am an old-fashioned man in an old-fashioned shop, in a street that is not the same as I remember it.' (32–3)

Like Mr Dombey, Uncle Sol identifies himself with his business. But the commodities he deals in are the work of his own hands, and he lives on the premises. The old-fashioned character of his business provides a foil to the bustling commercial activity associated with the firm of Dombey and Son in the early part of the novel. Indeed, the bankruptcy of Uncle Sol provides the occasion for the exhibition of Mr Dombey's greatness described above, as he lends the money to Walter to pay off the debt.

However, despite the fact that no customer ever makes a purchase from the shop throughout the entire novel, the business survives, and at the end of the novel, Captain Cuttle is taken into the enterprise as partner with Sol Gills, and the little Wooden Midshipman is newly painted. It seems that some undisclosed investments belonging to the ships' instrument-maker obviate the necessity for his shop to be commercially viable:

Not another stroke of business does the Midshipman achieve beyond his usual easy trade. But they do say, in a circuit of some half-mile round the blue umbrella in Leadenhall Market, that some of Mr Gills' old investments are coming out wonderfully well; and that instead of being behind the time in those respects, as he supposed, he was, in truth, a little before it, and had to wait the fulness of the time and the design. (731)

The wish-fulfilment shown in such an outcome is hard to deny. But criticism of its implausibility misses the point being made in the novel about the value of domesticity and the importance, therefore, of separating family and economic life. As Robert Clark explains, the Wooden Midshipman is a utopia 'where economy does not intrude'[23] and so it is not surprising that Sol Gills makes his money elsewhere. In some ways, the Wooden Midshipman looks back to the old-fashioned business of the Cheeryble brothers in *Nicholas Nickleby*, who spend most of their time engaged in charitable transactions apparently made possible by the income of a counting-house that thrives without any evidence of entrepreneurial energy. But while the mercantile activity of the Cheerybles is made benign by their old-fashioned but scrupulous fulfilment of 'feudal' responsibilities, the Wooden Midshipman derives its utopian character from the formation of separate spheres for family and economic life. The provision of a space free from the turbulence of capitalist activity aligns the Wooden Midshipman with the home of the Toodles, and is part of the novel's concern to show the restoration of the middle-class family as a haven of privacy.

The nexus of family and economic life is also explored in the portrayal of Mr Dombey's marriage to Edith Granger in the novel. His absolute identification of the family with the firm finds a parallel in his purchase of Edith, which involves a similar undermining of the boundary between the home and the marketplace. The commodification of Edith is yet another example of the extension of economic activity into the private realm. Like young Paul, whose destiny as the Son of the Firm has deprived him of a childhood, Edith has been subjected to an 'unnatural' upbringing by her rapacious mother, which has turned her into an object for sale in the marriage market. Since Mrs Skewton has had almost nothing else to live upon but 'the reputation of some diamonds, and her family connections' (242), her daughter's marketing has been the object of all her 'pains and labour' (364). Having been 'hawked and vended here and there, until the last grain of self-respect is dead within me', Edith tells her mother 'There is no slave in a market: there is no horse in a fair: so shown and offered and examined and paraded, Mother, as I have been, for ten shameful years' (333). All of her accomplishments have been acquired with a view to enhancing her exchange value, and that 'Colossus of commerce' (305), Mr Dombey, is her appropriate buyer. Belonging to an impoverished but aristocratic family, Edith offers Dombey the prospect of connecting himself with noble blood, and she is blunt in acknowledging his purchase:

> He sees me at the auction, and he thinks it well to buy me. Let him! When he came to view me – perhaps to bid – he required to see the roll of my accomplishments. I gave it to him. When he would have me show one of them, to justify his purchase to his men, I require of him to say which he demands, and I exhibit it. I will do no more. He makes the purchase of his own will, and with his own sense of its worth, and the power of his money; and I hope it may never disappoint him. (333–4)

Mr Dombey's purchase of Edith as a wife invokes a conception of female subjectivity which opposes the aristocratic woman to her middle-class, domestic counterpart. The aristocratic woman is a creature of display, whose value inheres in her social position and her serviceability in providing an heir. As Major Bagstock summarises her worth, Edith has 'beauty, blood, and talent' (315). The fact that she has already borne a son and is now 'not quite thirty' (244) augurs well for her reproduction of a new son, and Mr Dombey thinks 'no worse of her' for the fierce pride she displays: in fact, 'It flattered him to picture to himself, this proud and stately woman doing the honours of his house, and chilling his guests after his own manner. The dignity of Dombey and Son would be heightened and maintained, indeed, in such hands' (361).

In her pride, however, Edith retains a shameful consciousness of her objectification and a yearning for autonomy that cause her self-division, and reveal the way in which the ideology of separate spheres is implicated in the constitution of female subjectivity. While she submits to the financial arrangement that is her marriage, she does so refusing to accept any pretence about the nature of the transaction. Her contempt for the whole process of her commodification is clear, and the narrator empha-sises the self-division it entails: 'It was a remarkable characteristic of this lady's beauty that it appeared to vaunt and assert itself without her aid, and against her will. She knew that she was beautiful: it was impossible that it could be otherwise: but she seemed with her own pride to defy her very self' (246). Again, at the end of chapter xxx, on the eve of her wedding, the narrator describes Edith pacing up and down her room 'with an averted head, as if she would avoid the sight of her own fair person, and divorce herself from its companionship' (366). Edith is continually shown to maintain an 'air of opposition' towards herself, and this self-alienation is directly attributed to her commodification. Ashamed of the self that Mr Dombey has bought, her loathing and humiliation are vividly expressed in gestures of self-mutilation that spurn the signs of her position. For example, in chapter XL, entitled 'Domestic Relations', Edith sits before her imperious husband, 'still looking at him fixedly – turning a bracelet round and round upon her arm; not winding it about with a light, womanly touch, but pressing and dragging it over the smooth skin, until the white limb showed a bar of red' (473–4). Ironically, self-mortification is the only form of defiance available to Edith once she has internalised the values of a world that traffics in women. Far from embodying the internal consistency held to be an essential characteristic of female nature according to the middle-class ideology of separate spheres, Edith is self-divided as a consequence of her 'unnatural' upbringing at the hands of the ancient Cleopatra. Her commodification precludes her development of the kind of female subjectivity associated with the ideal domestic woman – the woman who is valued for her inner moral and spiritual worth, rather than her beauty and social position.

The connection between forms of female subjectivity and sphere ideology is reinforced by the parallel example of Alice Marwood and her mother. Like Edith, Alice's self-contempt is expressed in masochistic gestures of defiance. When she is comforted by the gentle Harriet, unknown sister of her seducer, in chapter XXXIII, she spurns the beauty that once gave her value: 'She held up her hair roughly with both hands; seizing it as if she would have torn it out; then, threw it down again, and flung it back as though it were a heap of serpents' (406). The prostitute is the figure who incarnates the transgression of the boundary between the family and the economy, between private and public life, in Victorian middle-class culture, because she turns sex into a trade. She is the example *par excellence* of the extension of the cash nexus into the home, selling herself to those with enough money to buy. Alice's 'wretchedness and ruin' are attributed to her upbringing by 'good Mrs Brown', who 'thought to make a sort of property' (629) of her daughter. Like Edith, she is another instance 'of mothers bringing up their daughters wrong, and evil coming of it' (630). Both daughters endure the transformation of their youth and beauty into saleable goods, and the parallel between them is highlighted by their hidden blood tie and by the role of Carker as the common agent of their ruin. The connection between Alice and Edith reveals the underside of commercial expansion and exploitation in the novel, as the fallen woman is shown to be a victim of imperial trade.

Edith's marriage is cast as a form of prostitution in which she has suffered herself 'to be sold, as infamously as any woman with a halter round her neck is sold in any marketplace' (639), and her near-seduction by Carker, the manager of the firm, is the logical development of a process of ruthless economic competition in which women are traded as commodities. Significantly, Mr Dombey first becomes aware of her resistance to his domination when she refuses to exert herself as hostess to entertain the 'sundry eastern magnates' (429) he has got together to celebrate their late nuptials. Alice's fate involves her transportation for robbery, and thus continues the pattern of extraordinary sea voyages which bring miraculous returns that is also traced in the lives of Walter Gay and Sol Gills. Like Magwitch in *Great Expectations*, however, Alice returns to the metropolis with a desire for retribution, and her story disturbs the optimistic narrative of imperial adventure associated with the success of Walter Gay. While Walter may live out the Whittington legend and form a family at the end of the novel with his master's daughter, and while Carker is killed, the closure of Alice's story with her penitence and death does not resolve the problem of her victimisation. The removal of Alice and Edith from the narrative paves the way for Florence to restore harmony through a reconstitution of the middle-class family; but the very failure of the narrative to assimilate these 'dark women' indicates the limits of familial ideology even as their deviance serves to highlight the virtues of the domestic woman.

Florence awakens Edith to the vestiges of a self that she retains despite her transformation into an object of exchange. She sees in Florence the woman she might have been, complaining to Mrs Skewton, 'Oh Mother, Mother, if you had but left me to my natural heart when I too was a girl – a younger girl than Florence – how different I might have been!' (365). Florence is characterised by her constancy throughout the novel. She is always patient and infinitely loving, as Mr Dombey comes to recognise when he has been chastened by the failure of his firm: 'He thought of her, as she had been that night when he and his bride came home. He thought of her as she had been, in all the home-events of the abandoned house. He thought, now, that of all around him, she alone had never changed' (702). Florence's constancy offsets the effects of the rapid change that is associated with industrial capitalism. She embodies an unchanging child-like innocence that represents the antithesis to the fallen adult world of sexuality and economic exploitation. Like Oliver Twist, when he is re-captured by Nancy and Sikes, she is momentarily threatened with defilement when she is lost in the city and caught by 'good Mrs Brown', who takes her clothes and dresses her in the garb of a pauper. Also like Oliver, however, Florence's disguise cannot conceal her true identity, and she is rescued in romance fashion by Walter Gay. Her goodness is held to be an essential part of her nature. It transcends the vicissitudes of experience, much as Oliver's innate goodness survives in the midst of London's underworld. But Florence's goodness takes the form of feminine devotion, and the naturalisation of her ideal femininity is an important part of the normative power of the middle-class family in the novel.

Florence's natural innocence and unremitting dedication to her roles as daughter and sister mark her virtue as the ideal domestic woman. Unlike Edith, who is tormented by self-division as a consequence of her complicity in blurring the distinction between home and marketplace, Florence shows the internal consistency held to define female nature according to the ideology of separate spheres. She undergoes no development through the course of the novel and is passive in the face of a range of experiences which merely serve to confirm her original nature. She embodies the virtues associated with the middle-class feminine ideal – self-sacrificing devotion, dependency, loyalty, and purity – and points towards an alternative source of value in a world obsessed with commercial gain. Her transcendent goodness protects her from the taint of Edith's fall,· preserving an ideal of female nature that derives from the ideology of domesticity and that triumphs in the restoration of the middle-class family at the end of the novel.

Florence's embodiment of the domestic ideal is initially demonstrated through her relationship with Paul. Rejected by her father, she devotes all her love and affection to her brother, showing a capacity for sisterly self-sacrifice that links her with Harriet Carker in the novel. While Paul is a baby, Florence is employed to amuse and enliven him; later, when Paul is sent to school at Dr Blimber's, she gets Susan to obtain copies of the books he is studying so that she might 'patiently assist him through so much as they could anticipate together, of his next week's work' (139). Her selfless and constant devotion as a sister parallels Harriet Carker's love for her ruined brother, John. Harriet is described as the 'slight, small, patient figure, neatly dressed in homely stuffs, and indicating nothing but the dull, household virtues, that have so little in common with the received idea of heroism and greatness' (399), who chose to accompany her brother in his shame to the outskirts of London, where they establish a house together that bespeaks her embodiment of the domestic ideal: 'It is a poor, small house, barely and sparely furnished, but very clean; and there is even an attempt to decorate it, shown in the homely flowers trained about the porch and in the narrow garden' (398).

Florence is unable to give full expression to her domestic virtues because of her repulsion by her father. But her desire to fulfil the role of dutiful and devoted daughter is shown in her gaze of longing at the family which occupies the house across the street. The eldest daughter attracts most of her attention:

The elder child remained with her father when the rest had gone away, and made his tea for him – happy little housekeeper she was then! – and sat conversing with him, sometimes at the window, sometimes in the room, until the candles came. He made her his companion, though she was some years younger than Florence; and she could be as staid and pleasantly demure with her little book or work-box, as a woman. (209)

Whether Florence's observation of the elder child's ministrations teaches her the arts of housewifery, or whether her possession of this domestic wisdom is inherited along with her native goodness, when she runs away to the Wooden Midshipman's shop in chapter XLIX, her skills are immediately apparent. Captain Cuttle is astonished 'at the quiet housewifery of Florence in assisting to clear the table, arrange the parlour, and sweep up the hearth' (571). Even more remarkable than these domestic feats, however, is her ability to mix 'a perfect glass of grog for him, unasked, and set it at his elbow' (571) and then to light the pipe he has just filled. Having daintily performed these daughterly offices, Florence resumes her place on the old sofa to enjoy the domestic bliss of Captain Cuttle's cosy hearth.

The snug retreat provided by the Wooden Midshipman recalls the warmth of the Toodles' hearth, where Polly presides as the apple-cheeked icon of nurturing and maternal devotion. In vivid contrast, the coldness and sterility of Mr Dombey's house are continually emphasised throughout the novel – most memorably, perhaps, in the chilling episode of Paul's christening. The guests at this affair return from the church to enjoy 'a cold collation, set forth in a cold pomp of glass and silver, and looking more like a dead dinner lying in state than a social refreshment' (48). Later in the novel, when Mr Dombey returns to London with his new wife, he holds what is ironically referred to as a 'Housewarming' party, at which *his* guests disagree with Mrs Dombey's guests, and the distance between the 'happy pair' is remarked by the narrator: 'the long plateau of precious metal frosted, separating him from Mrs Dombey, whereon frosted Cupids offered scentless flowers to each of them, was allegorical to see' (431). The house itself provides a symbolic comment on the married couple who reside within it, as the narrator comments ironically upon the stateliness and elegance of its appointments: 'what an altar to the Household Gods is raised up here!' (418)

Dickens frequently draws upon the image of the hearth as a potent symbol of the Victorian middle-class family. When Mr Dombey's failure as a father, husband and businessman culminates in his bankruptcy, his ruin is described in scenes which show the hearth being violated by brokers and other strangers:[24]

Then, all day long, there is a retinue of mouldy gigs and chaise-carts in the street; and herds of shabby vampires, Jew and Christian, over-run the house, sounding the plate-glass mirrors with their knuckles, striking discordant octaves on the Grand Piano, drawing wet forefingers over the pictures, breathing on the blades of the best dinner-knives, punching the squabs of chairs and sofas with their dirty fists, touzling the feather-beds, opening and shutting all the drawers, balancing the silver spoons and forks, looking into the very threads of the drapery and linen, and disparaging everything. There is not a secret place in the whole house. (696)

The sense of humiliation and exposure here is acute. The physical recoil from prying strangers is vividly expressed in the defilement suggested by the 'wet forefingers' and the 'breathing' of the 'vampires'. The auction of household possessions that follows from Mr Dombey's bankruptcy is clearly a violation of privacy, but the suggestions of desecration and pillage that emerge from the description owe their potency to the middle-class ideology of the family and its symbolic focus on the sacred hearth.

As an embodiment of the virtues associated with the domestic angel of middle-class ideology, Florence has the power to restore her father to a cosy hearth, and her service as surrogate daughter to Captain Cuttle foreshadows the role she will eventually play in presiding over a domestic haven that incorporates Mr Dombey, along with all the inhabitants of the Wooden Midshipman. Her first reward comes with the return of Walter Gay, whose dedication to hard work and self-improvement has enabled him to survive his testing at sea. He upholds the legendary example of Dick Whittington by proposing marriage to his master's daughter. Florence has always associated Walter with her dead brother, Paul, but her adherence to this quasi-sibling relationship is no impediment to their union. In chapter XVIII, even as she is sheltered within Walter's arm and weeps 'with happiness in such a refuge', Florence continues to think of Paul: 'The more she clung to it, the more the dear dead child was in her thoughts' (661). Florence marries her surrogate brother, and they give birth, in the course of time, to a second-generation sister and brother whom they name, not surprisingly, Florence and Paul.

The emphasis given to the sibling tie in these relationships is in keeping with the value placed upon childhood and upon constancy to the ideals associated with it in the novel.[25] Mr Dombey's redemption is effected through his rediscovery of a childlike state in which innocence is preserved, enabling him to enter the enchanted world of the Wooden Midshipman. But the prominence given to surrogate relationships of various kinds in the novel is in itself a significant feature of the operation of domestic ideology. The prevalence of surrogate family relationships is truly remarkable: Polly Toodle acts as surrogate mother to Florence and Paul, Sol Gills and Captain Cuttle act as surrogate fathers to Walter and Florence respectively, Florence is a surrogate mother for Paul, Walter is a surrogate brother for Florence, Edith is a surrogate mother for Florence (for a time), Miss Tox becomes a surrogate aunt to the Toodle family, and Cousin Feenix announces his intention of becoming a 'father' to Edith in the closing pages of the novel (729). Many of these familial substitutions reveal gaps or failures in the family. Obviously, the number of surrogate familial relationships in which Florence is involved is a sign of her emotional deprivation and rejection by her father. But the very formation of these surrogate relationships affirms the strength of the domestic ideal, and defines it as a form of family available to everyone. In contrast to the aristocratic model of the family associated with Mr Dombey's dynastic ambitions, the values of domesticity find expression in a range of substitute relationships that are shown to cut across class divisions in the novel. In this way, the ties of blood are shown to matter much less than the affective bonds of the middle-class family, which have been naturalised as universal human values.

The importance placed upon surrogate familial relationships in *Dombey and Son* is an index to the narrative's investment in the middle-class ideology of domesticity. The reconstitution of the family at the end of the novel follows upon the failure of the firm, and the removal of Carker, Edith and Alice from the narrative – through either death or exile. Mr Dombey's bankruptcy enables him to renounce the commercial world and embrace the values of the family hearth. His moral regeneration is achieved through a recognition of the domestic angel at his side, who has never flagged in her devotion to him: 'Unchanged still. Of all the world, unchanged' (705). The contrast between the rapid transformations of the marketplace and the consistency and stability of the home arranged by Florence is clear. Rather than reconciling the realms of commerce and domesticity, Florence works to achieve their separation, so that the sacredness of the hearth may be protected. Mr Dombey's fatal error throughout has been his failure to separate family and firm according to the requirements of domestic ideology. In his pride, he has clung to a dynastic ambition which has hastened the death of his son and finally brought about his own ruin, as he is driven by the desire 'to swell the reputation of the House for vast resources, and to exhibit it in magnificent contrast to other merchants' houses' (627). In this way, the novel aligns the bankruptcy of mercantilism with the demise of a concept of the family that is based on aristocratic premises. Genealogy gives way to domesticity in the resolution of the narrative, and the middle-class home that centres upon Florence is represented as a vision of family that supposedly transcends the divisions of class and gender.

The wish-fulfilment that directs this transcendent outcome is apparent, and the critique of mercantilism I have traced in the identification of Mr Dombey's family and firm is not sustained in the commercial fortunes of Walter Gay, whose return with Florence from their successful venture to China apparently coincides with a restoration of prosperity that is based on trade. Walter is appointed to a 'post of great trust and confidence at home', and he is said to be busily engaged in building 'an Edifice' that is 'perhaps to equal, perhaps excel' the old House of Dombey and Son (733). Presumably, he will not make the mistake of appropriating his family to the business, but will instead respect the privacy of his domestic hearth. After all, it is the maintenance of such a preserve that supposedly legitimates competition in the marketplace and mitigates the associated effects of self-alienation. However, none of these economic details is of major interest to Dickens in the closing chapters of his novel, which focus instead on the celebration of domestic values and the enchanted return to the innocence of childhood. Like *Oliver Twist*, *Dombey and Son* ends with the recovery of an apparently timeless realm that is sheltered from the vicissitudes of economic and social life. It is a realm in which the values of the middle-class family are generalised as transcendent ideals, and in this way, both novels contribute to the middle-class ascendancy that characterises Dickens's representation of the family in his later fiction.

CHAPTER 3

Dickens, Christmas and the family

During the 1840s, while his serial fiction began to show an increasing complexity in its analysis of contemporary society, Dickens embarked upon a new literary venture – the Christmas Book – which was to confirm his association with the middle-class family even further. Christmas is the great domestic festival we associate with Victorian society and Dickens was its specialist. Writing in *Blackwood's Magazine* in 1871, Margaret Oliphant described him as 'the first [writer] to find out the immense spiritual power of the Christmas turkey'.[1] Her wry comment refers to the kind of annual family festivity described in the sketch, 'A Christmas Dinner', published in Dickens's earliest work. Its narrator asks: 'Who can be insensible to the outpourings of good feeling, and the honest interchange of affectionate attachment, which abound at this season of the year? A Christmas family-party! We know nothing in nature more delightful! There seems a magic in the very name of Christmas.'[2] The narrator gives an account of the grand preparations for the event – the purchase of the bird, stirring of the pudding, and cleaning of the table ware – before the day itself is described, with its family reunions, games, songs, stories, and magnificent dinner of turkey, mince-pies, pudding, plum-cake and wine. As the annual ritual systematically developed for the expression of the middle-class ideology of the family, Christmas came to occupy a special place in Victorian culture, and the extent to which Dickens's name became synonymous with the celebration of Christmas during the nineteenth century can be gauged from the obituary tribute recorded by Theodore Watts-Dunton, who was walking down Drury Lane on the day that Dickens died and overheard a costermonger's girl exclaim, 'Dickens dead? ... Then will Father Christmas die too?'[3]

According to Watts-Dunton, the London populace had come to regard Dickens as 'the spirit of Christmas incarnate: as being, in a word, Father Christmas himself'.[4] As J. W. T. Ley wrote in the Christmas issue of the

Dickensian in 1906, 'Dickens and Christmas are well-nigh synonymous words; they are, at any rate, inseparable. Beyond question, it was Charles Dickens who gave us Christmas as we understand it to-day.'[5] G. K. Chesterton is often credited with (or blamed for) the promotion of a 'Christmassy Dickens'. Such twentieth-century tributes betray a glow of nostalgia. But Dickens's integral role in the formation of the Victorian middle-class Christmas was also acknowledged by his contemporaries. As Forster wrote in summarising the significance of *A Christmas Carol*, 'What was marked in him to the last was manifest now. He had identified himself with Christmas fancies. Its life and spirits, its humour in riotous abundance, of right belonged to him.'[6]

An 1869 reviewer defined Dickens's 'theory of life' as 'an expansion of the idea of Christmas':

It is a gospel of geniality that Mr Dickens sets himself to preach; the feelings and sympathies supposed to be evoked by the annual holiday are to be the ruling principles of life, the model keeper of Christmas, our guide and example. Joviality and high living; benevolence, good humour, and good fellowship – *sic itur ad astra*. There should also be a sprinkling of tender regrets for the dead and the absent – just enough to subdue part of the picture with a pleasing shade of darker colouring. Such is Mr Dickens's Utopia.[7]

Carlyle had made a similar point in objecting to Dickens's 'theory of life [as] entirely wrong': 'He thought men ought to be buttered up, and the world made soft and accommodating for them, and all sorts of fellows have turkey for their Christmas dinner.'[8] Dickens explicitly identified himself with this kind of philosophy in 1845 when he described his plans for a new periodical which was to be characterised by its 'Carol philosophy, cheerful views, sharp anatomisation of humbug, jolly good temper . . . and a vein of glowing, hearty, generous, mirthful, beaming reference in everything to Home, and Fireside.'[9] And in his well-known study of the social novel, Louis Cazamian sums up Dickens's outlook as 'la Philosophie de Noel'.[10]

As Carlyle's comment indicates, approval of Dickens's Christmas ideal was not universal, and a number of contemporary commentators criticised his secularisation of the season. The American reviewer, Edwin Whipple, wrote: 'He has put so much eating and drinking into [his Christmas] stories . . . but then he Christianises eating and drinking, and contrives to make the stomach in some odd way an organ of the soul . . . The glutton idolizes meat and drink; Dickens idealizes them.'[11] Whipple's remark acknowledges Dickens's ability to endow secular activities with a revitalising power that is akin to spiritual communion. Ruskin, however, observed that Dickens's Christmas 'meant mistletoe and pudding – neither resurrection from dead, nor rising of new stars, nor teaching of wise men, nor shepherds'.[12] Notwithstanding such criticisms, Dickens's reputation as the prophet of the season spread. Clearly, if Christmas was central to his work and outlook, Dickens's fiction was equally significant in shaping and popularising the Victorian Christmas as an institution, and analysis of this reciprocal relationship is crucial for any consideration of the representation of the family in his fiction.

'A Christmas Dinner' begins with the lament for a lost tradition that was commonly voiced in the early decades of the nineteenth century:

There are people who will tell you that Christmas is not to them what it used to be; that each succeeding Christmas has found some cherished hope, or happy prospect, of the year before, dimmed or passed away; that the present only serves to remind them of reduced circumstances and straitened incomes – of the feasts they once bestowed on hollow friends, and of the cold looks that meet them now, in adversity and misfortune. (220)

Dickens's narrator goes on to repudiate 'such dismal reminiscences' by regenerating the spirit of Christmas in a new urban setting, thus marking the shift from the old English Christmas (that was largely memory by the beginning of the nineteenth century) to the great Victorian domestic festival. Despite the sense of ancient tradition and the nostalgic spirit that invest observance of Christmas in the nineteenth and twentieth centuries, its celebration as the major family festival we know is actually a modern development. Leigh Hunt wrote a series of essays in the second and third decades of the nineteenth century on 'Christmas and Other Old National Merry-Makings Considered With Reference to the Nature of the Age, and to the Desirableness of Their Revival', in which he lamented a decline in the keeping of Christmas. In 1817, he wrote, 'Christmas is a dreary business, compared with what it used to be in old times; and scarcely one of the other national holidays is alive.'[13] He attributes this decay to three causes: the 'commercial and jobbing spirit', the growth of a 'superstition' which mistakes merriment for a vice, and a 'habit of trying everything by the test of common sense and utility'.[14] Hunt exhorts his readers to repair the nation's loss of the 'amiable title of Merry Old England' by reviving the spirit of Christmas:

Stir up your firesides, and your smiles, and your walks abroad; and consent to enjoy the happiness, which you have long been instinctively aware is not to be enjoyed by gain, or gloominess, or mere bustling, or shallow and grave egotisms, or worldliness of any sort, or, (as the secret of *most* people's religion may be called) *other*-worldliness. Every new pleasure added to your Christmas which you did not enjoy before, – every new and kind sociality, – every innocent enjoyment (and innocence has a much wider range of enjoyment, than ignorance would think, or malevolence would give it), – every additional dance, or song, or piece of music, – every fresh thing done to give a joy to a fellow-creature, – every festivity set a going among friends, or servants, or the village, – every fresh grappling with the hale pleasures of winter-time, – every meeting of the country-breezes out of doors, – every rub of one's own hands, and shake of another's, in-doors, – will be so much gain to the spirit and real happiness of the age.[15]

The beginnings of the Victorian revival of Christmas as a festival whose keeping is enjoined by its social purpose are evident here, and in subsequent articles Hunt describes a variety of customs peculiar to Christmas throughout the ages but 'now obsolete' in order to promote the festival as a contribution to social reform. These customs include the playing of 'rustic games', the singing of 'jolie carols', and the provision of a magnificent feast by the country squire for his tenants and neighbours.[16]

The nostalgic note distinguishing Hunt's vision of Christmas was also conspicuous in other early nineteenth-century representations of the festival. The Christmas Canto of Sir Walter Scott's *Marmion*,[17] first published in 1808, presents a similar ideal of Merry Old England, with its archaic language vividly recalling the 'wassel', 'plum-porridge', and 'blithesome din' of the carols. A year earlier, Robert Southey had remarked of Christmas, 'All persons say how differently this season was observed in their fathers' days, and speak of old ceremonies and old festivities as things which are obsolete.'[18] Even as late as 1842, Tennyson was lamenting the lost glory of the old-fashioned Christmas in the epic frame composed for 'Morte D'Arthur':

> The host, and I sat round the wassail-bowl,
> Then half-way ebb'd; and there we held a talk,
> How all the old honor had from Christmas gone,
> Or gone or dwindled down to some odd games
> In some odd nooks like this . . .[19]

But perhaps the most influential of the early nineteenth-century depictions of what G. K. Chesterton was later to call the 'feudal Christmas' was the account of the celebrations at Bracebridge Hall written by the American novelist, Washington Irving. His *Sketch Book of Geoffrey Crayon, Gent.* (1820) comprised a collection of tales and essays that contained a large section on English Christmas customs, later reprinted separately as *Bracebridge Hall* or *Old Christmas*. The best-known edition is that illustrated by Randolph Caldecott. Irving's nostalgic portrait is written in praise of a lost England, whose passing is observed with particular sorrow through his American eyes:

The English . . . were, in former days, particularly observant of the religious and social rites of Christmas. It is inspiring to read even the dry details which some antiquarians have given of the quaint humours, the burlesque pageants, the complete abandonment to mirth and good-fellowship, with which this festival was celebrated. It seemed to throw open every door, and unlock every heart. It brought the peasant and the peer together, and blended all ranks in one warm generous flow of joy and kindness. The old halls of castles and manor-houses resounded with the harp and the Christmas carol, and their ample boards groaned under the weight of hospitality. Even the poorest cottage welcomed the festive season with green decorations of bay and holly – the cheerful fire glanced its rays through the lattice, inviting the passenger to raise the latch, and join the gossip knot huddled round the hearth, beguiling the long evening with legendary jokes and oft-told Christmas tales.[20]

The separate reprinting of the Christmas sections from Irving's *Sketch Book* is in itself important evidence of the transformation the English Christmas underwent throughout the Victorian period. From an occasion 'scarcely worth mention' (according to Leigh Hunt) in the 1820s, when winter feasts and Christmas-like rituals took place sporadically and locally anywhere between All Hallow's Day on 1 November and Candlemas on 2 February, it became the single most important national festival in England and the major celebration of the family in Victorian culture. Clearly, a host of complex social and economic changes in the nineteenth century contributed to this transformation of the English Christmas. But all of these changes worked towards the evolution of the middle-class character of the festival. It is, of course, no mere coincidence that the rise of the domestic ideal, and the transformation of the English Christmas in the nineteenth century, were cultural developments that took place together. The rituals adopted to celebrate the season reflected middle-class values and preoccupations – including privacy, respectability, the importance of childhood and of family unity – but in such a way as to disguise the social and historical specificity of their origin. In

the words of a song of 'Christmas Mirth' printed in a broadside of
1823,

> This is the day that merits praise,
> Beyond all others in the year;
> It comfort gives, to all that lives,
> As well the poor man as the Peer.[21]

The values of Christmas provided the new 'truth' of goodwill and fellowship that could seem to unite individuals across class lines, healing the
divisions and conflicts between them. The discourse of Christmas
pervaded a variety of social forms and practices – holidays, songs, feasts,
gift-giving, games, decorations, religious observances and entertainment
– and it was arguably the most successful vehicle and expression of
middle-class cultural hegemony.

The extent to which the shape and popularity of the Victorian
Christmas might be attributed to the influence of Dickens can only be
conjectured. However, evidence of the growing importance of Christmas
gathers in the two decades which saw the publication of William Sandys's
Selection of Christmas Carols, Ancient and Modern in 1833 (the first significant
collection of old carols),[22] the publication of *Sketches by Boz* in 1836 and
Pickwick Papers in 1837, the introduction of 'that pretty German toy, the
Christmas tree' (as Dickens called it) by Prince Albert at Windsor in 1840,
the publication of *A Christmas Carol* and designing of the first English
Christmas card in 1843, and the invention of the Christmas cracker in
1846. The contrast between the representation of Christmas in *Pickwick*
and the *Carol* displays the process of transformation.

For the instalment of *Pickwick* published at the end of December 1836,
Dickens wrote 'A Good-Humoured Christmas Chapter, Containing an
Account of a Wedding, and Some Other Sports Beside, Which Although
in Their Way, Even as Good Customs as Marriage Itself, are Not Quite so
Religiously Kept Up, in These Degenerate Times'. The chapter begins
with reflections about 'the season of hospitality, merriment, and open-
heartedness ... Happy, happy Christmas, that can win us back to the
delusions of our childish days, that can recal [*sic*] to the old man the
pleasures of his youth, and transport the sailor and the traveller, thousands
of miles away, back to his own fire-side and his quiet home!' (334–5). But
the lament of the decline in the keeping of Christmas, incorporated in the
chapter title, echoes the regrets expressed by Leigh Hunt and Washington
Irving in the 1820s. Dickens later acknowledged his debt to Irving, and

their close friendship was an important consideration in his decision to visit America in 1842. He kept all that Irving wrote upon his bookshelves, he averred, and 'in his thoughts and in his heart of hearts'.[23] Indeed, one reviewer of *Pickwick* commented with asperity that 'Wardle's Manor House, with its merry doings at Christmas-time, is neither more nor less than Bracebridge Hall at second-hand'.[24]

In this fictionalisation of Christmas, Dickens focusses upon the 'invariable customs' of Dingley Dell on Christmas Eve. These begin with the assembly of the family in the kitchen – a custom 'observed by old Wardle's forefathers from time immemorial' (350) and designed to eliminate class differences in keeping with the spirit of the season. However, the narrator's reference to the antiquity of this ritual, and to its passage through succeeding generations of the Wardle family, immediately reintroduces the very hierarchical distinctions that the custom was supposed to do away with. Even the ceremony of kissing beneath the mistletoe, which commences once the gathering of the household is complete, betrays an ironic emphasis upon the removal of class distinctions. All take part in this scene of 'most delightful struggling and confusion', and the description of universal participation is meant to signify the special levelling-out of social differences. But while all take part, only certain combinations are permitted to form 'beneath the mystic branch': Mr Pickwick salutes the venerable 'old lady'; 'Mr Winkle kissed the young lady with the black eyes, and Mr Snodgrass kissed Emily; and Mr Weller, not being particular about the form of being under the mistletoe, kissed Emma and the other female servants, just as he caught them' (350–1). Meanwhile, the 'poor relations', who wish to please, are said to have 'kissed everybody', as if the social position they occupy is so ambiguous as to make discrimination a problem.

This sort of social differentiation in the representation of the Dingley Dell Christmas revels recalls the significance of the practices associated with the feudal Christmas. Daniel Maclise, a close friend of Dickens, captured the nostalgic image of the feudal Christmas in his 1838 painting *Merry Christmas in the Baron's Hall*.[25] The baron sits at table in the background of the picture with his guests and presides over the feast like Christ at the Last Supper. His inner position removes him from the plebeian orders who play Christmas games on the floor before the fire. The panorama includes a jester, juggler, fiddler, fortune-tellers, choristers and mummers; and while they rollick in the foreground, a procession descends the stairs to the right of the frame, bringing the boar's head into the middle of the painting.

Dickens looks back to some of the class considerations associated with this feudal Christmas in *The Chimes*, where the Spirits show Trotty Veck a vision of Bowley Hall on New Year's Day. The Hall is full of visitors and a great dinner is to be held at which that arch paternalist, Sir Joseph Bowley, 'in his celebrated character of Friend and Father of the Poor', is to make a speech, while 'certain plum-puddings were to be eaten by his Friends and Children in another Hall first' (149). Even more remarkable as a display of deference, suggests the narrator, is the fact that 'Sir Joseph Bowley, Baronet and Member of Parliament, was to play a match at skittles – real skittles – with his tenants!' (149–50).

A more subtle but nonetheless similar process of differentiation is at work in *Pickwick* in the description of the games which follow the ceremony with the mistletoe. Mr Pickwick genially takes part in the 'mysteries of blindman's buff, with the utmost relish for the game'; but the servility betrayed by the 'poor relations' elicits the narrator's irony: 'the poor relations caught just the people whom they thought would like it; and when the game flagged, got caught themselves' (351). Blindman's-buff is followed by snap-dragon and then a 'mighty bowl of wassail' is enjoyed around a log fire whose 'deep red blaze sent forth a rich glow, that penetrated into the furthest corner of the room, and cast its cheerful tint on every face' (351–2). Mr Pickwick compliments his host on these comfortable arrangements, and Mr Wardle replies: 'Every body sits down with us on Christmas eve, as you see them now – servants and all; and here we wait till the clock strikes twelve, to usher Christmas in, and while away the time with forfeits and old stories' (351–2), and he proceeds to regale his guests with a carol for 'Christmas old', and then a ghost tale which forms the next chapter: 'The Story of the Goblins who Stole a Sexton'.

As many critics have noted, this tale foreshadows the ingredients of *A Christmas Carol*. Gabriel Grub is a prototype for Scrooge in his ill-humour and solitude, and in his moral transformation as a result of the visions wrought by his encounter with supernatural agents. Also noteworthy, however, is the way in which the nesting of this tale inside a larger narrative of Christmas anticipates the relationship between Dickens's first Christmas Book and its cultural context. Storytelling (preferably by the fireside) was an important part of the Christmas tradition, and so the cultural function of the tale of Gabriel Grub is not confined to its exposition of the themes and values associated with the season: the tale itself forms a part of the ritual of the festival it is concerned to portray. This doubled function, apparent in the relationship between the tale and its framing narrative, foreshadows the way in which the Christmas Books make the season an object of representation, and simultaneously become a part of it through their commodification and consumption. Such a doubled function makes the Christmas Book a very potent cultural form.

In its stress on conviviality, and its characterisation as a communal celebration bringing together all those whose lives are centred upon the manor (whether they are kin or not), the Pickwickian Christmas looks back nostalgically to the 'feudal Christmas' whose passing was lamented by Hunt and Irving. As J. A. R. Pimlott comments, 'the celebrations at Dingley Dell might have been held in the eighteenth century'[26] – an observation that is hardly surprising given the literary origins upon which Dickens was drawing for this work. In contrast, the *Carol* focusses on the delineation of present social duties rather than on the evocation of nostalgia for a lost past. Its setting is the cottage rather than the manor-house, and its Christmas festivities are dedicated to a celebration of the domestic ideal.

This shift in focus from communal to domestic celebration, apparent in Dickens's fictionalisation of Christmas, was also occurring in other aspects of the developing institution, such as the games, food and family customs that were beginning to characterise the festival. In the interval between the publication of *Pickwick* and the *Carol*, Christmas was increasingly observed to concentrate itself into a timespan of two days – Christmas Day and Boxing Day – to bring its merrymaking indoors, and to become essentially a family festival, rather than a village event. A form of Christmas was being evolved to suit the requirements of the domestic ideal, and this process is evident in the variety of ways in which the Victorian middle classes tamed the spirit of misrule associated with the earlier pagan midwinter festivals from which Christmas derives. The domestication of a range of Saturnalian impulses and rituals of the season was a crucial step in the making of the Victorian Christmas. Already, the games of forfeits and blindman's-buff recorded in *Pickwick* represented an innocent replacement of the more raucous Twelfth Night activities pursued in the Regency period. The custom of 'topsy-turvy', where men dressed as women and women as men, was translated into the more restrained kind of role-reversal in which the head of the household would be asked to help stir the Christmas pudding mixture. In 'A Christmas Dinner' Dickens gleefully records the tradition in which 'grandmamma' 'insists, regularly every year, on uncle George coming down into the kitchen, taking off his coat, and stirring the pudding for half an hour or so, which uncle George good-humouredly does, to the vociferous delight of the children and servants' (222).

The custom of 'topsy-turvy' was also adapted for middle-class enjoyment through its transfer to the stage with the growth of the Christmas pantomime. Originally developed in the eighteenth century as an interlude of mime in plays, the pantomime became specifically associated with Christmas in the Victorian period. In his essay 'A Christmas Tree' Dickens reminisces about his childhood delight in watching the spectacular metamorphoses of pantomime:

the Pantomime – stupendous Phenomenon! – when clowns are shot from loaded mortars into the great chandelier, bright constellation that it is; when Harlequins, covered all over with scales of pure gold, twist and sparkle, like amazing fish; when Pantaloon (whom I deem it no irreverence to compare in my own mind to my grandfather) puts red-hot pokers in his pocket, and cries 'Here's somebody coming!' or taxes the Clown with petty larceny, by saying, 'Now, I sawed you do it!' when Everything is capable, with the greatest ease, of being changed into Anything; and 'Nothing is, but thinking makes it so.'[27]

As Nina Auerbach has noted, 'cross-dressing compounded this medley of identities'.[28] It was during the Victorian period that actresses took over the role of Principal Boy, while male actors played the role of the Dame. But this relegation of the custom of 'topsy-turvy' to the stage could effectively distance and contain the risqué role-reversals of old village custom for the enjoyment of the respectable middle classes.

The domestication of Saturnalian ritual involved in the Victorian middle-class version of 'topsy-turvy' is also evident in the introduction and subsequent popularity of the Christmas cracker. Its invention is attributed to a London sweet-maker, Tom Smith, who had introduced the French bon-bon into England in the early 1840s. In keeping with the homely sentiments of the developing institution, the legendary story of its origin is that Smith was inspired by a spark from his hearth with the idea to put the sweet inside a cracker. He discovered a way to control the explosion, and the fire-cracker sweets were so successful that he was later led to put paper hats and trinkets inside them. The cracker was a domesticated version of the communal bonfire ceremonies that had characterised the ancient pagan midwinter festivals, and its privatising function in the formation of the Victorian middle-class Christmas found a parallel in the introduction of the Christmas tree.

The institution of the illuminated fir tree derives from the ritual use of fire and evergreens to promote fertility and symbolise the continuance of life in the pagan midwinter celebrations. The Christmas-tree custom arrived in England with merchants and officials from the Hanoverian court in the 1820s, but did not flourish until the 1840s, when Prince Albert adopted the practice of having a tree at Windsor. In 1848, the *Illustrated London News* carried a full-page engraving of the Royal family encircling the Christmas tree at Windsor Castle; the engraving became widely known through its reprinting, and was accompanied by a description of the decorations used to adorn the tree and an explanation of its function in the Royal household. Clearly, the custom of the tree met the needs of the new Christmas that was in the making. It could be set up inside the home, the centre of the Victorian family Christmas, it was a vehicle for the giving of presents suited to the age and sex of their recipients and its decoration was a source of great appeal to the children who were rapidly becoming the focus of the institution.

Together with his description of the pantomime, quoted above, Dickens wrote an enthusiastic description of a Christmas tree in the same essay for *Household Words* in 1854, in which his characteristic narrative delight in the elaboration of heterogeneous detail is apparent in the profusion of gifts and trinkets decorating the tree (5). By the mid-1850s, the Christmas tree was firmly established as a convention of the middle-class Christmas, and ladies' magazines were proffering advice about which trees to buy and where to display them. Detailed instructions were given on its decoration and on the garlanding of the room in which it featured with holly, mistletoe and ivy. These ornaments, it was suggested, could be tastefully interspersed with hanging mottos – such as 'A Happy Christmas' or 'Pray You Walk In' – made of tinfoil or tiny everlasting flowers. All this decorative paraphernalia provided evidence of social status and generated the need for female industry within the home, requiring planning, purchasing, arranging and cleaning. It thus contributed to that formation of the private sphere – of the domain devoted to the reproduction of everyday life – so central to the rise of the middle classes. Similarly, the invention of the Christmas card by Henry Cole, in the same year that Dickens wrote *A Christmas Carol*, is another example of the way in which the festival was evolving to suit the requirements of the domestic ideal. The exchange of greetings by Christmas card provided a means of expressing goodwill to one's neighbour without disturbing the privacy of the family celebration.

The domestication of Christmas is also apparent in the evolution of the dinner held to mark the festival. The English Christmas of the sixteenth century was celebrated with a dinner consisting of all kinds of meats and several varieties of birds, together with Christmas pies (later called Yorkshire pies), mince-pies, wassail and plum-porridge. However, in contrast to the variegated and often communally celebrated feast of feudal times, the Victorian Christmas dinner was shaped to satisfy the appetites of its middle-class diners. Indeed, the rise of the turkey as the definitive fare of the Christmas dinner-table has been explained by its suitability to the size of the family Christmas gatherings of the middle classes.[29] But equally important was its social significance, since the means to purchase such fare were not available to all classes. Geese were a cheaper alternative and Goose Clubs, in which birds would be raffled just before Christmas, became a popular institution amongst the working classes in the 1840s. The distinction is drawn in *A Christmas Carol*, where much is made of the humble goose enjoyed by the Cratchits for their Christmas dinner – 'There never was such a goose. Bob said he didn't believe there ever was such a goose cooked. Its tenderness and flavour, size and cheapness, were the themes of universal admiration' (54) – and the conversion of Scrooge to the new Christmas spirit is marked by his decision to send the prize turkey from the poulterers around to the family of his impoverished clerk.

The loss of variation in the fare deemed suitable for Christmas dinner that the popularity of the turkey brought about is evidence of the way in which the class- and culture-specific customs of the Victorian middle-class Christmas became desirable for everyone. Regulating behaviour at both ends of the social scale, the Victorian middle-class Christmas helped to create an illusion of social harmony, establishing the values of the bourgeois family as a norm, and creating a sense of national identity. To celebrate Christmas in the appropriate way became an assertion of Englishness. (The use of Christmas to affirm national and imperial togetherness reached its climax in the inauguration of the Christmas royal message, the first of which was broadcast from Sandringham House in 1932 by George V, who described Christmas as 'the festival of the family' and the empire itself as 'one big family'.[30]) Indeed, in the latter decades of the nineteenth century, Christmas trees were decorated with Union Jacks and flags of the empire as the festival became a celebration of national unity; and the extraordinary tenacity with which expatriates in India or Australia persisted in keeping up those Christmas rituals designed for a genuine English winter attested to the function of the festival as a re-affirmation of Englishness and mark of national loyalty.

However, notwithstanding the zeal with which the customs and values of the middle-class Christmas were promoted, class differences survived to distinguish the social specificity of some festivities. Despite the popularity of the turkey associated with the middle-class domestication of Christmas throughout the nineteenth century, the boar's head ceremony (depicted in Maclise's painting as a relic of the feudal Christmas) is still kept up at Queen's College, Oxford, and is one of the few rituals showing the persistence of class differences in the celebration of Christmas. Another example of the survival of customs attesting to social difference is provided by a leader in *The Times*, published as late as Christmas Day 1877, in which the writer condemns the communal celebrations of the working classes:

Christmas is threatened by the multitude that choose to honour and observe it in their own way. There is no mincing the matter, nor is there disguising and no checking it either. Christmas for a large part of the people recalls the pagan Saturnalia without even the picturesque forms and social graces of paganism. The devotees reel about the streets, make nights hideous, turn their houses upside down, and crowd the police court ... Christmas indoors and Christmas out of doors, are very different things. One class regards it as a very different thing. One class regards it as a foretaste of heaven, the other is not capable of that sentiment, or that aspiration.[31]

In continuing to celebrate Christmas out of doors, working-class communities rejected the privatised family celebrations of the middle classes. But the generation of such forms of resistance is itself part of the hegemonic process, part of the creation of a cohesive middle-class identity through the categorisation of normality and deviance.

The assiduity with which Dickens's household kept up the festivities of the Christmas he was helping to form was famous amongst his contemporaries. One of Jane Carlyle's most delightful letters, written on 23 December 1843, records Dickens's energetic celebration of that Christmas. She had been invited to the birthday party of Macready's daughter, which fell on 21 December, and went with reluctance, having suffered a week of insomnia. Capturing the exuberance with which Dickens celebrated this particular Christmas, her description deserves quoting at length:

Dickens and Forster above all exerted themselves till the perspiration was pouring down and they seemed *drunk* with their efforts! Only think of that excellent Dickens playing the *conjuror* for one whole hour – the *best* conjuror I ever saw – (and I have paid money to see several) – and Forster acting as his servant. This part of the entertainment concluded with a plum pudding made out of raw flour, raw eggs – all the usual raw ingredients – boiled in a gentleman's hat – and tumbled out reeking – all in one minute before the eyes of the astonished children and astonished grown people! That trick – and his other of changing ladies' pocket handkerchiefs into comfits – and a box full of bran into a box full of – a live guineapig! would enable him to make a handsome subsistence, let the bookseller trade go as it please –! Then the dancing – old Major Burns with his one eye – old Jerdan of the Literary Gazette . . . the gigantic Thackeray, etc., etc. all capering like *Maenades*!! Dickens did all but go down on his knees to make *me* – waltz with him! But I thought I did my part well enough in talking the maddest nonsense with *him*, Forster, Thackeray and Maclise – without attempting the Impossible; however, *after supper* when we were all madder than ever with the pulling of crackers, the drinking of champagne, and the making of speeches, a universal country dance was proposed – and Forster, *seizing me round the waist*, whirled me into the thick of it, and *made* me dance!! like a person in the treadmill who must move forward or be crushed to death! Once I cried out 'oh for the love of heaven let me go! you are going to dash my brains out against the folding doors!' – to which he answered ... 'your brains!! who cares about their brains *here*? *let them go!*'

In fact the thing was rising into something not unlike the *rape of the Sabines*! . . . when somebody looked at her watch and exclaimed 'twelve o'clock!' Whereupon we all rushed to the cloakroom – and there and in the lobby and up to the last moment the mirth raged on.[32]

The Christmas celebration in which Jane Carlyle is made to join demonstrates the domestication of Saturnalian impulse characteristic of the Victorian festival. The spirit of misrule is translated into suitably private forms of revelry, such as conjuring, joking, pulling of crackers and dancing. But the zesty hint of forbidden pleasure remains in her half-blushing stress upon their 'madness' and uncontrollable mirth. In the keeping of his first Christmas after the writing of his first Christmas Book, Dickens was engaging in a performance of himself that anticipated the identification with Christmas he established later through his Public Readings. When he began his paid readings in 1858, the Christmas Books formed his original repertoire, although only the *Carol* was to remain a staple item. It has been read aloud ever since, including among its many famous readers Lionel Barrymore and Eleanor Roosevelt.[33] Not only was Dickens concerned to portray Christmas in his writings, his Christmas Books became a ritual element of the season.

According to Forster, the 'fancy' of writing *A Christmas Carol* first occurred to Dickens during a visit to Manchester in October 1843. He had been there to preside at the opening of its Athenaeum, where he spoke on the education of the poor, and the bearing he considered this to have upon the relations between workers and employers. Earlier in the year, he had been 'so perfectly stricken down' by the parliamentary report of the Children's Employment Commission that he thought of writing 'a very cheap pamphlet called An Appeal to the People of England in behalf of the Poor Man's Child'; and in September, he visited the Field Lane

Ragged School on behalf of Miss Coutts who was directing her charitable
efforts towards the relief of destitute children at this time. These circumstances inspired the social message of the *Carol*: its concern (among other
things) with the care of poor children, the link between ignorance and
poverty, and the need for relations of 'mutual duty and responsibility'
between employer and employee.[34]

However, Dickens's immediate motives were financial. Written in the
hope of offsetting the money lost on the poor sales of *Martin Chuzzlewit*, the
Carol was the work, says Forster, of 'such odd moments of leisure'[35] as were
left to him out of the time taken to write the novel. This sort of economic
expediency was in keeping with the commercialisation which accompanied the formation of the Victorian Christmas. Other writers were
already profiting from the season through their contributions to the highly
lucrative Christmas Annuals. These extremely popular collections of
fiction, poetry, essays and illustrations were published as gift books at the
end of each year to catch the Christmas market. Like the Annuals, the
printing and binding of *A Christmas Carol* were carefully planned with an
eye to the gift requirements of the season. The Christmas colours of red
and green were incorporated into the design of the title page, which shows
the title and author's name surrounded by a gold wreath of holly; the end-
papers were green, the pages had gold edges and the text was decorated
with eight illustrations by John Leech, four of them hand-coloured.[36]
Ironically, while these elaborate printing plans were designed to cash in on
the gift-giving market, their cost was not adequately covered by the price
of the book. Since Dickens had agreed to pay Chapman and Hall for its
expenses, he received only £230 profit from the first run of 6,000 copies
that sold on the first day; he had been expecting to clear £1,000.
Publication and printing arrangements were changed for the four succeeding books; but although they no longer carried the expensive coloured
etchings and title page, artists such as Daniel Maclise, Clarkson Stanfield,
Richard Doyle, and John Tenniel provided black-and-white illustrations
which enhanced their attractiveness as Christmas presents, and all five
retained the red cloth and embossed cover of the *Carol*.[37]

The marketability of the *Carol* was evident despite Dickens's initial
financial disappointment. Within twelve months, it had sold 15,000 copies
and attracted many plagiarisms. By February 1844, eight theatrical
productions had been mounted, including Edward Stirling's adaptation
at the Theatre Royal, Charles Webb's *Scrooge, the Miser's Dream* at Sadler's
Wells, and C. Z. Barnett's *A Christmas Carol; or, the Miser's Warning!* at the
Royal Surrey Theatre.[38] The first reviewers were warm in their praise:

Thackeray, for example, asking, 'Who can listen to objections regarding such a book as this? It seems to me a national benefit, and to every man or woman who reads it a personal kindness.'[39] Lord Jeffrey, founder and former editor of the *Edinburgh Review*, wrote to Dickens on 26 December 1843, 'you may be sure you have done more good, and not only fastened more kindly feelings, but prompted more positive acts of beneficence, by this little publication, than can be traced to all the pulpits and confessionals in Christendom, since Christmas 1842',[40] and other letters poured in from complete strangers telling Dickens 'amid many confidences, about their homes, how the *Carol* had come to be read aloud there, and was to be kept upon a little shelf by itself, and was to do them no end of good'.[41] Despite Carlyle's later objections to Dickens's 'Carol philosophy', he was so moved by 'visions of *Scrooge*' in 1843 that he was 'seized with a perfect *convulsion* of hospitality, and . . . actually insisted on *improvising two* dinner parties with only a day between'.[42]

In his exhaustive study of the cultural reconstructions of the *Carol* since its first publication, Paul Davis notes that until 1950 at least seventy-five dramatic productions were mounted, and he lists a further 225 live stagings, films, radio dramas and television plays since then.[43] Dickens chose the *Carol* for his first public reading in December 1853 and it was also the main item in the farewell performances he gave in New York (1868) and London (1870). These readings helped to ensure the fulfilment of Laman Blanchard's prophesy that this carol would be 'heard and remembered a hundred Christmasses to come',[44] and it has undoubtedly become institutionalised in a way that none of Dickens's other works have. The annual public reading of *A Christmas Carol* has survived into the 1990s as an important component of the celebration of the English Christmas. As Philip Collins remarked in 1970, 'since *George Barnwell* ceased to be performed on Shrove Tuesday, [Dickens] has provided the solitary seasonal item in our literature . . . Scrooge – so finely named for the purpose – has become part of the national mythology.'[45]

The status of the *Carol* as a national institution in part accounts for the nature of the critical response evident in early reviews of the book as well as in later scholarship: the view that the *Carol* transcends literary criticism, or is in some way an inappropriate text for such analysis. Thackeray's dismissal of 'objections regarding such a book as this' in his February 1844 review for *Fraser's Magazine* set aside the criticisms he imagined the *Quarterly*'s reviewer making, and complemented the remarks of Laman Blanchard in *Ainsworth's Magazine* that the *Carol* was a book 'not to be talked or written of by ordinary rules'.[46] Similarly, Forster concluded his account of its success with the claim: 'Literary criticism here is a second-rate thing, and the reader may be spared such discoveries as it might have made in regard to the *Christmas Carol*.'[47] Philip Collins has speculated that modern critics may 'have been put off by the *Carol*'s institutional status (one might as readily undertake a rhetorical analysis of the Lord's Prayer)'.[48] Whatever the explanation, this critical reverence or reticence helps to sustain the illusion of transcendence that distinguishes the *Carol*'s celebration of Christmas and sanctification of the hearth. The *Carol* works by affirming the possibility of reaching a position beyond the realm of class and politics, since its vision of Christmas is presented as available to everyone. By situating the *Carol* in a privileged domain according to the universality of its Christmas spirit, these early reviewers sought to confirm its message of transcendence. However, the special status given to the *Carol* in such contemporary reviews depends upon an opposition between the domain of politics and the realm of Christmas feeling that itself reproduces the gendered division of spheres involved in the middle-class ideology of the family. In this way, the critical reception of the *Carol* has been implicated in the formation of the middle-class Christmas represented in the tale.

From its first appearance, the *Carol* occupied a special place in Victorian middle-class culture. It carried the symbolic weight of the Christmas festival, implicitly requiring those who would criticise it to find themselves in league with the unreformed Scrooge. Authorised thus by the Victorian celebration of Christmas, the book simultaneously helped to shape and promote the festival upon which its marketability rested. It inaugurated a new publishing genre, flooding the market with Christmas Books resembling Dickens's that were designed to cash in on the gift-giving rituals of the season. Its status as commodity was clearly a significant element in the mutually authorising relationship that developed between the *Carol* and the Victorian middle-class Christmas. But this relationship was also fostered by the representational practices Dickens employed. He devised a narrative which appeared to determine its own mode of consumption at the firesides of the nation, exploiting and affirming the consumer culture and domestic ideology of the developing middle-class institution as part of his tale.

Together with the supernatural elements, worship of the family, and overt social purpose which characterise Dickens's Christmas Books, the intimacy of tone adopted by the narrator is a crucial defining feature. Michael Slater aptly describes the tone of the *Carol* as that of 'a jolly, kind-hearted, bachelor uncle, seated across the hearth from his hearers on some festive domestic occasion'.[49] The unmarried status of the narrator is important, for it frees him to construct a surrogate family among his readers. The jocularity and immediacy of address in the novel's opening establish the voice of the bachelor uncle, whose palpable presence as story-teller is most clearly insisted upon when Scrooge is confronted by the first of the three spirits: 'The curtains of his bed were drawn aside; and Scrooge, starting up into a half-recumbent attitude, found himself face to face with the unearthly visitor who drew them: as close to it as I am now to you, and I am standing in the spirit at your elbow' (27). The impression of physical proximity presented here seeks to determine the *Carol*'s mode of consumption. In his effort to produce a sense of oral narration, Dickens constructs the scene of reading in which the book is meant to be enjoyed. *A Christmas Carol* speaks not only for, but *from* the hearth, situating the reader – and the listener – in a domestic context that is projected by the tone and facilitated by the length of the work. Dickens apparently stressed this sense of fireside narration even more explicitly at his public readings of the *Carol*, on one occasion assuring his audience that 'nothing would be more in accordance with his wishes than that they should all, for the next two hours, make themselves as much as possible like a group of friends, listening to a tale told by a winter fire'.[50]

The scene of family reading, constructed by the mode of narration, accords with the supernatural element in the tale. According to Forster, in writing the Christmas Books Dickens was taking the 'fairy fancies' and 'old nursery tales' told to him during his childhood, and 'giving them a higher form'.[51] The fairy-tale themes, happenings and techniques that dominate the *Carol* help to produce the storybook atmosphere and to evoke the nostalgia associated with memories of childhood reading. But the intro-duction of the supernatural element carries political significance as well. The use of the spirits to unsettle Scrooge and challenge his hard empiricism is part of a larger epistemological enquiry generated by the fragmented experience of urban life shown in the tale. The spirits show Scrooge the inadequacy of his empirical attitude, pointing out the existence of a realm beyond the bounds of his immediate external experi-ence. However, the transcendence attributed to this supernatural realm is secured by obscuring the class specificity of the representation of Christmas and the family in the *Carol*. Scrooge's temporary freedom from spatial and temporal limitations enables him to see rural- and city-dwellers as part of a larger human family that is united by the spirit of Christmas. But it is precisely by managing to render its discourse invisible in this way that a class achieves hegemony.

A Christmas Carol charts Scrooge's conversion from a selfish, hard-hearted and miserly businessman into a jolly, charitable, surrogate father. The determination to keep Christmas and the absorption into the family that mark his transformation show the inseparability of Dickens's social purpose from his exaltation of family love. His message is the need for Christian *caritas*, for the spread of goodwill amongst all men, so that social misery might be alleviated by a national conversion to the Christmas spirit. Scrooge is the archetypal miser when the story begins: 'Hard and sharp as flint, from which no steel had ever struck out generous fire; secret, and self-contained, and solitary as an oyster. The cold within him froze his old features, nipped his pointed nose, shrivelled his cheek, stiffened his gait; made his eyes red, his thin lips blue; and spoke out shrewdly in his grating voice' (6). His association with the cold is ideologically significant in relation to the opposition between indoors and outdoors through which the domestic ideal is so often constructed in Dickens's fiction, and the fact that he carries 'his own low temperature always about with him' establishes an ominous parallel with the appearance of Marley's ghost, which is 'provided with an infernal atmosphere of its own' (19). Scrooge's struggle to blame the arrival of this spectre upon his own indigestion – 'You may be an undigested bit of beef' (19) – signifies his exclusion from those convivial feasters in Dickens's fiction (such as the members of the Pickwick club) whose capacity for fellow-feeling is manifested through the healthiness of their appetites. His choice of a 'little saucepan of gruel' (16) for his supper is a reflection of his parsimony, and contrasts sharply with the inexhaustible supply of edibles described with such verbal extravagance and relish elsewhere in the *Carol*.

However, as Paul Davis has shown, for the *Carol*'s earliest readers Scrooge was not the emotional centre of the tale. They saw the Cratchit family as the heart of the book, and dramatic adaptations during the Victorian period often assigned the lead role to Bob Cratchit rather than Ebenezer Scrooge.[52] The Cratchit Christmas dinner is the most celebrated of Dickens's domestic set-pieces, and contains all the essential ingredients for a happy Dickensian home: a clean snug house, a hot fire, good homely food and drink, a bustling little woman superintending the household, and a large number of obedient and well-washed children. The presence of the crippled Tiny Tim adds an element of sentimentality to the description which helps to evoke the shared emotional response in the audience that would unite them in a community of feeling. The depiction of Tiny Tim elicits the empathy amongst his readers that Dickens saw as essential to the Christmas spirit.

The Cratchits make the most of their limited resources, Mrs Cratchit being 'dressed out but poorly in a twice-turned gown, but brave in ribbons' (51). Like the meal itself, the narrative of their humble celebration is 'eked out' by the emphasis given to the delights of anticipation, to the glorious air of expectancy which grips the members of the family as they await the arrival of daughter Martha, father Bob (bearing Tiny Tim) and of the goose 'in high procession' (53). All of this excitement is quite mild, however, in comparison with the suspense which is generated as Mrs Cratchit poises the knife in readiness to carve the wonderful bird: '[Grace] was succeeded by a breathless pause, as Mrs Cratchit, looking slowly along the carving-knife, prepared to plunge it in the breast; but when she did, and when the long-expected gush of stuffing issued forth, one murmur of delight arose all round the board' (53). Similarly, much is made of the general trepidation which attends the momentous serving of the Christmas pudding, as the narrator assumes the perspective of the eager diners, who are tantalised by the sounds and smells proceeding from the kitchen which herald its coming:

Hallo! A great deal of steam! The pudding was out of the copper. A smell like a washing-day! That was the cloth. A smell like an eating-house and a pastrycook's next door to each other, with a laundress's next door to that! That was the pudding! In half a minute Mrs Cratchit entered – flushed, but smiling proudly – with the pudding, like a speckled cannon-ball, so hard and firm, blazing in half of half-a-quartern of ignited brandy, and bedight with Christmas holly stuck into the top. (54)

The dinner over and the clean-up completed, all of the Cratchit family draw together in a circle around the hearth. As a reviewer of Dickens's fourth Christmas Book wryly noted,

we feel convinced, [that] had Italy, or Spain, or any country nearer the tropics than ours produced [Mr Dickens], instead of describing lazzaroni, and maccaroni, and water melons, or Andalusian young ladies, and cigaritos, and chocolate, and mantillas, he would have migrated to our more northern shores for the sake of firesides, purring cats, boiling kettles, Dutch clocks and chirping crickets.[53]

In the *Carol*, the familial values of love, charity and good humour associated with the focus on the hearth are supplemented by the comfort and security of warm punch, compounded and dispensed by Bob, and crackling chestnuts. Shared in a family circle, food and drink represent physical, emotional and spiritual nourishment.

The domestic harmony celebrated in the scene of the Cratchit dinner is repeated in the portrait of the Peerybingles in *The Cricket on the Hearth*. The earnestness of Dot Peerybingle's love for the eponymous Cricket immediately indicates her embodiment of the domestic ideal. Like Mrs Cratchit, she is the bustling little woman essential to the provision of a happy home in Dickens's fiction. She is very young, although not a child-wife in the manner of Dora Copperfield, and her husband is 'a sturdy figure of a man, much taller and older than herself, who had to stoop a long way down, to kiss her' (190). Mrs Peerybingle's virtue is most clearly shown in her superintendence of the 'small snug home and the crisp fire' (188). She nurses the baby, makes the tea, and when John has eaten the supper of ham and bread and butter prepared for him, she arranges his great chair in the chimney-corner and fills his pipe with a skill which sends the narrator wild with admiration (211). These wifely ministrations are stressed by the Cricket on the Hearth in its defence of Dot against the false suspicions awakened in the breast of her husband by the cynical Tackleton. The Cricket presents John Peerybingle with a saving vision of home and of the Angel at its centre, calling upon him to 'Hear everything that speaks the language of your hearth and home!' (248–9).

The January and May theme, introduced in the Peerybingle marriage of male age to female youth, provides the occasion for the misunderstanding between husband and wife that is resolved by the influence of the Cricket's song. But this disparity in age also carries special significance for the representation of the domestic ideal. One of the key contradictions existing within the Victorian idealisation of womanhood was the idea of the adult woman who was also able to remain permanently childlike. The ambiguous combination of childlike innocence with the duties of wifehood and motherhood was a product of the doctrine of separate spheres, for as Deborah Gorham observes, the infantilisation of the ideal woman 'was a sign of the extent to which she was removed from the vicissitudes of the public sphere'.[54] The childishness of Dot Peerybingle is in this way an important part of the definition of privacy to which the Christmas Books so clearly dedicate themselves.

All of the Christmas Books establish a woman's embodiment of the domestic ideal as the grounds for her sexual appeal to the male. Indeed, the avuncular narrator is frequently characterised through his adoption of a January-like position with respect to the young women he describes, and this disparity in age makes his delight in their rosy charms more piquant.

In the *Carol* the narrator describes Scrooge's niece with an obvious relish for her childish appearance (61), and in foretelling the fate of Scrooge's lost love he observes her eldest daughter being 'pillaged' by the younger children of the family, and envies their sport with a zeal that is uncomfortably reminiscent of the lascivious Quilp (40–1). In the *Cricket*, it is Dot's small and childish stature and 'chubby little hands' (186) that elicit the narrator's admiration. He observes that she is 'something of what is called the dumpling shape', adding, 'but I don't myself object to that' (189). Dot is good enough to eat, and this association of female desirability with food is entirely in keeping with the gastronomic fervour of the Christmas Books, where everything is edible and offers itself to be eaten with a liberality that tantalisingly suggests a kind of sexual freedom. In the *Carol* the narrator describes the 'Norfolk Biffins' at the fruiterer's shop: 'squab and swarthy, setting off the yellow of the oranges and lemons, and, in the great compactness of their juicy persons, urgently entreating and beseeching to be carried home in paper bags and eaten after dinner' (48), and the French plums at the grocer's that 'blushed in modest tartness from their highly-decorated boxes' (49). In the representation of his anthropomorphic fruit and edible young women, Dickens domesticates the Saturnalian impulses traditionally associated with the Christmas season for a middle-class consumer culture.

The potency of the domestic set-pieces, which centre on women like Dot Peerybingle in the Christmas Books, is enhanced by the contrast drawn between indoor and outdoor settings and by the manipulation of narrative perspective. The *Cricket* begins with the description of a contest between two commonplace attributes of the hearth, which hum and chirp a 'song of invitation and welcome to somebody out of doors' until eventually, 'the kettle and the Cricket, at one and the same moment, and by some power of amalgamation best known to themselves, sent, each, his fireside song of comfort streaming into a ray of the candle that shone out through the window, and a long way down the lane' (189–90). The Cricket is invested with a special significance as the 'Genius' of the Peerybingle hearth and home (211). Its song becomes a measure of domestic harmony, so that the very mention of the curmudgeonly Tackleton is enough to stop the Cricket chirping. The point is made more explicitly when Tackleton betrays his affinity with the unreformed Scrooge by demystifying the value of the home: '"Bah! what's home?" cried Tackleton. "Four walls and a ceiling! (why don't you kill that Cricket? *I* would! I always do. I hate their noise.) There are four walls and a ceiling at my house"' (206). His view is echoed by the cynical Doctor Jeddler in Dickens's fourth Christmas Book,

The Battle of Life, who laughs away his daughter's grief over a story she had been reading, with the salutary reminder, 'a real home is only four walls; and a fictitious one, mere rags and ink' (319).

The indoor/outdoor opposition established in the 'song of invitation and welcome' put forth by the kettle and cricket is also a vital part of the exaltation of Home in the *Carol*. The scene of the Cratchit dinner is presided over by the Ghost of Christmas Present, and Scrooge is a privileged and secret witness to the festivities taking place within the home. His hidden viewpoint emphasises the allure of the private family celebration. A similar effect is apparent in the narrator's description of the coming night:

By this time it was getting dark, and snowing pretty heavily; and as Scrooge and the Spirit went along the streets, the brightness of the roaring fires in kitchens, parlours, and all sorts of rooms, was wonderful. Here, the flickering of the blaze showed preparations for a cosy dinner, with hot plates baking through and through before the fire, and deep red curtains, ready to be drawn to shut out cold and darkness. (57)

It is the fleeting vision, the stolen glimpse of a cosy place of privacy, that produces the impact of these scenes. In each of the vignettes presented by the spirits, Scrooge is the unseen observer, the witness who is excluded from being a participant in the action. This narrative dependence upon voyeurism itself inscribes the opposition between warm inside and cold outside through which the ideal of domesticity is largely constituted. In *The Battle of Life*, this opposition is invoked in the description of the day upon which Alfred Heathfield is expected to return to his foster-family:

A raging winter day, that shook the old house, sometimes, as if it shivered in the blast. A day to make home doubly home. To give the chimney-corner new delights. To shed a ruddier glow upon the faces gathered round the hearth, and draw each fireside group into a closer and more social league, against the roaring elements without. Such a wild winter day as best prepares the way for shut-out night; for curtained rooms, and cheerful looks; for music, laughter, dancing, light, and jovial entertainment! (330)

The emphasis upon protection, enclosure and security, associated with the interior of the home, asserts the value of privacy. This kind of spatial differentiation is also reproduced in the narrative frames of the *Carol* which position Scrooge as the unseen viewer, and the recurrence of these symbolic oppositions between inside and outside throughout the

Christmas Books promotes the separation of public and private spheres underpinning the ideal of domesticity. The framing devices help to reproduce the boundaries constituting middle-class ideology.

Dickens's choice of a businessman to embody his moral in the *Carol* enables him to make social comments about employer–employee relationships. But the significance of this choice is not restricted to the provision of commentary upon industrial relations. The unreformed Scrooge anticipates Mr Dombey in his failure to distinguish between his personal and business life – between 'family' and 'firm' – and his mistake is thus implicated in the definition of the domestic ideal. Scrooge lives in 'a gloomy suite of rooms, in a lowering pile of building up a yard' which is 'old enough now, and dreary enough, for nobody lived in it but Scrooge, the other rooms being all let out as offices' (14). Moreover, he begrudges his clerk the traditional holiday on Christmas Day, deriding it as an excuse 'for picking a man's pocket every twenty-fifth of December!' (13). And in seeking to do away with the work/holiday distinction, he demonstrates his rejection of middle-class family life.

Scrooge's domestic salvation is meant to serve as an emblem of social reform, the promise of a regenerated social system, although the wish-fulfilment of this fictional strategy is evident. Whether or not the cheering prospect of a wholesale change in human nature is convincingly represented, this substitution of individual moral transformation for social reform is, in itself, a politically significant gesture. It reaffirms the distinction between public and private realms, by translating social conflicts into personal problems that are solvable through an individual act of will. The sanctification of the home is reaffirmed in this provision of a private resolution to the wider social problems addressed in the narrative. The solution to social deprivation enjoined by Scrooge's moral transformation is a universal conversion to the values of the Victorian middle-class Christmas: the Christmas which celebrates the domestic ideal. Nina Auerbach has argued that 'Christmas in this tale means family, and society viewed as a family: Scrooge rejects not God incarnate but his own role as munificent father.'[55] But a more discriminating analysis of the conceptualisation of the family in the tale reveals an important distinction in its cultural message. Scrooge is not converted to a paternalistic ideal so much as to the values of domesticity. Rather than representing the family as a hierarchical model *for* social relations, the *Carol* advocates the spread of private, familial feeling and the virtues of the hearth *throughout* the social world. Dickens is concerned to view society not as '*a* family', but as composed of 'families', so that the ideal of domesticity might be spread throughout the commonwealth. And to this end the *Carol* projects itself into the hearth-side family circles of its readers. It asks to be purchased and read as a ritualised element of the Christmas celebration it is concerned to portray. Thus, in the closing lines of the *Carol* Dickens extends the benediction of Tiny Tim to his readers: 'it was always said of [Scrooge], that he knew how to keep Christmas well, if any man alive possessed the knowledge. May that be truly said of us, and all of us! And so, as Tiny Tim observed, God bless Us, Every One!' (90) Apparently breaching the boundary of the fiction, the narrator seeks to dissolve social differences in a moral vision which consolidates the middle class and generalises its values as available to everyone.

A similar effect is achieved at the end of Dickens's last Christmas Book, *The Haunted Man*, where he extends the motto that underlies the transformation of Redlaw as a benediction to his readers in the ending of the tale (472). In the original single-volume edition, text and picture merge in the tale's closing celebration of Christmas. The book's last sentence is completed by Clarkson Stanfield's illustration of the Christmas gathering in the Dinner Hall and a scroll below it bearing the motto in old English letters, 'Lord! keep my memory green!' This is the same motto that we are told decorates the portrait of an Elizabethan benefactor hanging in the Dinner Hall – a motto which Redlaw has learnt to appreciate through the suffering caused by the loss of his memory. With a similar scroll beneath it, Stanfield's illustration of the Christmas party is made to bear the moral significance of the portrait contemplated by the guests in the old Hall, and *The Haunted Man* thus exhorts its readers to interpret the phrase in the light of the Christmas scene it frames, and to embrace its message.

The peculiar impact of this injunction is lost in modern editions of the tale which fail to reproduce Dickens's original picture-and-text pages (although the use of the old English lettering in the World's Classics edition goes some way towards retrieving the effect). But the seasonal weight lent to the contents of the narrative is enhanced by foregrounding the relationship between reader and text in this way. In drawing attention to its participation in the festival it is concerned to represent, *The Haunted Man* repeats the gesture which closes the *Carol*. The self-consciousness with which the Christmas Books generally address their readers, asking to be read at the festive firesides of the nation, illustrates the way in which Dickens's fictional representations of Christmas helped to shape the institution which provided the occasion for their writing.

Dickens's awareness of the cultural functions served by his Christmas Books is suggested in a letter he wrote to Forster in September 1847. He had conceived the idea for *The Haunted Man* in 1846, but was having difficulties completing it with *Dombey and Son* still in progress. 'I am very loath to lose the money,' he wrote, 'And still more so to leave any gap at Christmas firesides which I ought to fill.'[56] This sense of having become an integral part of the Victorian celebration of Christmas was accommodated when the inauguration of *Household Words* in 1850 gave him the opportunity to publish a Christmas number each December and thus to fulfil his annual obligation in its pages. The practice was continued when he began *All the Year Round*, and lasted until 1868. Two of the titles that were considered for *Household Words* when he was planning the journal in 1849 indicate the centrality of Christmas to the ethos of these weekly publications which were designed for familial consumption – 'The Holly Tree' and 'The Robin' – and among those proposed for *All The Year Round* was 'Evergreen Leaves'. As Philip Collins notes, 'he had always associated his weeklies with the Christmas spirit'.[57]

Collins has attributed Dickens's '*Carol* philosophy' to his concern for 'the ordinary joys and sorrows of ordinary people': 'For Christmas [Collins argues] is as demotic, unsophisticated and classless an experience as can be: a festival celebrated much alike by duke and don and dustman. The one may drink wine, the other beer, but the turkey and crackers and Christmas tree, and the special concern for the children, is common to all.'[58] Such a description captures the spirit of Christmas Dickens was concerned to portray. But it also perpetuates the masquerading of middle-class values as universal norms that his Christmas Books enable. My analysis suggests that Dickens's fictionalisation of Christmas in the Christmas Books is thoroughly implicated in issues of class and gender. The attempt to disguise or downplay the significance of these categories of social difference is the very kind of gesture which secures the ubiquity of middle-class norms. Collins here identifies with Dickens in accepting the ideology of the middle-class Christmas which promotes itself as the universal celebration of home and family, and his comment is evidence of the normalising effect produced by the Christmas Books. But Dickens's fictionalisations of Christmas are not always so apparently dedicated to the reproduction of an essentially conservative ideology. In his two final attempts at the subject in his novels, the loving celebration of familial feeling and the delight in the material paraphernalia of Christmas are rendered in ways that expose the ideological significance of the festival.

The Christmas Eve chapter in *The Mystery of Edwin Drood* is ominously entitled 'When Shall These Three Meet Again?' and forms the prelude to

Edwin's murder. The descriptive emphasis there is upon death, rather than birth. Memories of childhood are awakened by the associations attached to familiar sights and sounds; but they serve only to remind those who revisit Cloisterham of their mortality. The gothic elements of the narrative displace the ebullient celebration of the Christmas spirit. However, if chapter XIV in *The Mystery of Edwin Drood* invokes a much more sombre Christmas scene, it is the description of Pip's terrifying Christmas Eve and miserable Christmas Day in *Great Expectations* which contrasts most compellingly with Dickens's earlier fictionalisations of Christmas. While the Christmas Books help to promote and shape the celebration from which they stem in ways that would seem to confirm its transcendence of politics and history, Dickens offers a much more subversive account of Christmas and the family in *Great Expectations*. There, the Gargery Christmas dinner can be seen to provide a site for the family's formation of class and gender differences. Pip's account of this celebration forms a vital part of Dickens's investigation of the relationship between respectable society – centred upon the family – and the underworld of the convict.

When Pip returns home at the beginning of chapter IV, following his rendezvous with Magwitch on the marshes, he finds his sister angrily 'getting the house ready for the festivities of the day' (21). He is alerted to the state of her temper by Joe, who 'secretly cross[es] his two forefingers' (22) as a warning signal to Pip. This secret communication – one of the many 'confidences' Pip and Joe are said to share – resembles Pip's conspiratorial alliance with Magwitch, which is also expressed by means of covert hand gestures. In this way, Pip's hidden involvement with the convict becomes an extension of the habits of secrecy developed in response to the brutal housekeeping of his sister.

The link between the child and the convict is strengthened by the issue of discipline and punishment. Pip and Joe are sent to church in a manner indicative of Mrs Joe's consistently punitive approach:

[Joe] emerged from his room, when the blithe bells were going, the picture of misery, in a full suit of Sunday penitentials. As to me, I think my sister must have had some general idea that I was a young offender whom an Accoucheur Policeman had taken up (on my birthday) and delivered over to her, to be dealt with according to the outraged majesty of the law. (22–3)

Mrs Joe's recital at dinner of Pip's misdemeanours is also reported in the language of the law. Pip notes that she entered on a fearful catalogue of all the illnesses I had been guilty of, and all the acts of sleeplessness I had committed, and all the high places I had tumbled from, and all the low places I had tumbled into, and all the injuries I had done myself, and all the times she had wished me in my grave, and I had contumaciously refused to go there. (27)

Again, Pip implicitly recognises the convict system as a logical extension of the discipline maintained by his sister within the family when he projects his fear of the imminent discovery of his guilt by the gathering at the Christmas dinner-table on to the appearance of the soldiers at the end of chapter IV.

Mrs Joe's preoccupation with punishment is informed by the kind of evangelical attitude to children expressed by Mr Hubble at this dinner, as he solves the 'moral mystery' of youthful ingratitude by concluding that they are 'Naterally wicious' (25): children and convicts are held to be one of a kind. But the identification is also confirmed by the way in which Pip is located in relation to the discourse of the elders here. He is made to occupy what he calls a 'false position' in the dinner-table dialogue, because although the discussion concerns him, he is implicitly forbidden to participate in it. He is situated on the margins of a discourse that nevertheless centres upon him. The contradictory position into which he is thrust by the members of the family group, who depend upon him for the expression of their supposed moral superiority, resembles the position occupied by Magwitch, the outlaw within a disciplinary society. For Magwitch represents the 'other' against which the middle-class subject distinguishes himself. The outcast's marginality is essential to the definition of middle-class respectability, so making him paradoxically central.

The operation of these ideologies of 'otherness' becomes particularly apparent in the institution of Christmas in *Great Expectations*. The chapter describing the Gargery Christmas dinner is set against the preceding account of Magwitch's desperate consumption of the food stolen for him by Pip. In chapter IV, Pip details the 'superb dinner' prepared by Mrs Joe, 'consisting of a leg of Pickled pork and greens, and a pair of roast stuffed fowls' (22). This main course is to be supplemented by a mince-pie and pudding, together with 'nuts and oranges and apples' and the notorious 'savoury pork pie' brought by Uncle Pumblechook. The ritualised serving of this special meal, and the relish with which individual items in the feast are consumed, contrast markedly with the dog-like way in which Magwitch devours his heterogeneous stolen meal of mincemeat, bread, meat-bone, cheese-rind and pork pie. And the food included in the

Gargery Christmas dinner is not selected solely with a view to the pleasure of eating it. Its value is social, as well as digestive. Thus Pip ends up with 'the scaly tips of the drumsticks of the fowls, and with those obscure corners of pork of which the pig, when living, had had the least reason to be vain' (25); and Uncle Pumblechook is 'sensible of having deserved well of his fellow-creatures' as a result of his 'delightful and delicious present' (29), the savoury pork pie. Indeed, the extent to which Pumblechook derives his standing from his gifts of food and wine is made apparent in the self-importance with which he responds to the flattery of the sergeant who leads the soldiers in chapter v by refilling his glass.

Uncle Pumblechook's gifts are presented to Mrs Joe, and Pip is clearly resentful of the way in which the masculine authority she exercises as the apparent owner of the household property is augmented by her role as hostess: 'Joe's station and influence [notes Pip], were something feebler (if possible) when there was company, than when there was none' (25). Notably missing in the description of this Christmas dinner is any mention of the carving ceremony conventionally performed by the Victorian father of the family, signifying his status as provider. On the contrary, Joe sits silent and powerless, mutely comforting Pip by spooning more gravy into his plate. However, despite the reversal of gender involved in Pip's representation of his sister and Joe here and elsewhere in his narrative,[59] Mrs Joe is still shown to depend upon her role as surrogate mother to Pip for her identity within the home and village. As Pip observes, she 'had established a great reputation with herself and the neighbours because she had brought me up by hand' (7–8), and her Christmas-dinner guests endorse this reputation by commiserating with her over Pip's 'misdemeanours' and by supporting her disciplinary methods (hence their comic discussion about pork as a subject with great potential for teaching young Squeakers like Pip a lesson – a debate in which the linguistic shifts from 'Pork' to 'Swine' are themselves evidence of the operation of class in the language of cooking and cuisine).

But if the food which forms the Christmas feast helps to articulate social distinctions, so too do the other conventions associated with the annual family celebration. To Pip, one of the most impressive of these is the unveiling of the parlour: 'Mrs Joe put clean white curtains up, and tacked a new flowered-flounce across the wide chimney to replace the old one, and uncovered the little state parlour across the passage, which was never uncovered at any other time, but passed the rest of the year in a cool haze of silver paper' (22). Similarly, the front door is unlocked for the company to enter by – ' (it never was at any other time)', notes Pip – and he has to admit the guests 'making believe that it was a habit of ours to open that door' (24). The pretence clearly amuses the narrator, and the status and lifestyle it is meant to imply are shown to be as fictional as the notion of the happy family which the holiday is supposed to celebrate. Pip likens the usage of the parlour to 'Joe's change from his working clothes to his Sunday dress' (24) and thereby links this Christmas ritual to the division between public and private that was part of the domesticated version of Christmas developed to suit the middle classes.

The narrative's focus on this ideological division is sharpened by the interruption to the festivities made by the entrance of the soldiers. They are at work – 'on a chase in the name of the king' – and, needing the services of a blacksmith, require Joe to break his holiday. The distinction between work and family life is again registered in the detail of Joe's clothing, as Pip notes that he 'had got his coat and waistcoat and cravat off, and his leather apron on, and passed into the forge' (31). But the disruption caused by the soldiers also discloses the relationship between the 'celebrating' family and the underworld of the convict. Posed as marginal to the unit which forms the ideal celebrant of Christmas, the convict helps the family to define itself and to identify its respectability. This ideological connection is made apparent in Pip's comment on the proceedings: 'As I watched them while they all stood clustering about the forge, enjoying themselves so much, I thought what a terrible good sauce for a dinner my fugitive friend on the marshes was. They had not enjoyed themselves a quarter so much, before the entertainment was brightened with the excitement he furnished' (32). Pip's acknowledgment of the family's indebtedness to the convict here identifies it as a privatised unit of consumption that is materially and ideologically dependent upon the outcast. The comment also links him with Magwitch, because the lip-smacking relish with which Pumblechook recounts the capture and execution of Pip as the pig in the homily on pork is not unlike the 'lively anticipation' with which the family gathering looks forward to '"the two villains" being taken' (32) in chapter v. In each case the intermingling of the literal and the figurative – Pip as pork and Magwitch as (presumably apple) sauce – generates peculiar suggestions of cannibalism. Recalling the personification of edibles in *A Christmas Carol*, the effect represents a much more equivocal version of the anthropomorphic descriptions of food found there.

Although the Christmas Books would suggest that Christmas is supposed to celebrate the middle-class family group whose solidarity comes from the affective ties held to obtain between its members, this is clearly not what is offered in *Great Expectations*. Pip's description of the Gargerys'

Christmas dinner parodies this ideal by exposing the tensions, power-games and domestic violence that actually characterise this family gathering, and by showing the way in which this ceremony relates to the plight of the convict. Here, the family becomes a crucial site for the production of class and gender differences. The visibility of its ideological implications makes this fictionalised Christmas a subversive representation of the very institution Dickens was so instrumental in shaping and popularising. 'Christmas *was* Christmas ... many, many centuries before Charles Dickens began to celebrate him in *Carols* and *Chimes*', wrote one commentator in 1849, reviewing Dickens's last Christmas Book.[60] But any examination of the making of the Victorian middle-class Christmas must challenge such a view. Whether or not the invention of this institution can be attributed to Dickens, his involvement in the process is clearly a significant part of the politics of the family in his fiction and in Victorian culture.

CHAPTER 4

Little Dorrit

Between the appearance of his last Christmas Book and the publication of
Little Dorrit in 1855–7, Dickens wrote three more novels: *David Copperfield,
Bleak House* and *Hard Times*. Engaging with a range of topics related to the
family – mothers, nurses, orphans, single-parent homes, young couples,
family bereavement and so on – *David Copperfield* shows how the hero's
quest to establish his social and sexual identity is bound up with the formation of a suitable family. As Chris R. Vanden Bossche has argued, in the
process David demonstrates the extent to which his middle-class identity is
dependent upon a commitment to the morality of domestic economy.[1]
Bleak House has a good deal to say about homemaking and housekeeping,
female sexual transgression, illegitimacy and the consoling function of
the middle-class family as a precarious site of privacy and personal
freedom (as analyses by D. A. Miller and Monica Feinberg show in
detail[2]), and Catherine Gallagher has demonstrated the importance of
the relationship between social paternalism and domestic ideology in
Hard Times.[3] However, the issues associated with the formation of the
family and middle-class self-making in these novels are dealt with in
more complex ways in Dickens's later fiction, and *Little Dorrit* provides a
particularly illuminating illustration of the narrative workings of familial
ideology.

The family and the prison are the two central metaphors of *Little Dorrit*
and their significance as part of Dickens's social and moral analysis is
widely recognised. What has not been duly acknowledged, however, is the
ideological function of the family in the novel's analysis of social and
economic transformation. While the perverted family relationships of the
Dorrits form a central focus in psychoanalytic discussions of the novel,
their wider political significance needs to be considered by noting the
cultural assumptions they entail. The normative definition of the family
implied in the very idea of perversion is, of course, culturally specific, and
is part of the process by which middle-class values gained ascendancy as

cross-class ideals in the Victorian period. Competing concepts of family shape the novel's representation of a changing social order where modern forms of power are being institutionalised in the formation of cultural knowledge. The ideology of domesticity upheld by the heroine, Little Dorrit, orders social life according to the doctrine of separate spheres and transforms bourgeois culture into 'universal nature'. But while the novel invokes a privatised domain that is held to transcend class-specific determination, this process involves a definition of the family that depends upon the existence of oppositional formulations.

As explained in the Introduction, the social history of the word 'family' reveals a shift in meaning from the seventeenth to the nineteenth centuries, involving a specialisation of the term to describe a small kin-group sharing the same household. But earlier conceptualisations of the 'family' persist in Victorian narrative, and in *Little Dorrit* they play an important role in the representation of social and economic change. In its portrayal of the Barnacles and Stiltstalkings, the novel makes use of the conceptualisation of the family as a tribe in order to satirise the nepotism and inefficiency of government bureaucracy; in its portrayal of the Father of the Marshalsea, the novel offers a critique of false paternalism; in the portrayal of its heroine, Little Dorrit, it provides an embodiment of domestic ideology and a normative vision of the family. These varying definitions of the family highlight the complexity with which Dickens interweaves the 'public' issues of economics and politics with 'private' affairs as part of his moral and social vision. The transformation of the old world into the new – famously characterised by Sir Henry Maine in 1861 as a 'movement *from Status to Contract*'[4] – is suggested in the novel by the deployment of shifting definitions of the family which political theorists such as Sir Robert Filmer and his major opponent, John Locke, had used to explain the origins of civil society.

The genealogical imperative governing the arrangement of civil administration in *Little Dorrit* and the paternalism shown in the character-isations of William Dorrit and Christopher Casby are forms of social organisation which derive from the theory of political right known as patriarchalism. Traditional patriarchal thought used the family and the authority of the father at its head as the model for all power relations, and was based upon what Sir Henry Maine described as 'the assumption that kinship in blood is the sole possible ground of community in political functions'.[5] The classic formulation of patriarchalism was articulated by Sir Robert Filmer in his *Patriarcha* (1636), where he claimed an identity between paternal and political power. Dickens's questioning of such 'rule by the fathers' is in keeping with the liberal sympathies he displayed earlier in the 1840s over the question of free trade, and his argument about true and false paternalism demonstrates *Little Dorrit*'s linkage of politics, economics and the family. His critique is related to the economic change recorded in the novel from older, familial forms of enterprise organisation based on personal relations towards the development of impersonal business corporations based on contractual relations. But this process of economic change – shown in the contrast drawn between the House of Clennam and Mr Merdle's bank – also raises questions of personal responsibility that challenge some of the assumptions about freedom and subjectivity underpinning liberal political theory. The figure of the family is therefore crucially implicated in the novel's ambivalent representation of social and economic change. According to the writings of the classic liberal theorists like Locke, the development of a modern form of political right is predicated upon the separation of spheres brought about by the creation of the civil or public world through the bonds of contract established between supposedly free and equal individuals. But while the freedom of the individual is thus defined through his[6] contractual relations, the new social order described by Dickens in the novel is deplored as a prison. *Little Dorrit* suggests that social and economic trans-formation entails problems that are indeed, as the novel's original title ironically declared, 'Nobody's Fault', but they are problems that may be mitigated by the healing powers of the domestic woman.

Dickens's indictment of government bureaucracy and social irresponsi-bility in *Little Dorrit* centres upon three families whose branches seem to stem from the one tree. The representation of the Barnacles, Stiltstalkings and Gowans involves a form of social organisation that is based upon the principle of genealogy. Their tribalism exemplifies an earlier definition of the family as the large kin-group, and they are devoted to the regime of power Foucault has associated with a 'symbolics of blood' – a juridical regime that came to be replaced by a productive model of power centring upon the action of the norm throughout the course of the nineteenth century.[7] Indeed, the juxtaposition of the worship of genealogy with the values of domesticity is one of the key mechanisms by which the novel effects the normalisation of the middle-class family. The economic and political significance of blood within the concept of family represented by the Barnacles is suggested in the ironic description of Mr Tite Barnacle, 'who was more flush of blood than money', and who 'had intermarried with a branch of the Stiltstalkings, who were also better endowed in a

sanguineous point of view than with real or personal property' (90). The
Barnacles are the vehicle for Dickens's satire on the Civil Service, which
was prompted by their maladministration of the Crimean War at the time
of the novel's writing, and the moral order appealed to in the narrative
continually demands that the members of this family be pried apart from
the ship of state to which they owe their metaphorical identity. Their
family name is synonymous with the Circumlocution Office not only
because they are responsible for the administration of this department at
the level of the plot, but also because the narrative techniques used to
represent them show the same self-reflexivity and verbal dexterity that
characterise the indefinite deferrals of civil administration.

This process is immediately apparent in the characterisation of Mr Tite
Barnacle. Arthur Clennam is admitted to his office in chapter x:

It was a comfortable room, handsomely furnished in the higher official manner;
and presenting stately suggestions of the absent Barnacle, in the thick carpet, the
leather-covered desk to sit at, the leather-covered desk to stand at, the formidable
easy chair and hearth-rug, the interposed screen, the torn-up papers, the
dispatch-boxes with little labels sticking out of them, like medicine bottles or
dead game, the pervading smell of leather and mahogany, and a general
bamboozling air of How not to do it. (90–1)

In this description, the office expresses the position expresses the man.
The room is full of furniture announcing its stately function, refuse which
supposedly constitutes evidence of business correspondence, and tools of
the trade, such as the 'dispatch-boxes'. But while Clennam reads these
details as signs of the 'absent Barnacle' – while he constructs a referent
for the contents of the room in which he is standing – it soon becomes
apparent that the relationship between sign and referent is not so straightforward or 'self'-evident. The Circumlocution Office thrives upon its
ability to 'bamboozle' its suitors with signs that are offered in lieu of
substance. The capacity of the Office to generate a proliferation of
documents, reports, memoranda, relays and endless referrals ensures its
own viability. This project of indefinite deferral is of the very nature of
textuality, since all signs refer to other signs in the system, and just as the
room of Mr Tite Barnacle 'suggests' its absent incumbent so, too, the
description of Mr Barnacle himself advertises his public office. Clennam
encounters the famous man at his 'gentlemanly residence' in Mews Street,
Grosvenor Square, and finds him to be precisely what his room was – 'the
express image and presentment of How not to do it':

He wound and wound folds of white cravat round his neck, as he wound and wound folds of tape and paper round the neck of the country. His wristbands and collar were oppressive, his voice and manner were oppressive. He had a large watch-chain and bunch of seals, a coat buttoned up to inconvenience, a waistcoat buttoned up to inconvenience, an unwrinkled pair of trousers, a stiff pair of boots. He was altogether splendid, massive, overpowering, and impracticable. He seemed to have been sitting for his portrait to Sir Thomas Lawrence all the days of his life. (93)

Mr Barnacle's aspect is indistinguishable from the institution he supposedly serves. He dresses himself almost to the point of immobility, and his deportment suggests all the unmanageability and obstructionism of the Circumlocution Office.

The identification of Mr Tite Barnacle with the Circumlocution Office is, of course, a development of that characteristic 'transposition of attributes' noted by Dorothy Van Ghent as 'the principle of relationship between things and people in the novels of Dickens',[8] and the effect of this technique of transposition in the presentation of the Barnacles is to expose the political effects of their tribalism. The 'branches' of the Circumlocution Department are shown to be coextensive with the 'branches' of the Barnacle family and it is this hold on power that Dickens objects to as much as to the bureaucratic principle of 'How not to do it'. Nepotism permits the Barnacles to administer a public institution for private gain by eliminating the distinction between these spheres of activity.

The most sustained attack upon this kind of corruption in Parliament and public administration is made by the narrator in the chapter describing the marriage of Pet Meagles (Book the First, chapter xxxiv). The wedding ceremony itself is glossed over in half a sentence after several pages of satiric description inveighing against the scandalous careers of the Barnacle wedding-guests. The apparent incongruity between the supposedly private nature of the occasion and the sharp political commentary provided by the narrator is significant, for this is a marriage that shores up, even as it transgresses, the principle of genealogy defining the Barnacle family. Clennam wonders, for example, whether Henry Gowan's 'notion of being disappointed in life' is not 'an assertion of station which the bridegroom brought into the family as his property' (337). Along with Mr Tite Barnacle and his family, Lord Decimus Tite Barnacle and William Barnacle, the narrator also describes the 'sprinkling of less distinguished Parliamentary Barnacles, who had not yet got anything snug, and were going through their probation to prove their worthiness' (341), in a long passage of satiric word-play which envisages the family as a large network

of kin that subsumes the individuality of any of its members. Like the
Boodles and Coodles that populate the government in *Bleak House*, any
differentiation between the Barnacles referred to in the narrative is less
important than their status as branches of the family tree. They are continually figured by collective nouns that suggest their alarming proliferation and the anonymity of the individual within the group. Chapter xxxiv
is entitled 'A Shoal of Barnacles', and while the 'sprinkling' of Barnacles
that attend the marriage of Pet Meagles belie their overall numbers (which
are said to be 'Legion'), they nevertheless form 'a swarm in the
Twickenham Cottage' (341).

The representation of the Barnacles in collective terms is set in ironic
counterpoint to the policy pursued by the 'heads of the family' who wish to
distinguish themselves from the 'swinish public' (263). At the dinner given
by Mrs Gowan in chapter xxvi, Clennam finds himself in the illustrious
company of a 'noble refrigerator' and an 'old lady with a high nose' who
discourse upon the 'evil days':

It was agreed that the country (another word for the Barnacles and Stiltstalkings)
wanted preserving, but how it came to want preserving was not so clear. It was
only clear that the question was all about John Barnacle, Augustus Stiltstalking,
William Barnacle and Tudor Stiltstalking, Tom, Dick, or Harry Barnacle or
Stiltstalking, because there was nobody else but mob. (263–4)

The ironic tension between the strategies of tribalism and the narrative
techniques used to represent them becomes evident in this passage. Mrs
Gowan's guests attempt to assert their identity as patricians in opposition
to the plebeian 'mob' by confining 'the question' to some half-dozen
individuals they name, and by regarding the rest of the nation as an
undifferentiated mass. But the attempt to individualise those Barnacles
and Stiltstalkings who may be charged with the preservation of the country is undercut by the comic reference to the generic 'Tom, Dick, or Harry
Barnacle or Stiltstalking' which completes the list. This narrative reluctance to individualise family members clearly contributes to the satiric
attack upon the tribalism of the Barnacles, Stiltstalkings and Gowans.
However, rather than simply harking back to the order of classic patriarchalism in which the tribe constituted the fundamental unit of society,
their representation looks towards the development of modern forms of
corporate identity. The tendency to subsume any individual Barnacle
within the tribe becomes a vehicle for the cultivation of impersonality – an
impersonality which gives rise to the dilemma that is 'Nobody's Fault'.

The nebulous operations of the Circumlocution Office thrive upon the 'anonymity' of its workers as part of a system which precludes personal responsibility. Such institutions constitute a radical challenge to the humanist self – the idea of a sovereign subject who possesses a unique individuality – which Dickens tries to fend off, as I will later show, through the recuperative domestic work of Little Dorrit.

It is no mere coincidence that the Barnacle family should occupy such a prominent place in the dinner-table conversation of Mrs Gowan. In a letter to Forster written while the novel was still in progress, Dickens noted: 'Society, the Circumlocution Office, and Mr Gowan, are of course three parts of one idea and design.'[9] This narrative design is evident in the kinship which links the Circumlocution Barnacles with the Gowans in the plot. Clennam discovers in chapter XVII that 'the Gowan family were a very distant ramification of the Barnacles; and that the paternal Gowan, originally attached to a legation abroad, had been pensioned off as a Commissioner of nothing particular somewhere or other, and had died at his post with his drawn salary in his hand, nobly defending it to the last extremity' (174). Some explanation for the persistence of such forms of nepotism and jobbery in the social world the novel represents is given earlier in the chapter, when Mr Meagles surprises Clennam by savouring the illustrious appearance of a Barnacle at his family dinner-party and thereby reveals his 'weakness'. Learning that Barnacle Junior's father is 'nephew to Lord Decimus', Mr Meagles 'luxuriously' repeats the phrase 'with his eyes shut, that he might have nothing to distract him from the full flavour of the genealogical tree' (172).

Mr Meagles's 'weakness' – one that the narrator notes 'none of us need go into the next street to find, and which no amount of Circumlocution experience could long subdue in him' (173) – helps to sustain the influence of that 'abstraction of Society' so worshipped by the Gowans and Merdles. The practice of 'Moving in Society' is introduced in the chapter of that title, where Fanny takes the Child of the Marshalsea to meet Mrs Merdle in Harley Street, Cavendish Square. This meeting is significantly preceded by Little Dorrit's visit to the theatre at which Fanny performs, where she finds backstage 'such a mixing of gaslight and daylight, that they seemed to have got on the wrong side of the pattern of the universe' (196). The bizarre and unreal scene that Little Dorrit encounters behind the proscenium arch foreshadows the kind of make-believe and pretence shown to be an essential part of 'moving in Society'. The confusion of props, machines, costumes and lights that so bewilders her here is alluded to again, four pages later, in the description of Mrs Merdle's 'spacious semicircular drawing room' (199). There, the two sisters find 'a parrot on the outside of a golden cage holding on by its beak with its scaly legs in the air, and putting itself into many strange upside-down postures' (200). Mrs Merdle makes her dramatic entrance through a curtained doorway, appearing before her audience as a lady who was 'not young and fresh from the hand of Nature, but was young and fresh from the hand of her maid' (200). The raucous parrot acts as an impertinent chorus throughout the interview, interrupting the genteel conversation of Mrs Merdle, whose theatricality is continued in the artfulness with which she 'compose[s] herself voluptuously, in a nest of crimson and gold cushions, on an ottoman' (200). Mrs Merdle's composition of her figure recalls the affectation of the appalling Mrs Skewton in *Dombey and Son*, who is usually found 'arranged, as Cleopatra, among the cushions of a sofa: very airily dressed: and certainly not resembling Shakespeare's Cleopatra, whom age could not wither' (245). Also like Mrs Skewton, who assures Mr Dombey that she is 'thrown away in society. Cows are my passion' (242), Mrs Merdle excuses her artifice and worship of Society by protesting a love of nature. She is charmed by pictures of 'Savages in the Tropical seas', laments the loss of 'our natural state' (201) and exclaims that 'A more primitive state of society would be delicious to me' (203). Her postulation of a natural condition that has been relinquished in the development towards modern civil society exploits the story told by the social contract theorists to explain the origin of political right. Her sadness at the loss of this state of nature is a fiction linking her regard for Society with the stories used to maintain social authority elsewhere in the novel.

As a convenient abstraction whose attitudes and practices can be invoked to serve the interests of a select group of families, Society is shown to underpin tribalism. Its operation is apparent when Mrs Gowan enlists the aid of Mrs Merdle in circulating her family fiction concerning Henry Gowan's marriage to Pet Meagles. The 'fable' created by Mrs Gowan in order to maintain 'her individual dignity, and the dignity of the blood of the Barnacles' (327) is that the Meagles are 'shrewd people', 'people of business' (266), who have ensnared her son for their daughter so as to profit from the 'honour' of such an alliance. Of course Gowan is marrying Pet for her father's money as much as her beauty, but after calling Arthur Clennam 'to bear witness to this fable', and 'impounding the family itself for the same purpose' (327), Mrs Gowan secures its currency by asking for the opinion of Mrs Merdle upon the proposed marriage because, as she assures her 'dear' friend, Mrs Merdle is able to 'represent and express Society so well' (328). According to the narrator, Mrs Merdle 'knew what

Society's mothers were, and what Society's daughters were, and what Society's matrimonial market was, and how prices ruled in it, and what scheming and counter-scheming took place for the high buyers, and what bargaining and huckstering went on', but 'perceiving the exact nature of the fiction to be nursed, she took it delicately in her arms, and put her required contribution of gloss upon it' (330). This perverse image of maternal care is part of the normalisation of domesticity through which the cultural dominance of the middle-class family is established in the novel, for questions of female subjectivity are central to the definition of the domestic ideal. Clearly, Mrs Merdle's 'bosom' is not put to its 'proper' womanly use. Its 'capaciousness' is a measure of its surface area, rather than a sign of its nurturing potential, and its utility as a 'show-window' (328) is in keeping with the understanding of 'Society's matrimonial market' as a stock-exchange trading in women. The values of womanhood proclaimed by the ideal of domesticity have no worth in this system, where social and financial position outweigh moral considerations, and marriage is shown to be a commercial and political contract.

Like the understanding of marriage as a business arrangement displayed in the union of Mr Dombey and Edith Granger in *Dombey and Son*, *Little Dorrit* demonstrates the way in which matrimonial traffic in women is bound up with questions of the family and female subjectivity. What makes a woman desirable depends upon the kind of familial economy in which she is exchanged. When the marriage market is regulated by the principles of tribalism, the construction of female desirability depends upon the genealogical and/or financial value of her alliance – the example of the Merdles indicating that money can buy many of the privileges of blood. The significance of the family connection and social privilege she helps to secure by the marriage are all-important. Pet Meagles's value to Henry Gowan is financial rather than genealogical, for what the gentleman 'gets' with the lady, as Mrs Gowan explains, is the payment of all his debts plus an allowance of 'three hundred a-year, or perhaps altogether something more' (330). But from Gowan's point of view, this payment is made in exchange for the family alliance he brings, and Pet continues to pay for it over and over again in ever after being made to feel 'sensible of being usually regarded as the wife of a man who had made a descent in marrying her, but whose chivalrous love for her had cancelled that inequality' (407). Their marriage confirms the power and privilege associated with the possession of blood by calculating it into the exchange. However, when the economy defining a woman's value is regulated by the ideal of domesticity, as in the case of Little Dorrit, her female subjectivity is what makes her desirable.

The analysis of Pet's value within the tribal economy of the Barnacles and Gowans is set against the stories of the rebellious Tattycoram and the embittered Miss Wade, for all of these women are shown to be objects of economic exchange. Tattycoram is 'taken' by Father and Mother Meagles from the Foundling Hospital in London to be 'a little maid to Pet' (15) in the wake of the death of Pet's twin sister. The Meagleses are inveterate travellers, and Tattycoram's status as an acquisition associates her with the extraordinary souvenirs that decorate the family home (163). Her name is as whimsical and miscellaneous as their collection of foreign bric-à-brac, but although its 'playful' choice is supposed to express the benevolent motives of the Meagleses, the act of renaming is still an act of possession.[10] The ambiguity of her position as both sister and servant fosters Tattycoram's rebellion against the cosy, middle-class paternalism of the Meagleses, and makes her a foil for Pet, because her acquisition helps to demystify the daughter's marriage, distinguishing the economic transactions which underlie the formation of families amongst those who aspire to 'move in Society'.[11]

Tattycoram's status as acquired property allies her with Miss Wade, whose story also challenges the domestic security of the Meagles family. She explains to Mr Meagles and Clennam in chapter XXVII that her 'influence' with the girl is 'founded in a common cause. What your broken plaything is as to birth, I am. She has no name, I have no name. Her wrong is my wrong' (278). The loss of name and exclusion from the family experienced by Miss Wade expose the way in which identity is constructed through the social codes of class and gender in the novel. Her illegitimacy is described in the remarkable chapter of first-person narrative, entitled 'The History of a Self-Tormentor'. Far from serving as a mere digression from the main narrative, this chapter crucially implicates Miss Wade in the exploration of the relationship between familial ideology and female subjectivity, telling the story of her experience as an adjunct to a succession of families. Her case is a parallel for the politics of familial exclusion practised by the Gowans and Barnacles. It is also a negative parallel for the novel's analysis of the domestic unit as a socialising institution designed to gender and stratify its members, for the female bastard is obviously defined by her *exclusion* from a legitimate family, and this position of deviance is held to embitter and pervert Miss Wade. The connection between her marginality and her 'self-torment' is established early in the narrative when she tells of discovering her orphanhood and illegitimacy.

'I carried the light of that information both into my past and into my future' (556), she bitterly declares. Her subsequent employment as a governess confirms the ignominy and insecurity of her social position.

The figure of the governess formed a focus for discussion of the domestic ideal in many novels and essays of the mid-Victorian period. M. Jeanne Peterson has identified the 'status incongruence' inherent in the governess's position.[12] As Elizabeth Missing Sewell observed in 1865 in *Principles of Education*, 'the real discomfort of a governess's position in a private family arises from the fact that it is undefined. She is not a relation, not a guest, not a mistress, not a servant – but something made up of all. No one knows exactly how to treat her.'[13] Miss Wade is clearly subject to the status incongruence characteristic of the Victorian governess, and this ambiguous position unites her with Tattycoram just as much as her illegitimacy does. If Tattycoram is troubled at being something between a sister and a maid, Miss Wade is bitterly aware that she is cast as a servant rather than a family member by her position as governess. (Significantly, Mrs General is careful to inform Mr Dorrit, with magnificent gravity, 'I am not, as I hope you are aware, a governess' (376), when he broaches the question of her remuneration later in the novel.)

In the family of the poor nobleman where Miss Wade first gains employment, she finds the mother of her pupils keen to acknowledge the governess as a social equal, but Miss Wade refuses to gloss over her status as acquired property. In the second employing family she enters, a nephew of the household begins to pay her attention. But Miss Wade finds her position as an object of courtship repugnant in just the same way that she deplores the governess's status as servant: '[He] caused me to feel among the rich people as if he had bought me for my looks, and made a show of his purchase to justify himself. They appraised me in their own minds, I saw, and were curious to ascertain what my full value was' (558). Her resentment eventually issues in a vehement denunciation of her employer, who 'seemed to think that her distinguished nephew had gone into a slave-market and purchased a wife' (560). According to Miss Wade, a wife is just as much bought by her husband as a governess is hired by her employer: both are forms of traffic in women in a market obsessed with 'moving in Society'. Pet Meagles's passage through the matrimonial market, in which she is allegedly sold for the honour of Gowan's alliance, is analogous to Miss Wade's experience of commodification in a family she describes as 'people of station and rich' (558), and this thematic link is reinforced by the plot revelation that Henry Gowan had a liaison with the governess before he married Pet. However, while this coincidence highlights the analogy between the oppression of the two women, it also explains away some of the subversiveness of Miss Wade's behaviour. The feminist implications of her rage are contained by its transformation into female jealousy and personal grievance.

In refusing to gloss over her anomalous position within each of the families into which she is introduced, Miss Wade helps to reveal some of the class and gender assumptions underlying their organisation, and provides a comment on the marriage of Pet Meagles through her assertion of an identity between the 'governess' and the 'wife' as positions similarly determined by the politics and economics of genealogical privilege. However, the force of this critique is also modified by the evidence of her self-torment, and her story is finally used to reaffirm the middle-class family through the restoration of Tattycoram to the Meagleses. Miss Wade enters the novel as a 'handsome young Englishwoman, travelling quite alone' (18), whose 'self-containment' and 'self-reliance' (19) establish her defiant spinsterhood. She reappears with Tattycoram in chapter XXVII, where she 'put[s] her arm about her waist as if she took possession of her for evermore' (277). Her fierce identification with Tattycoram carries implications which threaten familial ideology, challenging the logic of complementarity that regulates heterosexual relationships and underwrites the family in Victorian culture. Founded upon her bitter sense of their common oppression as female bastards, Miss Wade's ardent attachment to Tattycoram is condemned by Mr Meagles as 'perverted' (277) on these very grounds, and the justice of her grievances is obscured by Dickens's imaginative interest in the corrosive effects of her sadomasochism. As a lesbian, her defiance of the heterosexual imperative apparently removes her from the world of property-ownership and exchange regulated by the Barnacles and Gowans to the realm of the demonic and the alien.

Tattycoram's return to the Meagles in chapter XXXIII provides an ambiguous reaffirmation of the middle-class family. She places the box containing the Clennam documents at the feet of her old master and prostrates herself, crying 'Dear kind Master, dear kind Mistress, take me back again, and give me back my old name!' (676). The narrator treats Tattycoram's wish to serve as an expression of filial feeling, and comments, 'Father and Mother Meagles never deserved their names better, than when they took the headstrong foundling-girl into their protection again' (676). Through this gesture of surrogate parenthood, Tattycoram is transformed from an ungrateful servant into a family member. The narrative comment disguises any trace of the servant's appropriation, as the discourse of the middle-class family is used to hide its own politics. By welcoming Tattycoram as a daughter, the Meagleses appear to naturalise their entitlement to her possession, and to eliminate the question of her acquisition. However, it is precisely because the economic activity invested in Tattycoram is finally smoothed over in this way that she helps to identify Pet's commercial value within the systems of exchange which characterise the tribalism of the Barnacles and Gowans in the novel. While the emphasis upon the cosy, familial feeling of the Meagleses, conveyed by their names (Father, Mother and Pet) and by the depiction of their idyllic cottage at Twickenham, might suggest their embodiment of the domestic ideal, the place of peace removed from the public sphere of politics and commercial life, the case of Tattycoram is an inescapable reminder of their involvement in it.

The questioning of middle-class paternalism involved in Tattycoram's rebellion is elaborated further in the characterisations of Christopher Casby, William Dorrit and Arthur Clennam. Unlike the tribalism of the Barnacles and Gowans, where political authority is based upon the principles of genealogy and filiation, 'paternalism' describes a form of social organisation that works by way of analogy to the father's governance within the family. As part of its social critique, *Little Dorrit* explores the dimensions of true and false paternalism, showing how the structure of the family may be used to justify or disguise other power relations. Mr Casby is the landlord of Bleeding Heart Yard and he is given the title of 'The Last of the Patriarchs' by 'various old ladies' living in his neighbourhood (121). This title does not derive from his genealogical pretensions, however, but comes instead from the patriarchal image which earned him his former employment as town-agent to Lord Decimus Tite Barnacle. Looking 'so supremely benignant' with his 'shining bald head' and 'long grey hair at its sides and back, like floss silk or spun glass' (121), he was apparently an asset because 'nobody could suppose the property screwed or jobbed under such a man' (124). But Mr Casby's paternal image is yet another of the social fictions decried in the novel. He is 'a mere Inn signpost without any Inn' (124), a sign without a referent, belonging to the order of linguistic substitutions exemplified by the Barnacles. While the revelation of his 'emptiness' provides another attack upon social hypocrisy, it is also part of a critique of 'paternalism' itself as a model for social relations, exposing the attempt to naturalise social inequalities as an extension of the hierarchy within the family.

Like Mr Tite Barnacle, who 'seemed to be sitting for his portrait to Sir Thomas Lawrence all the days of his life' (93), Mr Casby's image as

'the last of the Patriarchs' is associated with the illusions created by
painters and their models. The narrator notes that during his calculated
appearances in Bleeding Heart Yard Mr Casby had been 'respectfully
solicited to become a Patriarch for painters and for sculptors' (121–2), and
Arthur Clennam muses that,

> whereas in the Royal Academy some evil old ruffian of a Dog-stealer will
> annually be found embodying all the cardinal virtues, on account of his eye-
> lashes, or his chin, or his legs (thereby planting thorns of confusion in the breasts
> of the more observant students of nature), so, in the great, social Exhibition,
> accessories are often accepted in lieu of the internal character. (124)

As part of his notorious attack upon Pre-Raphaelite painting, Dickens had
written an article for *Household Words* in 1850 ridiculing the artists' use of
models to assist in their pictorial attention to details rather than wholes.
Entitled 'The Ghost of Art' it describes the comical confrontation
between a 'bachelor' and an antiquated artist's model, who mysteriously
threatens to 'GROW ONE!' and returns later on with a beard, as 'the ghost of
art'.[14] The incongruity between the humorous, colloquial explanations of
his work given by the model, and the presumed sublimity of the portraits
he gives rise to, is echoed in Arthur's meditation upon the Dog-stealer
found to embody 'all the cardinal virtues'. This sort of gap between the
artist's model and the image he is used to represent is what defines Mr
Casby as a 'humbug'. He is simply the artist's model of a patriarch, and the
point is reinforced by the comical artifice which distinguishes his portrait
as a boy. Clennam notes that this portrait is one which anybody 'would
have identified as Master Christopher Casby, aged ten: though disguised
with a haymaking rake, for which he had had, at any time, as much taste or
use as for a diving-bell; and sitting (on one of his own legs) upon a bank of
violets, moved to precocious contemplation by the spire of a village
church' (121). All of these references to painting and portraiture in the
description of Mr Casby stress the constructedness of the representation
and the illusion created. The power of this illusion is noted again when the
Patriarch visits Clennam at his counting-house in the company of Flora,
and explains, 'being out, I thought I'd come also, thought I'd come also'.
Despite the inanity of the comment, the narrator observes, 'The benign
wisdom he infused into this declaration (not of itself profound), by means
of his blue eyes, his shining head, and his long white hair, was most
impressive. It seemed worth putting down among the noblest of sentiments
enunciated by the best of men' (227). Indeed, so powerful is his image, all

that is required to rout the Patriarch is the destruction of his accessories. Mr Casby is literally cut down to size in a symbolic castration by Mr Pancks, who snips off the 'sacred locks' that flow upon the shoulders of the Patriarch, and then trims down the broad-brimmed hat 'into a mere stewpan' (669). Whether the cropping of Mr Casby's locks can possibly effect any material change in the real power relations for which his paternalism was a guise is a question that is muffled by the laughter that sounds from Bleeding Heart Yard in this exhilarating moment of comic reversal.

Mr Casby's exposure as a false image of paternalism clarifies some of the ideological assumptions involved in this form of social organisation, and anticipates its historical decline. Although his paternalistic position is based upon landownership of a sort, his is purely a commercial venture in which the concept of 'real' landed estate – with its connotations of stability, solidity and history – gives way to the collection of ground rents as a more flexible form of property. Unlike the landowners who 'had deep roots in their localities and thus firm bonds with those dependent on them',[15] Mr Casby is simply a landlord concerned only about money, and who lacks the sense of duty towards his tenants upon which the viability of a paternalism based on property depended. Moreover, he employs Pancks specifically to avoid any personal ties of dependency in his relationship with the Bleeding Heart Yarders. In this way, his portrayal is part of the changing social order envisaged in the novel, for his business activity exemplifies the early nineteenth-century shift to a less paternalistic form of social organisation.

In his exposure as a hypocrite and renegade paternalist, Mr Casby functions as an important analogue for Mr Dorrit in the novel. In the Father of the Marshalsea, Dickens combines a satire on paternalism as a form of social organisation with an analysis of the domestic unit in a way that tests the division between public and private life upon which the middle-class ideal of the family appears to depend. Consigned to the Marshalsea as the result of a failed partnership (a form of business organisation that grew directly from the family household[16]), Mr Dorrit gradually becomes an institution in his own right – the Father of the Marshalsea – drawing upon the ideology of social paternalism to maintain his pretensions to gentility. His authority within the prison is founded purely and simply upon a 'tradition' which preserves the 'words' of the old turnkey who named the debtor, 'Father of the Marshalsea' (54). The basis to his paternal authority is no more substantial than a consensual belief in its existence – a collective fiction. In this respect, it resembles the legal fiction posited by some of the classic contract theorists and described by Sir Henry Maine: the patriarchal family as the original social form based paternal political right on an assumption of kinship that was false; the earliest families were 'constantly enlarged by the absorption of strangers', but the fiction was maintained that these persons were 'amalgamated into a family by their common descent' and 'common obedience to their highest living ascendant, the father, grandfather, or great-grandfather'.[17] Mr Dorrit's power and authority as Father are similarly maintained by a series of shared fictions, and the analogy implied between his rule within the Marshalsea and the conjectural history of political right described by the social contract theorists indicates the pervasiveness with which concepts of family are implicated in the political concerns of the novel.

According to the narrator, Mr Dorrit grows to be so proud of his 'title' that 'if any imposter had arisen to claim it, he would have shed tears in resentment of the attempt to deprive him of his rights' (54). His position as Father is assumed to be a 'natural' entitlement: less an acquired office than an inherited aristocratic distinction. He becomes involved in the institution of a series of rituals and ceremonies which recognise and consolidate his position. These include the reception of all newcomers, 'with a kind of bowed-down beneficence' (55), and the receipt of 'gifts' from departing collegians as 'tributes, from admirers, to a public character' (55). When tradition alone no longer proves to be strong enough to ensure the payment of the 'tribute' in a letter, Mr Dorrit 'established the custom of attending collegians of a certain standing, to the gate, and taking leave of them there' (55). Like the Barnacles who are paid to do little other than stick to their Parliamentary posts, Mr Dorrit is paid for doing nothing more than 'the honours of the place' – for simply being its Father.

The rituals and ceremonies which entrench the authority of the Father of the Marshalsea become more absurd as his residence in the prison continues. Book the First, chapter XIX, describes his habit of parading up and down the 'College-yard', observing a nice distinction between its 'Pump and Poor' sides, and on occasions of ceremony bestowing a Patriarchal benediction upon the 'young Insolvents with a benignity that was highly edifying' (185). Such gestures of condescension exhibit the aristocratic figure of paternalism Mr Dorrit is attempting to embody. Also important in this regard is the Father's attitude to Old Mr Nandy, the father of Mrs Plornish:

Mr Dorrit was in the habit of receiving this old man, as if the old man held of him in vassalage under some feudal tenure. He made little treats and teas for him, as if he came in with his homage from some outlying district where the tenantry were in a primitive state. It seemed as if there were moments when he could by no means have sworn but that the old man was an ancient retainer of his, who had been meritoriously faithful. When he mentioned him, he spoke of him casually as his old pensioner. (306)

Mr Dorrit's reliance upon the values of feudalism in his relationship with Mr Nandy situates him within the early nineteenth-century discourse of paternalism, which sought a revival of these values in order to regenerate society. However, rather than signifying an ideal for social reform, the model of feudal relations serves to express his nostalgia for a lost past, for the genteel lifestyle he imagines he once enjoyed. The narrator observes that Mr Dorrit always spoke of 'old Nandy' as 'an object of great antiquity, but he was two or three years younger than himself' (312). While the stress upon Nandy's old age, together with 'the relishing manner in which [the Father] remarked on the pensioner's infirmities and failings' (315), obviously provides a way of asserting his social and mental superiority, it also maintains the fiction of his fall from prosperity, of a world he has lost – a world where, he protests to his daughter, 'I was young, I was accomplished, I was good-looking, I was independent – by God I was, child!' (191). Mr Dorrit's construction of the spurious generational difference which supposedly distinguishes him from Old Nandy is a displaced expression of the nostalgia with which he mourns his 'vanished character' (192). Generational and class differences are articulated together here to sustain the fiction of paternal authority.

Mr Dorrit's use of the old man to shore up his own sense of self-importance is most memorably displayed in Book the First, chapter xxxi, when Mr Nandy is treated to afternoon tea. After recovering from his 'humiliation' at seeing his daughter enter the college arm in arm with 'a livery' (310), Mr Dorrit reaffirms his social position within the tiny room through the segregation of Mr Nandy, who takes his tea on the window-sill. The narrator's comment upon this proceeding draws an ironic distinction between two kinds of paternity: 'So, with a gulf between him and the good company of about a foot in width, standard measure, Mrs Plornish's father was handsomely regaled. Clennam had never seen anything like his magnanimous protection by that other Father, he of the Marshalsea; and was lost in the contemplation of its many wonders' (315). The distinction drawn here, between fatherhood and Fatherhood, is crucial to the representation of Mr Dorrit in the novel. Capitalisation is used consistently throughout the book to refer to Mr Dorrit in his 'public character' (55).

However, this 'character' is more often than not carried over into his 'private' life as well, so that the meaning of the terms 'public' and 'private' is brought under scrutiny. As the narrator outlines the history of the family in the early chapters, Little Dorrit's efforts to obtain schooling for her sister, brother and herself are attributed to her understanding that 'a man so broken as to be the Father of the Marshalsea, could be no father to his own children' (60), and this comment is the first of a series invoking Mr Dorrit's double identity as Father and father. Continuing the history of the family in chapter VII, the narrator observes of Mr Dorrit that 'the more Fatherly he grew as to the Marshalsea, and the more dependent he became on the contributions of his changing family, the greater stand he made by his forlorn gentility' (61). Again in chapter IX, when Little Dorrit is unwilling to prostitute her affections for the sake of the family gentility by accepting the attentions of Young John Chivery at her father's behest, Mr Dorrit initially responds with a wail of self-pity, but is eventually moved to 'say a word' of reconciliation to his daughter, and the narrator comments: 'O! Both the private father and the Father of the Marshalsea were strong within him then' (193). The ambivalence identified here by the narrator emerges in the mingled expression of a fatherly concern for Amy's 'life of hardship' with the Father's release of 'an irrepressible sound of self approval, the momentary outburst of a noble consciousness' (193).

Two concepts of the family are juxtaposed at these points where Mr Dorrit's double identity as father and Father is brought into focus. The social paternalism underpinning his position as Father of the Marshalsea is set against the values of fatherhood associated with the middle-class family, so that the ideology of domesticity may provide an index to Mr Dorrit's character. This narrative process enacts a shift in the meaning of 'fatherhood' – a movement that resembles the redefinition of the 'gentleman' in *Great Expectations* in terms of moral being, rather than social status. Such shifts in meaning demonstrate the power of language to constitute cultural knowledge, to materialise new ways of thinking and being in the world. The representation of middle-class ideals as universal moral values is part of the development of modern forms of power, which work through the production of subjectivity, and this process is evident in *Little Dorrit* where the values of domesticity appealed to in the portrayal of Mr Dorrit as an inadequate father appear to transcend the class pretensions maintained by his social paternalism. Although the distinction he makes between his private and public identity is initially cast as another of the Dorrit 'family fictions' and therefore dismissed as a pretence, the moral analysis involved in this reading is itself already informed by the logic of separate spheres. The distinction between private and public identity is reintroduced through the shift in the meaning of 'fatherhood', as domesticity is set against social paternalism to provide the normative vision of the family.

The normalisation of domesticity effected by the juxtaposition of the competing concepts of the family that define Mr Dorrit's 'fatherhood' is also apparent in the representation of Fanny and Tip. Fanny's condescension towards Little Dorrit is said to have 'a vast deal of the family in it', and in explaining her acceptance of the bracelet from Mrs Merdle in chapter xx, she begs her sister to '"consider what a thing it is to occupy my position and feel a consciousness of being superior to it. I shouldn't care," said the Daughter of the Father of the Marshalsea, "if the others were not so common. None of them have come down in the world as we have. They are all on their own level. Common"' (198–9). Fanny's social pretensions are presented as family traits which attest to her identity as the 'Daughter of the Father of the Marshalsea'. Lacking those qualities, held by Little Dorrit, which would make her an embodiment of the domestic ideal, she is only fit to be a Daughter, rather than a daughter, of the Father of the Marshalsea. Like Fanny, Tip also asserts the 'family gentility' 'by coming out in the character of the aristocratic brother' (179) and sneering at Young John Chivery's worship of Little Dorrit. His fondness for gambling and appreciation of horseflesh distinguish him as a poor imitation of the young rake. Thus Fanny and Tip prove themselves to be Daughter and Son, respectively, of the Father of the Marshalsea in a way which suggests that these 'public' identities are determined by their possession of family traits and represent a 'natural' inheritance.

But although they seem to be based upon the principle of genealogy, these genteel public positions are defined by a notion of family that is found wanting in the narrative. While Fanny's ironic description as 'Daughter of the Father of the Marshalsea' appears to do away with the distinction between public and private identity in its satiric extension of the model of social paternalism to a family member other than the father, the moral analysis implied in this designation relies upon the doctrine of separate spheres. Insofar as Fanny's identity as 'Daughter' unfits her to be a daughter, social status gives way to moral value in the narrative, and this value derives from the saving presence of a private sphere in which the domestic virtues Fanny lacks may be preserved and cultivated.

Fanny's ironic description as 'Daughter of the Father of the Marshalsea' contrasts with Little Dorrit's designation as 'Child of the Marshalsea' in the novel. The mediating role of the Father is significantly absent in the latter description, emphasising the virtual orphanhood of Little Dorrit. She is cast as a victim of paternal dereliction in her double identity as Child and child:

> With a pitiful and plaintive look for everything indeed, but with something in it for only him that was like protection, this Child of the Marshalsea and child of the Father of the Marshalsea, sat by her friend the turnkey in the Lodge, kept the family room, or wandered about the prison-yard, for the first eight years of her life. (57)

The successive titles to chapters VI and VII in Book the First – 'The Father of the Marshalsea' and 'The Child of the Marshalsea' – suggest a structural equivalence in the positions of the Father and Child; but in contrast to Mr Dorrit, who claims his title by right of 'more than twenty years of residence' (55), the public position of the Child is thrust upon her as she is quite literally 'handed down among the generations of collegians, like the tradition of their common parent' (56). Unlike the Father, who constantly exploits his paternal identity to maintain the fiction of his gentility, the Child trades on her title only to obtain employment for her siblings and herself.

As well as sharpening the focus upon the nature of Mr Dorrit's paternalism in the novel, Little Dorrit's designation as Child of the Marshalsea contributes to the satire on the tribalism of the Gowans and Barnacles. Her 'public identity' captures the imagination of Young John Chivery's parents, leading them to favour his suit. Their absurd social ambitions form a comic parallel to the more sinister machinations of the 'gipsies of gentility' in the novel, the language of patrilineage being used to describe their aspirations: 'His father hoped, in the fulness of time, to leave him the inheritance of an unstained key; and had from his early youth familiarised him with the duties of his office, and with an ambition to retain the prison-lock in the family' (177–8). Like the Gowans and Barnacles, who show a similar concern for the principle of genealogy, Mrs Chivery recognises the significance of marriage alliances as entrées to power:

> Mrs Chivery, a prudent woman, had desired her husband to take notice that their John's prospects of the lock would certainly be strengthened by an alliance with Miss Dorrit, who had herself a kind of claim upon the College, and was much respected there. Mrs Chivery had desired her husband to take notice that if, on the one hand, their John had means and a post of trust, on the other hand, Miss Dorrit had Family; and that her (Mrs Chivery's) sentiment was, that two halves made a whole. (179)

Having 'Family' increases Little Dorrit's value in a marriage market ironically paralleling that in which Pet Meagles is sold, and the economic character of the situation is only reinforced by Mr Dorrit's hints that his daughter might prostitute her affections for the sake of her father.

Arthur Clennam acts as a foil for the Father of the Marshalsea in the stance he adopts towards its Child. The contrast drawn between these 'fathers' is made salient by the middle-class ideal of the family which defines 'true' paternalism in the novel. While Mr Dorrit's paternalism is a social outlook held in order to confirm his gentility, Clennam's paternalism is shown to arise, in the first instance, from his sense of compassion; but it is also symptomatic of the psychic wound his Calvinistic upbringing has inflicted, and is fed by his sense of guilt. Mrs Clennam's harsh authority has had the effect of emasculating Arthur, with the result that he abandons the hope of loving Pet Meagles and regards himself as 'a very much older man who had done with that part of life' (281). His tendency to infantilise Little Dorrit and watch over her with paternal care is prompted by recognition of her family's dereliction and his own experience of parental neglect. But it also makes visible some of the assumptions informing the middle-class feminine ideal and its basis in the ideology of separate spheres. While Mr Dorrit's 'false' paternalism serves primarily to entrench class as a category of difference, Clennam's 'true' paternalism, which takes a daughter, rather than an institution, as its object, constructs the distinctions of gender. 'Diminutive', 'fragile', and 'defenceless' (146–7), Little Dorrit embodies the Victorian ideal of femininity in Clennam's eyes, awakening in him an impulse to offer her protection, comfort and succour. 'Thinking of her' on the way to Twickenham in chapter xvi, he yearns for the change in circumstances which 'might enable him to be such a friend to her as he wished to be, by altering her whole manner of life, smoothing her rough road, and giving her a home', and he regards her 'in that perspective, as his adopted daughter, his poor child of the Marshalsea hushed to rest' (159).

But the compassion informing Clennam's paternalism is also compromised by the resemblances discernible between his attitude to the Child of the Marshalsea and the attitude of her family. While he condemns the complacency with which they accept her services – the fact that 'they were lazily habituated to her, as they were to all the rest of their condition' (77) – and deplores the effects produced by their acquisition of a prison mentality, his Calvinist upbringing seems to have imposed constraints upon his own thinking which place him within the same carceral framework. This becomes clear when Clennam is unpleasantly surprised to discover that Little Dorrit has a 'lover'. According to the narrator, 'he found it disappointing, disagreeable, almost painful, to suppose her in love with young Mr Chivery in the back yard, or any such person' (216), and his response to Mrs Chivery's news acknowledges the very fault of 'habituation' he had detected in the attitude of the family towards Little Dorrit in chapter IX: '"I have been so habituated," returned Arthur, at a loss, "during the short time I have known her, to consider Little – I have been so habituated to consider Miss Dorrit in a light altogether removed from that in which you present her to me, that you quite take me by surprise"' (215). In his sensitivity to the effects of parental dereliction, Clennam idealises Little Dorrit in his imagination, attaching to her 'an interest that removed her from, while it grew out of, the common and coarse things surrounding her' (216). His psychological need to infantilise and idealise her sets a limit to his thinking that resembles the way in which the family fictions upheld by the Dorrits provide evidence of their prison mentality: 'It was the family custom to lay it down as family law, that she was a plain domestic little creature, without the great and sage experiences of the rest. This family fiction was the family assertion of itself against her services. Not to make too much of them' (197). While Clennam is not charged with such hypocrisy in the narrative, his need to regard her as 'his innocent friend, his delicate child, his dear Little Dorrit' (434) shows a confinement within his own point of view that links him with the Dorrit family.

The narrator associates Clennam's paternalism with 'the habit, begun on the night when the roses floated away, of considering himself as a much older man than his years really made him' (434) and this habituation fore-shadows his eventual supplanting of the Father of the Marshalsea. When Clennam is consigned to the jail, he not only occupies the room that belonged to Mr Dorrit, but enjoys the same devoted ministrations of his daughter upon her return from abroad. In his illness, he re-enacts the inverted father–daughter relationship that characterised Little Dorrit's care of the Father of the Marshalsea. Her voice takes him back to the knee of Mother Nature, where he 'dwelt in his youth on hopeful promises' (679), and this association of paternalism with regression to a vanished past in the treatment of the relationship between Clennam and Little Dorrit recalls the nostalgia and retrospection shown by the Father of the Marshalsea. In its representation as a reversionary outlook, paternalism is set against another definition of the family centring upon the domestic ideal. In this way, *Little Dorrit* uses the family to imagine an historical shift in power away from the aristocracy to the middle classes, as paternalism is associated with the regressive, feudal attitudes and practices of an earlier social order. In the moral scheme of the novel, any hope for the future, however fragile, must lie with the ideal of domesticity promised by Little Dorrit, who restores Arthur to health and happiness.

As the 'universal' norm against which individual families and familial relations are measured, 'domesticity' provides the hegemonic definition of the family in the novel. Exemplary representations of the domestic ideal are as rare in *Little Dorrit* as they are in the rest of Dickens's later novels, but the Plornish family illustrates some of its requirements. (The other possible example, the Meagles family, is more like a satire on the ideal as its idyllic aspect is qualified from the outset by the spoiling of Pet and the threatening intrusions of Henry Gowan and Miss Wade.) Despite their poverty, the Plornishes maintain a tiny cottage in Bleeding Heart Yard whose parlour is 'poetically heightened' by the painting of one wall 'to represent the exterior of a thatched cottage' (478). Mrs Plornish's 'little fiction' proclaims the values of pastoral simplicity and domestic harmony and depends for its effect upon the characteristic opposition between interior and exterior so central to the cult of domesticity. While housed beneath the one roof, the parlour is separated from the shop by the extra-ordinary mural of an imaginary cottage, and it is Mrs Plornish's delight to 'come out into the shop after it was shut, and hear her father sing a song inside this cottage' (479).

But the fiction of a contrast between inside and outside that distinguishes the notion of the family as a cosy enclave in which the virtues of domesticity are preserved also informs the representation of the prison in *Little Dorrit*. As Doctor Haggage, 'an old jail-bird', argues in chapter VI,

We are quiet here; we don't get badgered here; there's no knocker here, sir, to be hammered at by creditors and bring a man's heart into his mouth. Nobody comes here to ask if a man's at home, and to say he'll stand on the door mat till he is. Nobody writes threatening letters about money, to this place. It's freedom, sir, it's freedom! (53)

Doctor Haggage's ironic invocation of the contrast between inside and outside usually associated with the domestic ideal is only one of the ways in which the family and the prison are figured together in the novel. In its representation of the Dorrit and Clennam families, the novel aligns these institutions as part of a mutually illuminating critique. Clearly, Mr Dorrit's identity as 'Father of the Marshalsea' figures the prison as a family, and so his release from the jail is described in a chapter appropriately entitled,

'The Marshalsea becomes an Orphan'. His 'public' identity is an assertion of paternal authority that depends upon the application of the family's benevolent hierarchy as a model for power relations within the prison. But the identification of the Dorrit family with the Marshalsea is much more pervasive than this analogy would suggest, for the prison is not only an arena for the display of Mr Dorrit's social paternalism, but his home, with all that this implies about his 'private' self. The representation of the Marshalsea becomes inseparable from questions about the formation of identity of each of the Dorrits, for the prison displaces the family as the primary agent of socialisation in the novel, rewriting the narrative of child development and figuring upbringing as a form of incarceration. For example, Mr Dorrit's familiarisation of himself with the Marshalsea in the early chapters of the novel is described as a kind of 'familialisation': 'He had unpacked the portmanteau long ago; and his elder children now played regularly about the yard, and everybody knew the baby, and claimed a kind of proprietorship in her' (53). Indeed, the induction of new inmates into the Marshalsea is marked by the acknowledgment of its Father and Child, a discovery of a quasi-kinship, the narrator noting that it was 'almost a part of the entrance footing of every new collegian to nurse the child who had been born in the college' (56).

The assimilation of the Dorrit children into the life of the prison is shown in a number of ways. Little Dorrit's doll, for instance, which she sits dressing by the side of her friend the turnkey, is said to have come 'to be unlike dolls on the other side of the lock, and to bear a horrible *family resemblance* to Mrs Bangham' (57, my emphasis). Mrs Bangham, the Marshalsea's charwoman and messenger, 'was not a prisoner (though she had been once), but was the popular medium of communication with the outer world' (51). Ominously, the narrator observes that when she 'began to be infirm, and to be found oftener than usual comatose on pavements, with her basket of purchases spilt, and the change of her clients ninepence short', Little Dorrit's brother, Tip, 'began to supersede Mrs Bangham, and to execute commissions in a knowing manner, and to be of the prison prisonous, and of the streets streety' (54). This change is described as a 'succession' (62) to the business, linking the familial concepts of blood and upbringing – nature and nurture – in the question of Tip's development. Further evidence of the shaping effects of the prison family on the formation of Tip's identity is provided by the narrator's observation that

Wherever he went, this foredoomed Tip appeared to take the prison walls with him, and to set them up in such trade or calling; and to prowl about within their narrow limits in the old slip-shod, purposeless, down-at-heel way; until the real immovable Marshalsea walls asserted their fascination over him, and brought him back. (63)

Just as the effects of the Court of Chancery upon Richard Carstone are represented as an example of poor parenting in *Bleak House*, so, too, the Marshalsea prison is a disastrous substitute for the family as an agent of Tip's socialisation.

The integral connection between the family and the prison continues in the portrayal of the Clennams. When Arthur returns to his home in London on a gloomy Sunday evening in Book the First, chapter III, his Calvinist upbringing is vividly recalled as an endless course of discipline and punishment (24). His home is described as a prison in which his mother, 'stern of face and unrelenting of heart', would wield the Bible as if it were 'a fortification against sweetness of temper, natural affection, and gentle intercourse' (24). The importance placed upon corporal punishment as part of his upbringing associates Arthur's family tutelage with the form of discipline Foucault has identified as characteristic of an earlier, more openly coercive, mode of power. But Arthur's retrospective account of his childhood also shows evidence of the extent to which his thinking is structured by the discourse of the prison, thereby demonstrating the modern form of power, identified by Foucault, that works through the production of subjectivity. His memory is set within a carceral framework, and the description of his socialisation in the family explains his development of another kind of prison mentality. Recognition of the 'mind-forged manacles' which constrain Mrs Clennam is commonplace in critical discussions of the novel: in Book the Second, chapter XXXI, she stands in the Marshalsea 'looking down into this prison as it were out of her own different prison' (658). But Arthur is also shown to carry the prison within his consciousness, his upbringing having induced an obsessive sense of guilt and a belief in his own obsolescence. His internalisation of the prison demonstrates the distorting effects of the family on the formation of identity, and exemplifies the technology of subjection Foucault associates with the development of modern forms of power.

The discourses of religion and commerce play a significant role in the portrayal of the Clennam family as a prison. Arthur's overwhelming sense of guilt in the wake of his father's death leads him to raise the question of 'reparation' with his mother, but she rejects it, invoking her confinement 'in prison, and in bonds here' as penance for her sins, and credit for 'balancing her bargain with the Majesty of heaven' (41–3). This narrative link between religion and commerce is in keeping with Weber's well-known and much-disputed formulation of the Protestant ethic. Weber attributed the development of the modern economy in the Western world to a 'spirit of capitalism' which he saw as a psychological by-product of Calvinism.[18] According to his thesis, the Calvinist subject's doubt as to his own salvation leads him to engage in intense worldly activity as a means of carrying out his calling in the secular sphere. Such constant, systematic work in one's calling was the readiest way to glorify God and to 'prove' the certainty of salvation. In this way, religion consecrated the money-making motive, for as the sign that the endless task of proving one's election had been successfully accomplished, the accumulation of capital became a moral and spiritual imperative.

Mrs Clennam's stark embodiment of the Protestant ethic is well recognised. What has not been acknowledged in critical discussions of the novel, however, is the way in which the relationship between ethics and economics in *Little Dorrit* also depends upon the representation of varying forms of enterprise organisation and business activity as part of its concern with a changing social order. The novel details a range of commercial activities alongside its redefinition of the family in such a way as to implicate the ideological work of domesticity in the development of corporate capitalism. Two of the most important forms of commercial enterprise represented in the novel are evident in the contrast drawn between the sort of business in which the Clennams are involved, and the economic activity of Mr Merdle.

Arthur's inheritance is a share in the family business which, upon his return to London from the East, he relinquishes in opposition to the wishes of his mother. The discussion of this business is entered upon in the chapter entitled 'Family Affairs', where Arthur speaks to his mother of their 'House' as a dying concern, and of the 'old house' itself as 'an instance of what I say. In my father's earlier time, and in his uncle's time before him, it was a place of business – really a place of business, and business resort. Now, it is a mere anomaly and incongruity here, out of date and out of purpose' (37). Noting that their 'consignments have long been made to Rovinghams' the commission-merchants', he asks whether Mrs Clennam's 'judgment and watchfulness' with respect to his father's resources could not have been equally influential if she had 'lived in any private dwelling' (37). Arthur argues here for the distinction between home and workplace that was part of the regulation of class and gender differences in middle-class ideology. His comments register a shift in conceptions of business procedure and enterprise organisation away from the notion of an 'establishment' to a differentiation of family and business firm. According to Leonore Davidoff and Catherine Hall, the term 'establishment' was 'used to connote the combined enterprise and family/household' in the late eighteenth and early nineteenth century.[19] The anachronism associated with the House of Clennam therefore derives not only from the narrator's vivid descriptions of the age of the building it occupies, but also from its demonstration of that interweaving of economic organisation, finance, training and personnel with domestic affairs, identified by Davidoff and Hall as characteristic of late eighteenth- and early nineteenth-century business activity. The family frames the form of enterprise established in the House of Clennam, and Jeremiah Flintwinch's assumption of Arthur's share in the House maintains its familial character, given his status as 'an old and faithful servant' (44) of the Clennams.

In contrast to the family form of enterprise represented by the House of Clennam, and its dealings in commodified property, the economic activity of Mr Merdle is characterised by the abstractions of shares and credit. He is described as 'one of England's world-famed capitalists and merchant-princes' (209), 'a commercial Colossus' (466), and is said to be waved about on the trunk of the elephantine Lord Decimus 'as Gigantic Enterprise, the Wealth of England, Elasticity, Credit, Capital, Prosperity, and all manner of blessings' (578). The function of Mr Merdle in the novel's critique of the commercial scandals of the 1850s has received widespread critical comment. However, little attention has been given to the way in which his business activity enters into the novel's eventual formation of a domestic estate through the contrast set up with the House of Clennam. His career highlights the significance of the connection between changes in economic structure and forms of family in the novel – a connection that Dickens had explored earlier and with a different emphasis in *Dombey and Son*.

Davidoff and Hall trace a shift in economic structure throughout the nineteenth century from enterprises in which the fortunes of family and firm were so closely tied as to be indistinguishable from one another to the development of 'impersonal forms' of enterprise organisation. The controversy associated with the introduction of limited liability, discussed in chapter 2, was part of this process. Resistance to its introduction was largely based upon adherence to the principle of personal responsibility – a legacy of an earlier form of business organisation that was enshrined in the identification of family and firm. Such a principle assumed the reliance of legitimate economic activity upon the moral integrity of the family. However, in *Little Dorrit* this sort of assumption is undermined by the behaviour of the Clennams. Their questionable morality illustrates the consequences of continuing to tie the family to the fortunes of the enterprise in a way that gives a new twist to the relationship between ethics and economics identified by Weber. The vulnerability of the Clennam establishment emerges in the inseparability of its moral and financial affairs, which are, in turn, shown to have implications for the survival of both family and firm. However, the historical development of modern forms of business association depended upon the eventual abandonment of the principle of personal responsibility in favour of limited liability. The raising of investment capital was severely restricted by the risks involved for small entrepreneurs under the conditions of unlimited liability, and this situation fuelled the agitation surrounding the Limited Liability Act of 1855, which made shareholders of 'limited' companies liable only for the unpaid portion of their shares. *Little Dorrit* appeared in the thick of this controversy, its topical concern with economic change linking the development of corporate capitalism to the systemic irresponsibility it exposes everywhere else. The novel's 'Preface' situates the Marshalsea Prison – that most notorious institution established to enforce personal responsibility for debt – in a bygone era; and the distinction drawn between the period of the novel's setting, and the time of its publication, highlights for its first readers the transformation in economic activity forecast in the narrative. Arrest for debt on mesne process had been abolished in 1838 and, according to Barbara Weiss, 'by the middle of the nineteenth century, imprisonment for debt had been all but eliminated'.[20]

The world of *Little Dorrit* – set, in the opening words of the narrator, 'Thirty years ago' (1) – bears a prophetic resemblance to the world of its first readers, a world of modern institutions in which economic irresponsibility permits rapid capitalist expansion. But while the business affairs of Mr Merdle look towards an age in which personal responsibility for commercial ventures can be evaded, Dickens also uses Mr Dorrit to suggest that the obligations of debt are inalienable, thereby establishing an irreducible ground for moral identity. The novel appears to deplore the impersonality of corporate capitalism, punishing all those contaminated by the Merdle epidemic, and to exploit instead the old-fashioned identification of family and firm implied in the morality of Mr Dorrit's imprisonment for debt and inability to escape from his past. Yet it was the introduction of limited liability which gave economic sanction to the distinction between public and private identities so crucial to the ideology of domesticity by shielding the family from business failure, and it is this middle-class concept of the family that underwrites the satiric exposure of the Father of the Marshalsea. The ideological function of the family in the representation of economic change in the novel is thus ambivalent, contributing both to the critique of moral and social irresponsibility, and to the normalisation of the domestic ideal and the familial roles it defines. While the nineteenth-century development of impersonal forms to encompass the enterprise may, on the one hand, serve to segregate the middle-class family and protect its privacy, on the other it turns business failure into a deplorable situation which is 'Nobody's Fault'.

The fortunes of the House of Clennam are clearly inseparable from family affairs. The precariously balanced house, which, many years ago, 'had had it in its mind to slide down sideways' so that it required propping up by 'some half dozen gigantic crutches' (25), is an obvious symbol for the ominous situation of the family and firm. For Clennam, the house is enveloped in an atmosphere of secrecy which is ultimately traced to the twin secrets of his illegitimacy and Mrs Clennam's withholding of the will which would confer the legacy upon Little Dorrit. The revelation of these secrets coincides with the collapse of the house and explanation of the 'mysterious noises' heard by Affery. The fracturing of the family originally effected by Arthur's father in his mistaken marriage thus issues in the Fall of the House of Clennam. The Fall is preceded by another business failure with which it forms a contrast. Like the House of Clennam, the economic affairs of Mr Merdle also end in ruin in the novel. However, his downfall does not depend upon the kind of identification between family and firm associated with this earlier form of enterprise organisation. Indeed, both Mrs Merdle and Mr Sparkler manage to survive the crash, the former 'causing it to be understood that she was even more incensed against the felonious shade of the deceased than anybody else was' (671). There is an essentialism evident in the representation of the House of Clennam that is significantly missing in the representation of Mr Merdle's capitalism. The moral transgressions of the Clennam family issue in the Fall of the House in a way that ties business failure to family respectability. However, Mr Merdle's commercial activity appears to rely upon liquid assets and the notion of credit, rather than real property or the possession and exchange of commodities. His fortune is finally shown to be as vacuous as the 'abstraction' of Society in whose interests it was supposedly amassed. It consists of a capacity to keep money in perpetual circulation, like the jugglers in *Our Mutual Friend* who traffic in shares. His wealth is a clever fiction, an illusion of presence that only risks being seen as such when the mechanisms of circulation which 'bamboozle' the investors begin to break down. The magic name of Merdle exerts a signifying power that depends upon the arbitrary nature of the sign – a systemic power that resembles the nebulous bureaucratic authority wielded by the Barnacles.

According to Davidoff and Hall, the removal of the principle of personal responsibility in the organisation of nineteenth-century economic activity was compensated for by the evolution of public auditing of accounts and the formal registration of companies, and these changes parallel other shifts within the development of industrial capitalism: 'The separation of individuals and their dependants from personal implication with the main economic form, limiting their rights and responsibilities to that of the formal contract as either managers or shareholders, can be seen as analogous to the shift from personal service to the wage contract in the working class.'[21] The contrast drawn between the economic activity of the House of Clennam and of Mr Merdle is thus consistent with the novel's critique of Mr Dorrit's social paternalism as a regressive form of social organisation. The personal ties of dependency, cultivated by Mr Dorrit and which form the basis for his pretensions as Father of the Marshalsea, belong to an earlier social order in which the principle of personal responsibility regulated business activity and the family was identified with the firm. The transformation in economic life recorded in the novel implicates evolving conceptions of the family in this historical shift away from a feudal pattern of social relationships.

Offsetting the destabilising effects of social and economic change, however, is the unremitting domestic labour of Little Dorrit. The story of the novel's progress from 'Nobody's Fault' to *Little Dorrit* is well known. As Dickens came to realise that the social problems he deplored were systemic – that they were indeed 'Nobody's Fault' – the irony of the original title was lost and Little Dorrit in effect stepped in to remedy the 'false start' already made. The vacuous institutions represented in the novel, like Society, the Circumlocution Office and Mr Merdle's wonderful Bank, project problems that cannot be localised or attributed to individuals. The original title lives on, however, in the descriptions of Mr Merdle's extraordinary power and influence, which seem to be based on nothing more substantial than a form of collective ignorance: 'Nobody, as aforesaid, knew what he had done; but everybody knew him to be the greatest that had appeared' (476). Like Mr Dorrit's authority as Father of the Marshalsea, Mr Merdle's power rests upon a shared fiction, a consensual belief in its existence. And it is in opposition to the systemic and unaccountable nature of this power that the 'solution' provided by the union of Little Dorrit and Clennam is located.

The closure of the narrative with the union of Little Dorrit and Clennam situates domesticity as the familial goal towards which the novel has been moving. This union entails Arthur's abandonment of his paternalism and his submission to the moral guardianship of a domestic woman. It follows immediately upon Little Dorrit's declaration of her loss of fortune in the Merdle collapse, clearing the way for Clennam to mark his appreciation of her true worth in marriage. Unlike Pet Meagles, whose dowry tellingly defines her as an object of desire in the eyes of Henry Gowan, Little Dorrit's value lies in her female subjectivity – her loving capacity to supervise and service a household, her filial dutifulness, her purity – in short, her embodiment of the Victorian middle-class ideal of femininity. Her possession of these moral depths is perhaps most forcefully suggested by the contrast drawn between Little Dorrit and Mrs Merdle in the narrative. Mrs Merdle's identity is constituted by the magnificent bosom she displays, so that she is rendered entirely as a creature of surface. Even her marriage is determined by this capacity to exhibit, Mr Merdle having recognised that 'It was not a bosom to repose upon, but it was a capital bosom to hang jewels upon', and since 'Mr Merdle wanted something to hang jewels upon ... he bought it for the purpose. Storr and Mortimer might have married on the same speculation' (207). Clearly, what made Mrs Merdle desirable was her value as an object of aristocratic display; hence she had, and still has, no value as a female subject. According to Nancy Armstrong, this sort of emphasis upon putting the body and its adornments on display is 'a carry-over from the Renaissance display of aristocratic power',[22] and it contrasts with the value Little Dorrit is held to embody in the novel. Her diminutive stature, silence and the invisibility of her work are all part of an attempt to withdraw attention from her material body.

When the Dorrits accede to 'Riches' in the second part of the novel, Mrs General is specifically hired to 'varnish' the daughters of the family. Fanny is shown to be adept at forming a 'surface'. But Little Dorrit proves to be a more intractable subject, for she persists in seeing beyond façades, and deplores the ascendancy of 'Prunes and Prism' on their tour of Rome, where 'Everybody was walking about St Peter's and the Vatican on somebody else's cork legs, and straining every visible object through somebody else's sieve. Nobody said what anything was, but everybody said what the Mrs Generals, Mr Eustace, or somebody else said it was' (428). Little Dorrit is continually reproved by her father and sister for 'reviv[ing] the topic' (399) they wish to repress, for 'systematically reproduc[ing] what the rest of [the family] blot out' (400), for bearing the traces of the place in which 'she was born and bred' (400), but these traces are the signs of her female subjectivity. Unlike the visible trappings of wealth worn by Fanny, they provide evidence of her virtue as a domestic woman. In her inability to assume 'that graceful equanimity of surface which is so expressive of good breeding' (398), Little Dorrit continues to demonstrate the womanly devotion and duty defined by the middle-class ideology of the family. She exemplifies a shift, identified elsewhere by Nancy Armstrong, 'from an earlier form of power based on sumptuary display to a modern form that works through the production of subjectivity'.[23] For, in contrast to the illusory freedom gained upon the family's release from the Marshalsea, Little Dorrit submits to a less visible (although apparently more benign) mode of power by becoming morally responsible. In situating Little Dorrit as the saviour of Clennam and the hope of the novel, Dickens contributes to the cultural ascendancy of the middle-class definitions of the family and female identity.

The recuperative effects produced by Little Dorrit's embodiment of the feminine ideal situate middle-class domesticity as the normative vision of the family against which the problems associated with the tribalism of the Barnacles and the social paternalism of Mr Casby and Mr Dorrit are set. This sort of analysis refines existing critical considerations of the prison/family metaphor in the novel by demonstrating the complexity and pervasiveness of the relationship between these two institutions, and by uncovering the ideological work their connection enables. For example, *Little Dorrit* appears to give power a local habitation by situating its operations within a disciplinary institution such as the Marshalsea Prison, and this presentation of power as an institutional site of constraint or oppression suggests the existence of a place outside it, a realm of freedom in which privacy and identity may be recovered. However, the illusion of a place outside power, of the possibility of an escape into domesticity, is dispelled by the utility of the family as a figure for the prison in the novel. While the portrait of the Father of the Marshalsea produces his perversion of the family as a form of deviance, and so contributes to the normalising effects of middle-class ideology in the novel, the representation nevertheless depends upon a continuity between the family and the prison that threatens the opposition between them which is being asserted. A similar ambivalence distinguishes the representation of Clennam's paternalism, which is both bound up with his prison mentality and at least residually present in the January-and-May union he forms with Little Dorrit. Closing with their marriage, the novel resorts to a private solution, managing the destructive effects of institutions like the Circumlocution

Office, Mr Merdle's Bank and the Marshalsea Prison through the agency of a woman who embodies the domestic ideal. As the figure whose female 'nature' renders her the ideological guarantor of truth, meaning, male identity and the middle-class family, Little Dorrit promises respite from the vicissitudes of a changing social world that the novel cannot otherwise imagine how to overcome.

CHAPTER 5

A Tale of Two Cities

When he began writing the weekly parts of *A Tale of Two Cities* for his new journal, *All the Year Round*, in 1859, Dickens complained about 'the time and trouble of the incessant condensation' required by this form of publication.[1] His second attempt at 'historical fiction', the novel lacks the dense social atmosphere and proliferation of 'unnecessary' detail that characterise the 'big books' like *Bleak House* and *Little Dorrit*. But notwithstanding the relative tautness and economy of its narrative, *A Tale of Two Cities* shares the fascination with the family shown by the more expansive works. As Dickens explained in another letter recorded by Forster, part of his intention in the novel was to contrast the 'feudal cruelties' of the *ancien régime* with the 'new philosophy' espoused by Charles Darnay: 'With the slang of the new philosophy on the one side, it was surely not unreasonable or unallowable, on the other, to suppose a nobleman wedded to the old cruel ideas, and representing the time going out as his nephew represents the time coming in.'[2] This contrast involves the juxtaposition of two different conceptions of the family, as the Marquis's 'good breeding' (144) and concern for 'the power and honour of families' (145) are set against the Victorian middle-class domestic ideal to which his anglicised nephew is committed. Critical discussions of the family in the novel have often focussed upon the relationship between the Marquis St Evrémonde and Charles Darnay as a version of the generational rivalry between fathers and sons that is evident elsewhere in the relations between Darnay and Doctor Manette, Carton and Stryver, and Young Jerry and his father. Albert D. Hutter has analysed the novel in these terms, arguing that 'As much as any other work of 1859, *A Tale of Two Cities* demonstrates the correlation between family and nation, and it uses the language of psychological conflict and psychological identification to portray social upheaval and the restoration of social order.'[3]

But rather than offering another psychoanalytic account of relationships between fathers and sons in the novel, my analysis focusses upon the way in which concepts of the family and female identity are invested in Dickens's appalled and yet fascinated response to the French Revolution. The novel uses gender difference – defined by the Victorian middle-class ideal of domesticity – to represent its political conflicts in a narrative strategy designed to universalise the horror of the crisis. Dickens characteristically rejects politics in favour of a personal, familial resolution; but the dissemination of the ideal of domesticity in his fiction that this narrative procedure entails has a normalising effect that is, nonetheless, politically significant. Dickens genders the Revolution, turning its overtly political conflicts into questions of sexual difference. Posing the political crisis as a threat to the values of the English middle-class family, the novel performs a larger cultural function by participating in the development of forms of knowledge and power based upon a model of sexual difference. In *A Tale of Two Cities*, this process is primarily shown in the sustained effort to identify the French Revolution with female deviance in the narrative.

Dickens's primary source for the novel was Carlyle's great narrative, *The French Revolution*. Like Carlyle, Dickens uses a prophetic voice to discover order in the apparent anarchy of the French Revolution. His narrator fashions a coherent account of events to explain the past and apprehend the truths of history. Carlyle's charting of the 'cycles and seasons' in the progress of the Revolution is an attempt to identify the ordering principles of history that resembles the providential design evident in *A Tale of Two Cities* – the pattern recognised by Charles Darnay according to which, he says, 'All things have worked together as they have fallen out' (413). Carlyle recognised the importance of the imagination in understanding the past: he sought to resuscitate dead facts into a living reality in a process that cast history as an act of imaginative projection and identification, and turned its writing into a work of literary creation. And to this end his personal pronouns and use of the present tense situate the reader in the midst of the revolutionary turmoil, as he focusses upon the role of heroic individuals in the course of the conflict.

Like Carlyle, Dickens attempts to provide an imaginative reconstruction of this historical conflict. But rather than finding a way out of revolutionary chaos through hero-worship, he relies upon the saving power of the middle-class family, conceived as an ideal transcending social and national differences. Dickens's moral aim is expressed in the novel by Charles Darnay in his determination to return to France that he may try 'to do something to stay bloodshed, and assert the claims of mercy and humanity' (297). The novel's apparent goal, suggested in the opening antitheses which mock attempts to define the age, is to universalise the action – to emphasise the commonality of human experience everywhere – and the representation of the family is central to this process, because the domestic ideal is invoked as a norm ostensibly beyond the contingency of historical difference. Dickens uses the idea of the family in an attempt to depoliticise and dehistoricise the events recorded in what one might expect to be the most overtly political and historical of his novels.

A number of commentators have criticised Dickens for posing private answers to the public problems of history and failing to provide an adequate analysis of the Revolution in *A Tale of Two Cities*. Lukács provided the most well known of these criticisms in his study of the historical novel, where he objects that Dickens uses the events of the French Revolution merely as a 'romantic background' to the lives of his fictional characters.[4] However, rather than betraying Dickens's failure to provide a satisfactory historical investigation of the revolutionary process, the novel's use of private lives to explore public conflicts should itself be seen as a historically significant strategy. In *A Tale of Two Cities*, the Victorian middle-class family appears to promise a haven of true love and humanity in the midst of the Revolution that transcends the turmoil of class conflict and national difference, and grounds identity in the locus of the domestic hearth. This account of the family provides another example of the representation of middle-class ascendancy.

The event which precipitates the major actions of the plot of *A Tale of Two Cities* is a crime against the domestic family. The younger of the Evrémonde brothers rapes a young peasant girl, the daughter of one of his tenants. Her young husband had previously been worked to death in a harness and her father's heart had 'burst' (403) at the news of her capture. When her brother, who recounts these events, attempts to punish the ravisher, he is mortally wounded. Only one member of the family escapes – a younger sister – who turns out to be Madame Defarge. In the account of this precipitating crime recorded by Doctor Manette, aristocratic *droit de seigneur* is defined as a violation of the family whose integrity and purity are identified with female chastity. Social exploitation and sexual violence are yoked together. The use of this figure of female/familial violation to characterise the *ancien régime* has important consequences for the portrayal of the Revolution in the novel, for if the aristocratic oppression of the French peasantry which leads to the Revolution is represented as a rivalry between men over the possession of a woman, in a process of signification which grounds itself in the apparent timelessness of gender arrangements beneath the vicissitudes of social conflict, the depiction of the Revolution itself also involves a displacement of class on to gender. The Revolution is represented as a kind of Amazonian 'misrule'. It is gendered, and set in opposition to the idealised domestic family in the narrative, enabling Dickens to offer an ostensibly apolitical analysis of his subject.

The gendering of the Revolution in *A Tale of Two Cities* is primarily brought about through the concentration of the narrative upon the figure of Madame Defarge, 'leader of the Saint Antoine women' (271). In the cover design created by Hablôt Browne for the part issues,[5] Madame Defarge is set in opposition to Lucie on the left-hand side of the page, clearly signalling their juxtaposition in the text. The symmetry of their pairing is part of a set of parallels drawn between England and France, designed to bridge national differences in the interests of rendering universal human nature. Other parallels included in this set are the 'Two Cities' of the title, the crowds in England and France, the trials of Darnay in each country, and the pairing of Stryver and the Marquis St Evrémonde through their respective relationships with Carton and Darnay. However, as the careful juxtapositioning of Madame Defarge with Lucie Manette in the novel shows, the universal human nature which Dickens is attempting to portray through these techniques of parallelism takes gender as the transhistorical constituent of identity, and yet, at the same time, grounds it in the ideology of the Victorian middle-class family. For the definition of female identity produced through the opposition between these two women hinges upon the wider formation of domestic ideology and the propagation of the values of home in Victorian middle-class culture. The fear of social disintegration generated by the hostility of class difference is apparently allayed through the commonality of a belief in shared familial values that define the activities of Madame Defarge as deviant. However, the family proves to be a problematic mechanism for easing bourgeois anxieties about the consequences of class conflict, since its use in the novel is informed by the very social differences it was supposed to transcend.

The characterisation of Madame Defarge carries strong echoes of the portrayal of her compatriot, Mademoiselle Hortense, from *Bleak House*. Hortense is described as 'a large-eyed brown woman with black hair; who would be handsome, but for a certain feline mouth, and general uncomfortable tightness of face, rendering the jaws too eager, and the skull too prominent' (143). Like the 'universal watchfulness' (302) that characterises the inhabitants of revolutionary France, Hortense has a 'watchful way of looking out of the corners of her eyes without turning her head, which could be pleasantly dispensed with – especially when she is in an ill-humour and near knives' (143). As a double for Lady Dedlock, she blends the threat of violence with the threat of female sexuality. When Mr Bucket informs her of his wife's part in her capture, Hortense, 'panting tigress-like', exclaims:

'I would like to kiss her!' . . .
'You'd bite her, I suspect,' says Mr Bucket.
'I would!' making her eyes very large. 'I would love to tear her, limb from limb.'
(652)

Esther makes the connection with Madame Defarge even more directly when she remarks 'a lowering energy in [Mademoiselle Hortense's] face . . . which seemed to bring visibly before me some woman from the streets of Paris in the reign of terror' (286).

However, Madame Defarge is distinguished from Hortense by her beguiling steadiness of demeanour. Until the moment for rebellion arrives, she remains outwardly calm and imperturbable. While Hortense cannot help betraying her passionate anger, Madame Defarge is remarkable for the success with which she conceals her rage. Indeed, it is the extraordinary tension between her hidden fury and her façade of equanimity that makes her so fascinating and formidable. The narrator refers repeatedly to her astonishing 'composure'. On her first appearance in Book the First, chapter v, she is described as 'a stout woman of about [30], with a watchful eye that seldom seemed to look at anything, a large hand heavily ringed, a steady face, strong features, and great composure of manner' (37). Clearly, her 'watchful eye' suggests a capacity for dissimulation that worries the narrator, whose cautious and tentative account of her behaviour conveys a sense of hidden menace. Her gipsy-like attire adds to the dubiousness of her moral status and suggestively casts her as something of an outlaw, as exotic and 'other'. Andrew Sanders notes that the manuscript of the novel reveals a change from the original paragraph in which Dickens had portrayed Madame Defarge as a 'little woman' intent on her needlework.[6] These assertions of Madame Defarge's freedom from the norms and restraints of English middle-class femininity sit oddly and ironically with the narrator's conventional reference to Monsieur Defarge as 'her lord'. The incongruity makes apparent the way in which the normalising discourse of Victorian domesticity underlines cultural difference here, and provides a means for evaluating and containing the revolutionary threat.

Much of the menace surrounding Madame Defarge in these early descriptions obviously comes from the ominousness of the narrator's inordinate attention to her every movement and expression. The most trivial details and innocent gestures – Madame's habit of picking her teeth, slight coughs, raising her eyebrows by nicely calculated degrees – are loaded with hidden meaning as they are repeatedly particularised and dwelt upon in the narrative. Of course, the knitting of Madame Defarge is the most famous of these secret codes. The threat posed by her knitting draws on the symbolism of the Three Fates which is made explicit at the end of Book the Second, chapter VII. When the Marquis attempts to make token reparation for running over the child of Gaspard by contemptuously flinging two gold coins to the bereft father, he is incensed to find the money thrown back into his carriage:

'Hold!' said Monsieur the Marquis. 'Hold the horses! Who threw that?'

He looked to the spot where Defarge the vendor of wine had stood, a moment before; but the wretched father was grovelling on his face on the pavement in that spot, and the figure that stood beside him was the figure of a dark stout woman, knitting. (132)

The substitution of wife for husband at the side of Gaspard foreshadows the gender reversal which is used to represent the revolutionary threat in the narrative. After the child's body is taken away by its father, Madame Defarge remains by the fountain, knitting on 'with the steadfastness of Fate' (133).

Madame Defarge's knitting associates her with the notorious *tricoteuses*, the patriotic knitting-women of Paris, who are described in Carlyle's *The French Revolution*. She knits a register of all the oppressors belonging to the *ancien régime*, dooming them to destruction. Her knitting is an unalterable chronicle, a grim history which records the past in a mysterious female language that only she and her sister-knitters can decipher. It forms an analogue for omniscient narration in the novel, contrasting with Dickens's apparently more fluid and sympathetic handling of history.[7] But perhaps the most important thematic and ideological function of her inexorable knitting is its relevance to the representation of domesticity and the feminine ideal in the novel. The knitted register produces a shock in its implicit linkage of images and emotions normally opposed in Victorian middle-class ideology. The creativity, nurture and maternal affection, conventionally associated with knitting, are connected here with vengeance, violence and death. The incongruity is given a darkly comic expression in a brief conversation witnessed by the 'mender of roads' during his excursion to Versailles with the Defarges. A bystander remarks on her knitting:

'You work hard, madame,' said a man near her.
'Yes,' answered Madame Defarge; 'I have a good deal to do.'
'What do you make, madame?'
'Many things.'
'For instance –'
'For instance,' returned Madame Defarge, composedly, 'shrouds.' (209)

The striking mixture of domestic activity and public violence involved in the knitted register finds its climax in the description of the *tricoteuses* who encircle the guillotine and sit 'knitting, knitting, counting dropping heads' (225). This overriding of the boundary between public and private realms in the deadly knitting of the patriotic women defies the Victorian middle-class ideals of femininity and domesticity. It shows not only Madame Defarge's failure to conform to the normal 'requirements' of her gender, but her strategic use or abuse of these requirements as a guise for her sinister activities. A related example is to be found in the rose which she pins in her head-dress as a warning-signal to her compatriots in Book the Second, chapter XVI. While the function of the rose as an emblem of England is relevant here, it is also significant that the aesthetics of feminine adornment are deployed in the service of the Revolution. Rather than observing the rules of fashion in an effort to attract the admiration of male onlookers, Madame Defarge uses the trappings of female finery as a code for political intrigue. The ritual expression of beauty and sexual attractiveness becomes a guise for the subversive activities of the revolutionaries.

The subversion of gender promoted by the knitting of Madame Defarge is extended in other aspects of her characterisation. Traits of masculinity are suggested in the narrator's observation of her 'large hand', 'steady face' and 'strong features' in Book the First, chapter V, and this impression is confirmed in the depiction of her relationship with Monsieur Defarge. There is more than a hint of the reversal in power-relations, shown elsewhere by such comic Dickensian partners as Mr and Mrs Snagsby, Joe and Mrs Joe, and Mr and Mrs Wilfer, in the portrayal of the Defarges, husband and wife. The circumspection shown by Madame in managing the trade of the wine-shop is not unlike the thriftiness and vigilance manifested by her fictional English counterparts, and Monsieur Defarge's reaction finds a similar parallel in the behaviour of their meek English husbands: 'All this while, Defarge, with his pipe in his mouth, walked up and down, complacently admiring, but never interfering; in which condition, indeed, as to the business and his domestic affairs, he walked up and down through life' (214–15). However, the masculine authority apparently assumed in these matters by Madame Defarge does not provide the only test to the limits of gender entailed in her characterisation. This scene in Book the Second, chapter XVI, draws upon Victorian ideals of wifely duty which enjoined a woman to comfort and counsel her partner, but does so only to show Madame Defarge abusing and undermining them. The counsel she gives her husband is to sustain his rage and discontent in secret, and the comfort she offers is the promise of vengeance and retribution. Her strategy in this discussion is to insinuate a charge of cowardice against her husband, and his 'weakness' is implicitly contrasted with her own courage and deadly determination. The scene recalls the dialogue between Lady Macbeth and her faltering husband in its questioning of the attributes of gender. Echoing something of the shock generated by Lady Macbeth's violent repudiation of maternity, Madame Defarge's routine actions, in knotting up into her handkerchief the small moneys taken in the shop, are seen as a series of executions. Her conversation with Monsieur Defarge is punctuated by narrative comments on her sinister delight in this occupation: 'She tied a knot with flashing eyes, as if it throttled a foe' (216). The discussion between husband and wife ends with Madame exhorting her partner to sustain himself without needing 'to see [his] victim and [his] opportunity': 'Madame enforced the conclusion of this piece of advice by striking her little counter with her chain of money as if she knocked its brains out, and then gathering the heavy handkerchief under her arm in a serene manner, and observing that it was time to go to bed' (217). The relish of imagined murder is incongruously combined with the routine preparation for bed, reinforcing the link with Lady Macbeth that is clear in the verbal echo here.[8] Madame Defarge is (appropriately) childless, and she admonishes her quailing husband, who characteristically 'stand[s] before her with his head a little bent, and his hands clasped at his back, like a docile and attentive pupil before his catechist' (216).

The reversal in the power-relations between husband and wife becomes more pronounced as the novel progresses. This subversion of gender differences signifies a breakdown in male authority – an overthrowing of social order – and it gathers momentum around the question of the respective fates of Lucie, Charles and Doctor Manette. When the marriage of Lucie and Charles is made known to the Defarges by Barsad in Book the Second, chapter XVI, Monsieur Defarge finds himself 'rather pleading with his wife to induce her to admit' the 'strangeness' of the fact that Lucie and her father should be proscribed under her hand after

having been the objects of their sympathy. His 'pleading' proves to be
ineffectual, and when this discussion recurs in Book the Third, chapter XII,
Monsieur Defarge is reduced to feeble protests in the face of his wife's
implacable wrath: 'Defarge, a weak minority, interposed a few words for
the memory of the compassionate wife of the Marquis; but only elicited
from his own wife a repetition of her last reply. "Tell the Wind and the Fire
where to stop; not me!"' (421). The narrator's reference to Defarge as a
'minority' indicates not only a difference in the opinions of the husband
and wife, but a change in the dynamics of the household and in its
decision-making procedures. The male–female pairing ratified by
marriage has apparently been cut across by new relationships and
alliances formed in the pursuit of revolutionary goals. Madame Defarge's
closest ally is no longer her husband, but a female friend who was introduced in Book the Second, chapter XXII, as one of Madame's 'sisterhood'
– one who sits faithfully beside her, knitting, and who 'had already earned
the complimentary name of The Vengeance' (271). The terms of endear-
ment repeatedly exchanged between Madame and her lieutenant are
given a ghoulish aspect by the murderous sentiments which are shown to
prompt them. Madame's relishing assertion of her power over the fate of
Lucie – '"Let me but lift my finger – !" She seemed to raise it . . . , and to let
it fall with a rattle on the ledge before her, as if the axe had dropped' (420) –
provokes The Vengeance to embrace her Chief and cry 'She is an Angel!'
In return, Madame Defarge acknowledges the devotion of her passionate
friend by addressing her in a travesty of tenderness as 'my little
Vengeance' (420).

The bond between these two women is shown to become more close
and deadly as the Revolution gathers momentum. Madame Defarge holds
'darkly ominous council with The Vengeance and Jacques Three of the
Revolutionary Jury' in Book the Third, chapter XIV, to plot the execution
of Lucie and her child. The secret council measures the extent of the rup-
ture between husband and wife, as Madame condemns his 'weaknesses',
explains that she 'dare not confide to him the details of my projects' and
announces her decision to act for herself (444). This transfer of confidence
and loyalties from her husband to her revolutionary comrades is the most
obvious sign of a fracture in the family. However, there is also something
particularly sinister about the emphasis upon the alliance between the two
women here. Jacques Three is full of praise for Madame and is said to
vie with The Vengeance 'in their fervent protestations that she was the
most admirable and marvellous of witnesses' (445). But his rivalling
acclamations and gestures serve to underline the threat posed by the

homosocial bond between the two women, who embrace one another with melodramatic fervour. The Vengeance is entrusted with the safe-keeping of the fatal register, and the blood-lust shared by the two women here represents perhaps the Revolution's most significant challenge to patriarchal authority and order. Both The Vengeance and the Juryman, looking after Madame Defarge as she walks away, are said to be 'highly appreciative of her fine figure, and her superb moral endowments' (447). Clearly, the narrator's irony emphasises the moral chaos implied by such an approving estimation of ruthlessness. But the equivalence of their admiration also disrupts the structuring of sexual relations associated with Victorian middle-class ideology. The relationships shown to obtain between these revolutionary citizens are not 'properly' refracted by gender. There is no differentiation between the underlying bonds of desire joining Madame Defarge to her male and female comrades. And this failure to preserve the difference between heterosexual and homosocial relationships represents a challenge to the patriarchal social structure that characterises not only the *ancien régime* in France, but the social order of Victorian England. Directed against an oppressive patriarchal system, the sisterly solidarity of Madame Defarge and The Vengeance is therefore especially threatening.

The Vengeance is characterised throughout the novel by an exhibition of extreme passion and violence bordering on insanity. When the lynching of Foulon commences in chapter XXII, she 'tears' from house to house, rousing the women, 'uttering terrific shrieks, and flinging her arms about her head like all the forty Furies at once' (272). She 'screeches' admiration for Monsieur Defarge in the midst of Darnay's trial, and when the President rings his bell, 'shrieks' defiance of his warning (392). She is equally vehement in her affection for her 'Chief', 'kissing her cheek' (447) and lavishing extravagant epithets of praise upon her. Madame Defarge is occasionally required to moderate the enthusiasm of The Vengeance – '"Peace, little Vengeance," said Madame Defarge, laying her hand with a slight frown on her lieutenant's lips, "hear me speak"' (443) – and these cautions emphasise the barely controlled madness in her behaviour. The crazed passion of The Vengeance betrays a fundamental loss of rationality that is part of the novel's feminisation of the Revolution, and that is suggested elsewhere in the imagery of natural disaster used to portray the rising of the people. Madame Defarge's reply to her husband's plea in Book the Third, chapter XII, 'Tell the Wind and the Fire where to stop; not me!' (371), invokes the resistless forces of nature to identify her implacability with the impulse of the Revolution, which is also described as the working-out of catastrophic natural history.[9] The coming of the Revolution and its intrusion into the lives of Lucie and Doctor Manette are heralded in the electrical storm which interrupts the family gathering seated beneath the plane-tree at the Doctor's lodgings in Soho in June 1780 (the fictional event coinciding with the timing of the Gordon Riots), and the storming of the Bastille nine years later is described as an all-destroying ocean, the rising of a 'living sea' (263).

Dickens was drawing upon a well-established apocalyptic tradition for the imagery he used to portray the Revolution. But this representation of the Revolution in terms of catastrophic natural history is also part of the novel's exploitation of sexual difference to represent political conflict. The history of the concept of reason in Western philosophical thought has been characterised by the use of oppositional formulations in which men have been distinguished by their rational capacity and women have been defined as irrational and associated with the uncontrollable forces of nature.[10] In a similar way, the characterisation of the revolutionary mob in *A Tale of Two Cities* as an irresistible natural force locates its violent activity outside the realm of patriarchal culture and helps displace political conflict on to gender conflict. The description of the emblematic wrath of Saint Antoine as a relentless natural force in Book the Second, chapter XXI – a 'sea of black and threatening waters, and of destructive upheaving of wave against wave', containing 'faces hardened in the furnaces of suffering until the touch of pity could make no mark on them' (268) – is echoed in the later portrait of Madame Defarge as a figure 'absolutely without pity', and one whom 'the troubled time would have heaved ... up, under any circumstances' (447). As a movement that is mindlessly passionate and dangerously unpredictable, the Revolution suggests the chaos associated with the idea of female insubordination. As Dickens's sympathies shift from the revolutionaries to their victims in *A Tale of Two Cities*, the representation of the Revolution itself is increasingly shaped by the nature/culture dichotomy so prevalent in the Western philosophical and literary traditions, and embodied, for example, in *King Lear*, where Lear's relinquishment of his patriarchal power to his diabolical daughters is shown to issue in natural and civil disorder.

Dickens emphasises the role of the women in the French Revolution as evidence of a violation of the sexual hierarchy. Even that most notorious instrument of revolutionary justice – La Guillotine – is female. It is a 'devouring and insatiate' (459) monster, a rapacious woman whose appetite can never be satisfied: 'Lovely girls; bright women, brown-haired, black-haired, and grey; youths; stalwart men and old; gentle born and peasant born; all red wine for La Guillotine, all daily brought into light from the dark cellars of the loathsome prisons, and carried to her through the street to slake her devouring thirst' (338). Adding to this effect of 'unnatural' female blood-lust, the melodramatic vision of the revolution-aries' lynching of Foulon, given in Book the Second, chapter XXII, uses the transgression of gender norms to describe the social disorder:

[T]he women were a sight to chill the boldest. From such household occupations as their bare poverty yielded, from their children, from their aged and their sick crouching on the bare ground famished and naked, they ran out with streaming hair, urging one another, and themselves, to madness with the wildest cries and actions. Villain Fouln taken, my sister. Old Foulon taken, my mother. Miscreant Foulon taken, my daughter. Then, a score of others ran into the midst of these, beating their breasts, tearing their hair, and screaming, Foulon alive. (272)

In an effort to convey the horror of the mob, the narrator focusses upon the abandonment of domestic responsibilities, and the violence and mad-ness that seem to possess the women. The mixture of free direct speech with narrative comment and description is used to convey the chaos of the scene. The passage draws upon historical accounts describing the Eumenides of the Revolution. In particular, it was the Parisian women in their march to Versailles to demand bread from the king and the National Assembly who were condemned by English observers as 'furies', 'harlots', and 'shrews'.[11] One of Dickens's sons later remembered his father naming

two scenes in literature which he regarded as being the most dramatic descrip-tions he could recall . . . The first was the description of the Woman in White's appearance on the Hampstead Road after her escape from the asylum in Wilkie Collins's famous book *The Woman in White*. The other was the stirring account of the march of the women to Versailles in Carlyle's *French Revolution*.[12]

The violation of gender norms illustrated by the women who cry for the blood of Foulon is repeated in the description of two other set scenes of the Revolution: the Terror and the Carmagnole. Dickens encapsulates the Reign of Terror in the emblem of the blood-smeared grindstone in Book the Third, chapter II, which is turned by two men whose faces

were more horrible and cruel than the visages of the wildest savages in their most barbarous disguise. False eyebrows and false moustaches were stuck upon them, and their hideous countenances were all bloody and sweaty, and all awry with

howling, and all staring and glaring with beastly excitement and want of sleep. As
these ruffians turned and turned, their matted locks now flung forward over their
eyes, now flung backward over their necks, some women held wine to their
mouths that they might drink; and what with dropping blood, and what with
dropping wine, and what with the stream of sparks struck out of the stone, all
their wicked atmosphere seemed gore and fire. (321)

Smeared with blood, the men who shoulder one another in an effort to get
at the grindstone are 'devilishly set off with spoils of women's lace and silk
and ribbon, with the stain dyeing all those trifles through and through'. As
the men work at the grindstone while the women supply them with drink,
gender differences appear to be preserved only in order to set off their
obliteration elsewhere in the indiscriminate frenzy of blood-lust. The
revolutionaries are characterised by their violence and passion, and the
disgust of the narrator is strikingly registered in the brutal frankness
with which he intrudes at the end of the passage, seeking to 'petrify' the
'frenzied eyes' of the mob 'with a well-directed gun' (322). Images of
barbarism and sexual perversion convey the horror of the scene. Instead
of being portrayed as a cataclysmic natural force – a living sea, raging fire
or earthquake – the revolutionaries are figured here as the members of a
degenerate race. The gathering of the throng is like a crazy primitive
ritual, a carnal scene of blood, sweat, filth and dissipation. Nineteenth-
century depictions of revolution commonly fantasised the conflict as
a reversion to cannibalism,[13] and here the metaphor of cannibalism is
literalised in the syntax, which identifies the 'dropping blood' with the
'dropping wine', bringing this scene together with the earlier account of
the spilt wine outside the shop of Monsieur Defarge (33). But whereas the
breaking of the wine cask is represented as an opportunity for innocent
conviviality, the activity around the grindstone is represented as the work
of degeneracy. The perversion of gender identity evident in the ghastly
appearance of the revolutionaries is an important part of this critique.
According to Andrew Sanders, there is no reference to the 'false eyebrows
and false moustaches' of the revolutionaries in any of Dickens's likely
sources for this section, and he attributes the description to Carlyle's
account of the murder of the Princess de Lamballe at La Force in 1789,
noting that Dickens does not seem to have read, or remembered, the
original French which appears to have been available to him.[14] In
Mercier's account, one of the assassins of the Princess cut off her pubic
hair and made himself moustaches of it. Whatever Dickens knew of this
incident, the detail adds to the promiscuous mixing of genders in the scene

of carnality described. The signs of parodic cross-dressing are yet another example of the way in which a violation of the sexual hierarchy is used to represent the social upheaval of the Revolution.

These images of the Terror anticipate the description of the Carmagnole in Book the Third, chapter v. Near the shop of the wood-sawyer on the outskirts of La Force, Lucie encounters a throng of people dancing, 'in the midst of whom was the wood-sawyer hand in hand with The Vengeance':

Men and women danced together, women danced together, men danced together, as hazard had brought them together. At first, they were a mere storm of coarse red caps and coarse woollen rags; but, as they filled the place, and stopped to dance about Lucie, some ghastly apparition of a dance-figure gone raving mad arose among them. (342)

The description emphasises the incongruous mixture of organised ritual and violent anarchy evident in the fiery patriotic dance. A primitive patterning is evident in the recurrence of gestures, and the movements made in unison. But these signs of order are offset by the violence and overt sexuality of the performance: 'Such grace as was visible in it, made it the uglier, showing how warped and perverted all things good by nature were become,' says the narrator. Partnering in the dance ignores the rules of sexual difference, leaving the combinations to 'hazard', and the suggestion of promiscuity implicit in this defiance of convention is compounded by the stress upon the unrestrained energy and physicality of the dancers, who 'strike', 'clutch', 'tear', 'spin' and 'scream'. The Carmagnole is a 'fallen sport', a 'something, once innocent, delivered over to all devilry'. Social disorder is expressed through the loss of female purity shown by the 'baring' of 'maidenly bosoms', the 'distracting' of 'pretty' heads, and the 'mincing' of 'delicate feet' in 'this slough of blood and dirt'. The narrator is both appalled and fascinated by the sight. His description of the Carmagnole assumes the grounding of gender difference in 'nature' in order to distinguish the perversions of this 'disjointed time'. But in identifying the revolutionary turmoil with female deviance, and dwelling upon its description in such scenes of mob frenzy in the novel, the narrator also seems to reveal a repressed fascination with the horrors he so strenuously deplores.[15] It is as if he cannot evade the implications of the model of heterosexual desire upon which his representation of female subjectivity is founded. This sexual tension in the narrative recalls the ambiguous imaginative interest Dickens shows elsewhere in 'fallen' women like Edith Granger and Lady Dedlock, and is further evidence that his attitudes towards the middle-class ideals of femininity and family were never entirely straightforward.

The link between political violence and sexual anarchy in Dickens's representation of the Revolution was not new. Edmund Burke had used the image of the Furies to represent the political threat in his *Reflections on the Revolution in France* (1790).[16] Revolutionary activity in France and America provided feminists of the Enlightenment, like Mary Wollstonecraft, with encouragement in their call for equality between the sexes. The language of political libertarianism was adapted for the articulation of a feminist position, and it is no coincidence that in the midst of this exciting atmosphere of change women became more politicised. A number of female clubs and societies were formed in France which initiated women into public life and gave them a forum for discussing their demands for justice and education. So it is hardly surprising that Dickens should associate the overthrow of government there with female insubordination. Dickens's original for Madame Defarge was Théroigne de Méricourt, who was active as a feminist in the last years of the constitutional monarchy and a member of the 'Société fraternelle des patriotes des deux sexes'. She took part in the October 1789 march to Versailles, and is described by Carlyle's narrator as 'the brown-locked, light-behaved, fire-hearted Demoiselle Théroigne'.[17] Carlyle indicates the transgression of gender norms evident in the behaviour of Théroigne, and Dickens develops this suggestive combination of violence and sexual attraction in his portrayal of Thérèse Defarge. In pursuit of Lucie, she is described as a 'tigress', a woman 'absolutely without pity':

Such a heart Madame Defarge carried under her rough robe. Carelessly worn, it was a becoming robe enough, in a certain weird way, and her dark hair looked rich under her coarse red cap. Lying hidden in her bosom, was a loaded pistol. Lying hidden at her waist, was a sharpened dagger. Thus accoutred, and walking with the confident tread of such a character, and with the supple freedom of a woman who had habitually walked in her girlhood, bare-foot and bare-legged, on the brown sea-sand, Madame Defarge took her way along the streets. (448)

Like Mademoiselle Hortense, Madame Defarge's perversion of female nature is predictably expressed in her identification with the wild animal which epitomised, for the Victorians, the greatest threat to be feared from the animal kingdom and from restive human subordinates: the tigress.[18] But what is most striking about this description is the way in which the danger represented by Madame Defarge is combined with hints of sexual fascination. Just as the accounts of the grindstone and Carmagnole reveal undercurrents of sexual horror and fascination, the characterisation of Madame Defarge shows a peculiar tension between feelings of attraction and repulsion in the narrator's stance. Given the informal censorship associated with the practice of 'family reading' amongst the Victorian middle classes and dominant assumptions about women's sexuality during the period, any description of the female body in Victorian domestic fiction treads on dangerous ground; and the portrait of Madame Defarge dwells upon bodily details that were specific sites of sexual signification in Victorian middle-class culture: her hair, bosom, waist and legs. There is something rather tantalising about the narrative emphasis given to the deadly weapons hidden in these erotogenic zones upon the body of Madame Defarge – the pistol secreted in her bosom, the dagger at her waist – despite their function as evidence of her 'unwomanly' activities. The emphasis given here to her 'confidence' and 'supple freedom' accords with the loud assertion of female independence that accompanied the Revolution. Mary Wollstonecraft's *A Vindication of the Rights of Woman* was published in the first year of the new Republic, and Madame Defarge's alliance with The Vengeance in the novel may well owe something to the reputation of Théroigne de Méricourt as a member of the 'Société fraternelle' and an advocate for the formation of a women's militia company in February 1792.[19]

Albert D. Hutter has noted an interesting change in the illustration of Madame Defarge since the novel's first publication in 1859. In the original 'Phiz' drawings, she is shown as a strong, young woman, with a beautiful but determined face, and dark hair. The illustrations set her in contrast with the blond-haired beauty of Lucie Manette. However, many subsequent versions of Madame Defarge in film and illustration have made her a witch. According to Hutter, the Harper and Row cover to *A Tale of Two Cities*, for example, 'shows a cadaverous old crone, gray-haired, hunched over her knitting, with wrinkles stitched across a tightened face'.[20] In the 1935 film, starring Ronald Colman, Madame Defarge is a rather haggard and plain-faced woman, with dark circles beneath her eyes, whose grim appearance contrasts with the fair complexion and rosy lips of the beautiful Lucie.

This change in the visual representation of Madame Defarge denotes a cultural shift in the construction of female subjectivity from the nineteenth to the twentieth century, and highlights Defarge's function in the novel. As a crucial part of the novel's effort to solve the problems posed by the Revolution, Madame Defarge serves as the monstrous female 'other' against which the norms of Victorian middle-class femininity and domesticity can be invoked. She is characterised as dangerously sexual and violent, oblivious of her wifely role and domestic responsibilities, lacking the feminine virtues of meekness, compassion and purity shown by Lucie and ominously intimate with like-minded women. All of these traits are informed by a Victorian middle-class conception of female subjectivity. Later representations showing Madame Defarge as a witch provide evidence of a historical change in the significance of femininity and domesticity as cultural norms. In order to continue serving as the 'other' woman, Madame Defarge is represented as old, ugly and deformed, because overt sexual attractiveness, assertiveness and freedom from convention have become attributes of the new twentieth-century heroine. These traits no longer function as signs of female deviance.

Madame Defarge's ruthless behaviour is shown to be driven by the vengeance she seeks for the original crime against her family perpetrated by the Evrémondes. But her defiance of gender norms is nevertheless condemned for its 'unnaturalness'. When her husband expresses sympathy for 'the compassionate wife of the Marquis' (421) in Book the Third, chapter XXII, Madame Defarge remains implacable in her revenge. Dickens juxtaposes the contrasting behaviour of two wives here: one is 'a good, compassionate lady' (409), according to the testimony of Doctor Manette, the other a pitiless 'wife of Lucifer' (452–3), in the words of Miss Pross. What redeems the wife of the Marquis St Evrémonde is her embodiment of the Victorian ideal of womanhood. Her class and connection with the *ancien régime* are overridden by her gender in the narrative. Doctor Manette's hidden diary provides the most direct portrait of the Marquise in the novel, and he describes her anguish at the cruelty of the Evrémonde brothers and her desire to comfort their victim: 'Her hope had been, she said in great distress, to show her, in secret, *a woman's sympathy*' (408, my emphasis). Learning that the girl is dead, the Marquise wants to make reparation by helping the young sister of the victim, and she therefore enjoins her son, Charles, to atone for the family's suffering:

'What I have left to call my own – it is little beyond the worth of a few jewels – I will make it the first charge of his life to bestow, with the compassion and lamenting of his dead mother, on this injured family, if the sister can be discovered.'

She kissed the boy, and said, caressing him, 'It is for thine own dear sake. Thou wilt be faithful, little Charles?' The child answered her bravely, 'Yes!' I kissed her hand, and she took him in her arms, and went away caressing him. (409)

The Marquise's call upon her son to repair the injury done to the family fractured by the Evrémonde brothers, together with her display of maternal affection and devotion, shows her embodiment of the Victorian middle-class ideals of domesticity and womanhood. She indicates the novel's investment in the middle-class family and forms a foil for Madame Defarge, the very sister she had hoped to assist. For in contrast to the Marquise St Evrémonde, Madame Defarge is represented as a female who lacks femininity.

Even more important as a foil for the behaviour of Madame Defarge, however, is the devotion shown by Lucie Manette as daughter, wife and mother. One of the most obvious points of comparison is the contrast drawn between Madame Defarge's knitting in the service of the Revolution and Lucie's busy winding of 'the golden thread which bound her husband, and her father, and herself, and her old directress and companion, in a life of quiet bliss' (256). While the handiwork of one promotes violence and destruction, the other toils only to secure peace and domestic harmony. The significance of their juxtaposition for the novel's construction of female subjectivity is evident in the description of their encounter in Book the Third, chapter III. Madame Defarge accompanies her husband when he delivers a note to Lucie from her imprisoned husband. Thrown into a 'transport' by the tidings, Lucie's instinctive response is a 'womanly' one: 'she turned from Defarge to his wife, and kissed one of the hands that knitted. It was a passionate, loving, thankful, womanly action, but the hand made no response – dropped cold and heavy, and took to its knitting again' (327). Lucie assumes the existence of a fellow-feeling between herself and Madame Defarge, based on their common gender. She automatically expects Madame Defarge to identify with her joy *as a woman*. The realisation of her mistake strikes her with 'terror' and leads to the admission – 'We are more afraid of you than of these others' – which Madame calmly receives as 'a compliment' (328). Notwithstanding the evidence of the fierce Frenchwoman's failure to conform to the womanly ideal she herself upholds, Lucie appeals once more for mercy, crying to Madame Defarge, 'O sister-woman, think of me. As a wife and mother!' (329). Lucie demonstrates an ardent faith in the overriding power of gender as the natural determinant of female identity. Her supreme appeal is to the sanctity of the Victorian middle-class family and to the status of women as relative creatures within it. Surely, implies Lucie, Madame Defarge is at one with her in her reverence for these fundamental truths; surely she has a woman's 'nature'.

Lucie's appeal to a shared belief in the value of familial roles as determinants of female identity is, of course, shown to be useless, and its failure confirms Madame Defarge's repudiation of the norms of femininity and domesticity. The worship of the middle-class hearth is shown to be of little importance to one who is bent upon reversing the hierarchies of a patrilineal order. Indeed, her motives are based upon a different notion of family altogether. Already subject to censure in the narrative for her violence, overt sexuality and sisterly solidarity, she is finally condemned by her ironic dedication to the sovereign power of genealogy for which the aristocracy of the *ancien régime* is overthrown. Madame Defarge is motivated by the blood-ties of a 'race'. When she explains to her comrades, in Book the Third, chapter XII, the reason for having 'this [Evrémonde] race a long time on my register, doomed to destruction and extermination', she repeats the secret previously disclosed to her husband:

'[T]hat peasant family so injured by the two Evrémonde brothers, as that Bastille paper describes, is my family. Defarge, that sister of the mortally wounded boy upon the ground was my sister, that husband was my sister's husband, that unborn child was their child, that brother was my brother, that father was my father, those dead are my dead, and that summons to answer for those things descends to me!' (421)

Madame Defarge stresses the fact of kinship here, rather than the affective ties that one might expect to be uppermost in her memory of her lost 'loved ones'. Her inheritance of the 'summons' is determined by the very pattern of descent that she would seek to overthrow. Ironically, she now invokes the language of the law – that most patriarchal and aristocratic of institutions – to ratify her inheritance.

The reactionary stance implied in her ironic capitulation to the very principle of genealogy set up as a distinguishing trait of the aristocracy sits oddly with the more subversive activities undertaken by Thérèse Defarge, as a revolutionary worker and as a woman, in the novel. But such inconsistency only enhances her function as the monstrous example of female deviance with which the horror of the Revolution can be identified. As she is finally brought down in the text to be punished and eliminated, some of the threat posed by the alien realm of revolutionary France is symbolically diminished. And it is for this reason that the nemesis chosen for Madame Defarge is the otherwise unlikely figure of Miss Pross.

Miss Pross is described in terms which evoke the stereotypical Victorian old maid. She is a comic grotesque, 'A wild-looking woman, whom even in his agitation, Mr Lorry observed to be all of a red colour, and to have red hair' (30). Despite her masculine strength and her spinsterhood (and her red hair), Miss Pross represents no challenge to the norms of femininity and domesticity. On the contrary, she is assimilated into the family by her devotion as a surrogate mother to Lucie. But her wiry strength and characterisation as a decidedly *English* grotesque also make her a fit opponent for Madame Defarge. While Madame Defarge represents a repudiation of the ideals Miss Pross so vigilantly protects in the person of her 'Ladybird', it is primarily the national differences between the two women that determine their fateful encounter. As the two of them are set face to face in the narrative, other categories of difference – gender, generational and class difference – are ostensibly overridden by the opposition of nationalities. What distinguishes the struggle between Madame Defarge and Miss Pross is not its commonly proclaimed thematic function as 'a contest between the forces of hatred and love',[21] but its characterisation as a confrontation between France and England. The significance of Miss Pross's defence is expressed in her vow, 'you shall not get the better of me. I am an Englishwoman' (453). This proud assertion of national identity informs her behaviour throughout the episode. Each woman speaks in her own language – English, of course, being privileged in the narrative anyway – and Miss Pross's words have a peculiarly idiomatic flavour that complements Dickens's literal translation of French idioms into English in order to represent the speech of the francophones in the novel. For example, she responds to the unintelligible exclamations of Madame Defarge with a peculiarly English image of defiance: '"If those eyes of yours were bed-winches," returned Miss Pross, "and I was an English four-poster, they shouldn't loose a splinter of me. No, you wicked foreign woman; I am your match"' (453). And so she is. In spite of the novel's conscientious effort to condemn the revolutionaries' desire for revenge, Miss Pross's victory over Madame Defarge brings with it all the satisfaction of an exacted retribution. An unmistakable note of triumph informs the narrator's ironic adjurations to The Vengeance in the final chapter to 'cry louder' for the missing Thérèse at the site of La Guillotine (462).

With the defeat and death of Madame Defarge, the salvation of Lucie Manette and her family is secured. Their survival, together with the ideals they represent, is of course exactly what Miss Pross fights for. But while 'eccentric' figures like Miss Pross (and Sydney Carton) play such an important role in enabling the representative Victorian middle-class family to withstand the assault of the French Revolution, its initial formation is entrusted primarily to Lucie. Whether or not Lucie's description is based upon Ellen Ternan as Michael Slater suggests,[22] she has the 'short, slight, pretty figure', 'quantity of golden hair', and 'blue eyes', that typically distinguish those heroines who embody the feminine ideal in Dickens's fiction. More important than the details of her appearance, however, although in fact culturally inseparable from them, is her function as a home-maker. On visiting the Doctor's lodgings, Mr Lorry is charmed to detect evidence of Lucie's silent presence everywhere:

The disposition of everything in the rooms, from the largest object to the least; the arrangement of colours, the elegant variety and contrast obtained by thrift in trifles, by delicate hands, clear eyes, and good sense; were at once so pleasant in themselves, and so expressive of their originator, that, as Mr Lorry stood looking about him, the very chairs and tables seemed to ask him, with something of that peculiar expression which he knew so well by this time, whether he approved? (110–11)

This household bespeaks the loving superintendence of a model domestic economist. Its objects are signs of the taste and 'good sense' of the woman who cares for them – as if Lucie's identity were coterminous with the domestic space she inhabits. Simple, reassuring, and, above all, utterly familiar, Lucie's home is set up as a haven in contrast with the foreign turmoil of revolutionary France. And like Ruskin's 'true wife' whose 'home is always round her',[23] Lucie arranges the 'little household' in Paris, while Charles is imprisoned, 'exactly as if her husband had been there': 'everything had its appointed place and its appointed time' (338–9). Indeed, given her French birth, Lucie seems to reconcile national differences in her own person. She helps to define a norm of respectable femininity that supposedly cuts across the conflicts generated by class and national differences.

Lucie's womanliness is shown to have rescued her father from the psychological trauma induced by his imprisonment in the Bastille, and she continues to fulfil this function in the wake of her marriage to Charles Darnay, 'Ever busily winding the golden thread that bound them all together, weaving the service of her happy influence through the tissue of all their lives' (257). Her role at the centre of the home, winding the thread of domestic harmony and cohesion, obviously sets her in contrast with Madame Defarge, whose activities and attitudes fracture the family. However, while the representation of the domestic ideal in Victorian culture depends upon the supervision of the home exercised by the Angel at its centre, it also requires the support of an appropriate personification of manhood, one who will manifest the virtues of industry and self-reliance necessary for the achievement of middle-class independence and respectability. As Leonore Davidoff and Catherine Hall have shown, the concept of occupation became an integral part of masculine identity in the nineteenth century, requiring middle-class men to wrest economic independence and public status away from the personal ties of dependency involved in the performance of service for a patron.[24] The emerging concept of middle-class manhood was thus implicated in the shift to a less paternalistic social order in which domesticity would become the dominant definition of the family. In *A Tale of Two Cities*, the ideal of domesticity Lucie embodies is thus appropriately complemented by her marriage to a self-made man. Charles Darnay's subscription to the values of middle-class self-making is clearly indicated in the description of his employment as 'a higher teacher of the French language' (155) in England. He shows 'great perseverance and untiring industry' (155), and as a result, he prospers. Samuel Smiles's *Self-Help* was published in the same year as *A Tale of Two Cities*; and Charles Darnay embodies its ideal of the self-made man who achieves success through his diligence and thrift. He holds a 'new philosophy', one that is based upon a distaste for aristocratic privilege and a belief in individual effort. While his uncle preaches 'repression' as 'the only lasting philosophy' (146), Charles renounces his heritage and embraces England and the doctrine of middle-class self-making instead.

A Tale of Two Cities recalls another historical novel, Thackeray's *The History of Henry Esmond* (1852), in its record of a historical shift in the form of the family, from the portrait of a rakish French aristocratic 'race' to the emergence of an English middle-class domestic circle. Like Henry Esmond, who renounces his title once his identity as the legitimate heir of the Castlewoods is known, and marries the woman who has embodied the values of middle-class domesticity throughout the novel, Charles Darnay relinquishes the Marquisate, withdraws to England and marries a domestic Angel. When he returns temporarily to France in Book the Second, chapter IX, the remonstrance made to his uncle opposes bourgeois to aristocratic conceptions of the family. The Marquis St Evrémonde stands for the 'grandeur of the family' (146), receiving the 'dark deference of fear and slavery' deplored by his nephew as a compliment to its greatness. When Charles bitterly attributes his freedom to the disgrace which has kept his uncle from obtaining a 'letter *de cachet*', the Marquis excuses these notorious documents as 'little instruments of correction, ... gentle aids to the power and honour of families' (145).

In his analysis of the historical movement from a government *of* families to a government *through* the family in the development of social discipline during the eighteenth and the nineteenth centuries, Jacques Donzelot explains the role played by the practice of *lettres de cachet*. Under the *ancien régime*, he argues, social power was exercised through a collaboration between the state administration and families, thus effecting a direct insertion of the family into the political sphere:

> The notorious *lettres de cachet de famille* derived their significance from this regulated exchange of obligations and protections between the public agencies and family authority, playing alternately on the menace to public order constituted by an individual who had broken with religion and morality, and on the threat to the family interest posed by the disobedient acts of one of its members.[25]

The taking of the Bastille, where many of those detained through the procedure of *lettres de cachet* were confined, marks for Donzelot the symbolic destruction *par excellence* of the old government of families.[26] It ushered in a new form of family that was regulated internally by moral norms, providing a more flexible organisation of ties and obligations than was available under the old juridical regime. In other words, the outlawing of the practice of *lettres de cachet* was an integral part of the historical transformation of the family as a mechanism of social discipline. As a supporter of the system of *lettres de cachet* – of the 'manner in which the family has sustained its grandeur' (146) – the Marquis clings to an older form of family authority. But Charles's conception of the 'honour' of the family is quite different:

> '[Death] has left me,' answered the nephew, 'bound to a system that is frightful to me, responsible for it, but powerless in it; seeking to execute the last request of my dear mother's lips, and obey the last look of my dear mother's eyes, which implored me to have mercy and to redress; and tortured by seeking assistance and power in vain.' (147–8)

Charles's dedication to discharging the sacred trust of the dead Marquise expresses a middle-class worship of motherhood. The holiness of a woman's function as mother was a central tenet of the ideology of domesticity, as the thrashing delivered by the normally passive Oliver Twist to the cringing Noah Claypole in chapter VI of *Oliver Twist* makes clear.

Charles Darnay's devotion to this middle-class ideal leads him to renounce France and the Marquisate, to anglicise his name, and to practise the virtues of self-making in his adopted country. His determination shows the shaping force of the middle-class family already at work in the construction of gender in the narrative, providing the norms against which aristocratic deviance and excess can be evaluated. And of course it is precisely by assuming such ground that the ascendancy of the middle classes is represented.

As a result of his mother's injunction to repair class conflict, Charles Darnay forms a new middle-class family in England. But this form of family is threatened when the Revolution breaks out by the many invasions and public expositions of the private that are part of its progress. Doctor Manette is put on show 'to a chosen few' by Monsieur Defarge (43), and Lucie is later brought before Madame Defarge under the pretence that Madame 'wishes to see those whom she has the power to protect at [turbulent] times, to the end that she may know them – that she may identify them' (327). The Revolution is characterised by images of the gaze: Madame Defarge always 'looks steadily', the Gorgon's Head surveys the château of Monsieur the Marquis, and a 'universal watchfulness' encompasses Charles on his return to France. Moreover, it is an ordinance of the Republic that on the door of every house the names of its inmates must be inscribed (356). This exposure of the domestic and private to public gaze adds to the more explicit assaults upon the middle-class family made by the Revolution. A parody of the ideal of family unity is presented in the wood-sawyer's grim imitation of La Guillotine, cutting off the heads of 'All the family!' (341). Similarly, the judgment of the President overseeing the Paris Tribunal before which Charles is brought in Book the Third, chapter x, is a grotesque elevation of patriotic over paternal feeling. Fearful for the loss of his own head, he rules that Doctor Manette 'would doubtless feel a sacred glow and joy in making his daughter a widow and her child an orphan' in order to root out 'an obnoxious family of Aristocrats' (411).

The comment of the President brings into focus the opposition between the domestic and the genealogical family that constitutes Doctor Manette's dilemma. The personal history he writes and conceals in his Bastille cell provides the explanation of the events which drive the novel's plot, and it contains a solemn denunciation of the Evrémondes, 'them and their descendents, to the last of their race' (410). The memorial unwittingly implicates him in the dominance of the very regime he would seek to overthrow, by affirming the power of lineage. His obsession with the 'race' resembles Madame Defarge's capitulation to the metaphysics of blood. This surrender to the aristocratic principle of genealogy is brought into conflict with the wish to save his son-in-law in the narrative. Newly formed bonds of affection and devotedness are set against blood-ties, as the Doctor struggles to assert the value of the roles and relationships of the domestic family over the facts of consanguinity. He fails in this effort, and it is left to Sydney Carton to save Charles Darnay and defend the ideals of the middle-class family.

At first sight, Sydney Carton seems an unlikely figure to be associated with the defence of the middle-class family. In many ways, he stands outside the domestic sphere in the novel and calls it into question. His marginal position is suggested early on in Book the Second, chapter IV, when Carton remains aloof from the 'congratulatory' group gathered around the aquitted Darnay: 'Another person, who had not joined the group, or interchanged a word with any one of them, but who had been leaning against the wall where its shadow was darkest, had silently strolled out after the rest, and had looked on until the coach drove away' (94–5). His anonymity and association with the shadows here combine with Carton's subsequent characterisation as a 'self-flung away, wasted, drunken, poor creature of misuse' (181) to set him outside the domestic circle. While Lucie strives to use her influence to 'save' and 'recall' him 'to a better course', his 'fixed despair of himself' (181) defeats her. Revealing the limits to the redeeming power of the domestic Angel, Carton embodies something of the transgressive desire that is evident elsewhere in Dickens's fascination with ambivalent figures like Steerforth or Eugene Wrayburn, who also pose a threat to the family. Physically similar to Charles Darnay, the two are opposed in terms of personality and character, and look forward to other pairings such as Pip and Orlick in *Great Expectations* or Wrayburn and Headstone in *Our Mutual Friend*.[27] Dickens's strong identification with the alienation and self-division that Carton represents is indicated by his passion for playing the role of Richard Wardour in the Wilkie Collins's play, *The Frozen Deep*, which gave him the 'main idea' for his story. As he writes in the Preface of this idea and its shaping: 'Throughout its execution, it has had the complete possession of me; I have so far verified what is done and suffered in these pages, as that I have certainly done and suffered it all myself' (xxvii). Richard Wardour is the rejected suitor who dies in the arms of the woman he still loves at the end of the play after saving the life of his rival. This moment of consummation is matched in the novel by the 'confidence' Carton reposes in Lucie on the single occasion when he opens his heart to her in Book the Second, chapter xii – a confidence that is not shared with her husband, but that is licensed by the impossibility of her ever returning Carton's love.

Carton's marginal relation to the middle-class family would seem to call its efficacy into question. While he acknowledges the good influence of Lucie's domestic devotion – 'I have not been so degraded but that the sight of you with your father, and of this home made such a home by you, has stirred old shadows that I thought had died out of me' – his love for her remains ineffectual, described as a fire 'inseparable in its nature from myself, quickening nothing, lighting nothing, doing no service, idly burning away' (182). Not even the loving compassion of a domestic Angel is enough to restore his bitterly divided self. He asks the newly married Darnay for permission 'to come and go as a privileged person here; that I might be regarded as an useless . . . piece of furniture, tolerated for its old service, and taken no notice of' (253) and he remains a disengaged observer throughout, despite the 'strange sympathy' Lucie's children have with him (258). While his final sacrifice asserts the transcendent value of his complete devotion to Lucie, it also expresses his profound alienation and his conviction, grimly put to Stryver in Book the Second, chapter xi, 'I have no business to be, at all, that I know of' (167). However, it is precisely because he *cannot* be domesticated that Carton is available to sacrifice himself and therefore ensure the survival of Darnay's family. Ironically, the triumph of the representative middle-class family is secured through an instance of its own failure.

Notwithstanding Carton's self-estrangement and alienation, however, he also assists in reaffirming the dominance of domestic ideology, for the fact that two such different men as Carton and Darnay, constituting opposed sides of a single ego, can take the same woman as their object of desire, demonstrates the unifying power of the domestic woman in Victorian culture. Nancy Armstrong has analysed the function of the domestic woman as a figure used to establish horizontal connections between the members of a heterogeneous economic group by embodying a norm – a figure used 'to generate the belief that there was such a thing as a middle class with clearly established affiliations before it actually existed'.[28] In *A Tale of Two Cities*, the rivalry between Carton and Darnay for the love of Lucie strengthens the authority of the ideal she represents by demonstrating its ability to attract and accommodate such diverse desiring subjects.

Furthermore, Carton's scheme of self-sacrifice stems from a notion of family and identity that depends upon the ideology of domesticity, rather than blood-relatedness – not simply because it is done for the love of

Lucie, but because it is an endorsement of *surrogate* familial relationships. The genealogical family does not concern itself with the provision of substitute kin. Its interest is in blood-ties, rather than surrogate relationships. In contrast, the domestic ideal is preoccupied with the fulfilment of familial roles and duties, whether these coincide with the relations of consanguinity or not. According to this ideal, the provision of fatherly and motherly care, for example, is of far greater importance than the facts of blood-relatedness, and Carton's sacrifice ratifies this principle of familial substitution. The narrator's record of his final words offers a vision of a new kind of lineage based not on blood, but on commemoration of his devotion to Lucie and all that she represents. The name that is passed on to subsequent generations is the Christian name, rather than the patronymic, and the story that is told to the child who bears this name continues the translation of public into private history begun by Dickens's novel.

The sacrifice of Sydney Carton closes the narrative. Dickens would seem to have epitomised the progress of the French Revolution in the story of the Evrémondes and Defarges in order to draw the oft-quoted moral, which opens the concluding chapter, concerning the dire consequences of 'crush[ing] humanity out of shape' (459). History is shown to unfold causally in his narrative, and its effects are traced through the representation of the family. The novel finds an exemplary impetus for the Revolution in the practice of *droit de seigneur*. As the Evrémonde brothers violate the family of Madame Defarge, they sow the seeds of a violent harvest. In turn, the overthrow of the *ancien régime* threatens to fracture the family of Lucie and Charles.

Dickens manages the turmoil of the French Revolution by its gradual identification with the activity of Madame Defarge and her knitting sisters throughout the narrative. Revolutionary violence becomes an exhibition of female deviance. By constructing the desires of the revolutionaries as transgressive of gender, the novel apparently makes them 'other' and clears a safe space for the English middle-class subject. This strategy of displacement and denial is part of a normalising technique which enables the reproduction of respectable femininity and domesticity as the mutually authorising and dominant definitions of female identity and the family. However, at the same time, the use of a male omniscient narrator to gender the Revolution makes the instability of this rhetorical and ideological strategy apparent. The figures of female deviance with which the Revolution is identified threaten to exercise an allure that would undermine the project of narrative containment they ostensibly enable.

The narrator's denunciation of the revolutionary mob remains haunted by a fascination with its frenzied forms of power. The feminisation of the French Revolution is thus not an unequivocal strategy of consolation, for this narrative gesture is inhabited by the kind of unruly desires it would seek to restrain and exclude.

CHAPTER 6

Great Expectations

Despite being hailed by its first reviewers as a return to the 'flowing humour' and 'old manner' of Dickens's 'earlier fancies',[1] *Great Expectations* is distinguished by a pervading pessimism about the bourgeois male plot of aspiration and upward mobility. While its title promises an orientation towards the future, the novel is preoccupied with a return to the past and the exploration of its determining influences upon the development of identity. It combines the self-determination of a narrator who is constantly engaged in revising or reinterpreting his conception of himself, with an apprehension of profound self-alienation. Pip's sense of who he is depends upon his perception of the plot his story will follow and, in misreading his role, he is left radically displaced from the centre of his own narrative. Despite being set earlier in the century, his story is a record of mid-Victorian anxieties about male identity in a period of rapid industrial change and rampant individualism.

Under the influence of post-structuralist theory, critical discussion of *Great Expectations* in recent years has focussed upon the problems of identity associated with autobiographical narration. Concerned to demonstrate the ways in which the novel examines the relationship between self and language, self and society, these studies have challenged essentialist views of the subject, using a neo-Freudian framework to consider the question of identity and to expose the psychological effects of repression and internalised guilt. For example, Peter Brooks remarks the appearance in the opening chapter of 'the problem of identity, self-consciousness, naming, and language, that will accompany Pip throughout the novel';[2] Steven Connor describes *Great Expectations* as a novel provoking 'questions about the relationship of consciousness and language';[3] and Anny Sadrin identifies it as 'an oedipal novel with Telemachus in the leading role'.[4] These readings tend to assume that the individual, the self, is gender-neutral, or to ignore the historical specificity of the family's form and cultural meaning. However, any consideration of the role of the family in the novel immediately raises the issue of sexual difference and its historical definition in the formation of subjectivity. In *Great Expectations* the question of Pip's identity is necessarily bound up with his masculinity, his shifting class position and their determination by the system of family relationships in which he is caught. As a novel about writing the self, the narrative of Pip's progress is shaped by his representations of family and female identity (the two are inseparable). The opposing incarnations of womanhood to be found in Estella and Biddy locate Pip's movement between competing conceptualisations of the family, and between competing views of the 'gentleman' as a figure distinguished by birth or merit. Together with the inadequate mothers so prevalent in his narrative, these representations of women are used to create the effect of Pip's development.

Despite the assertion of autonomy implied in Pip's self-naming on the novel's opening page, the determination of his identity by a familial context and the difference made by gender in these arrangements are made apparent in his contemplation of the family tombstones. The tombstones represent the members of an absent family, and his engagement in speculation about what they were like is combined with a reconstruction of the relationships between them. The authority of the father is confirmed by the way in which the inscriptions upon the tombstones of his wife and children refer back to his own, depending upon it as an origin of meaning: while Philip Pirrip is described as 'late of this parish', Georgiana is identified as 'wife of the above' and Alexander, Bartholomew, Abraham, Tobias and Roger are also identified as 'infant children of the aforesaid' (3–4). Philip is both the source of meaning here – the named subject needed to make sense of the terms 'above' and 'aforesaid' – and the mediator between his family and the parish, between the private and the public spheres (an ideological division that will be thematised more fully in the portrait of Wemmick). The tombstone text inscribes divisions of power within the family which are registered in Pip's reading, and indicate that the process of identity-formation expressed here is not conducted in some neutral linguistic medium. The language Pip works with is already gendered.

Indeed, Pip's interpretation of the appearance of his lost parents from the shape of the letters in their epitaphs curiously accords with Victorian stereotypes of masculinity and femininity. He derives contrasting impressions of his father and mother, giving ironic expression to Victorian middle-class assumptions about gender complementarity. He has an 'odd idea' that his father 'was a square, stout, dark man, with curly black hair', while he concludes that his mother 'was freckled and sickly'. The terms of the contrast suggest the stereotypical oppositions between vigour and debility, hardness and softness, strength and weakness, darkness and fairness, that characterised middle-class ideals of manhood and womanhood, and the determining effects of sexual difference shown here continue to pervade the narrative of Pip's childhood.

In a novel that is filled with defective parents and dysfunctional families, Mrs Joe stands forth in Pip's account of his upbringing as the first in a series of inadequate mothers. The satire of the older Pip, who records the injustices suffered by his younger self, complicates the representation of the family, for his portrait of Mrs Joe betrays the internalised guilt of the adult narrator. Dickens had told Forster on the delivery of the novel's first instalment that he would 'not have to complain of the want of humour' in this new serial: 'I have made the opening, I hope, in its general effect exceedingly droll. I have put a child and a good-natured foolish man, in relations that seem to me very funny.'5 But the novel's comedy is often black – tinged with anxiety and unease – and its representation of the family is equally ambivalent, as the adult narrator is torn between self-justification and self-condemnation, between the impulses of desire and guilt, in the account of his childhood.

On the one hand, Pip's portrait of his sister invokes a missing familial ideal, an expectation of maternal devotion that she fails to embody. Her representation helps to define a norm of motherhood and domesticity that was an important part of the affirmation of middle-class values in the nineteenth century. Pip's narrative is dominated by families showing a deviation from the domestic ideal, and by mothers who fail to fulfil their proper duty. The representations of the Gargery and Pocket families, and of the perverse parenting provided by Miss Havisham, are three crucial sources for the production of the ideology of domesticity in the novel. On the other hand, however, Dickens seems to challenge and subvert the middle-class ideal of the family through the comic violence and black humour of Pip's satire. The narrator exacts a kind of revenge for the cruel treatment he is shown to have received from Mrs Joe, deriving a retributive satisfaction from the satire used to portray her. The amusing naivety of the child's point of view is often used to license the highly unflattering portrait of his sister, as in the young Pip's speculation about her 'prevailing redness of skin' and whether 'she washed herself with a nutmeg-grater instead of soap' (8). However, while the revenge enjoyed by the adult narrator is hidden behind the 'innocent' perspective of the child here, it has the potential to undermine the moral analysis that justifies his satiric attack. Pip's account of his sister shows something of the very savagery he complains about. As an exemplary 'bad mother', Mrs Joe is exposed with a salutary purpose; but the critique of motherhood and family is presented with a bad conscience, like so much of Pip's story. The imaginative relish with which Mrs Joe's atrocities are recorded, and the comic delight with which her pretensions are displayed for ridicule, have the effect of throwing the moral discourse of the adult narrator into question.[6]

Mrs Joe is very clearly defined by her lack of maternal qualities and her perversion of domestic values in Pip's narrative. The 'coarse apron' she wears, with its 'square impregnable bib in front, that was stuck full of pins and needles' (8) is a facetious allusion to her pride in hand-feeding, as well as a comic form of self-martyrdom, and not only repels any movement towards an embrace, but is worn as a 'reproach' to the husband. The description of the way in which she feeds her family is informed by similar judgments about her inadequacy as a mother-surrogate, as Pip's account of her 'trenchant way of cutting our bread-and-butter for us' (10) emphasises the physical aggression and parsimony which characterise her serving of meals. She is seen as a monstrous mother, a figure of deviance, feeding her family without love or due ceremony.[7] The point is made again when Pip describes the vigorous ablutions which precede his visit to Satis House: 'my face was squeezed into wooden bowls in sinks, and my head was put under taps of water-butts, and I was soaped, and kneaded, and towelled, and thumped, and harrowed, and rasped, until I really was quite beside myself'. Pip's idiomatic reference to the effects of his sister's assault, which leave him 'beside himself', will gather added significance in the context of his gradual displacement from the centre of his own narrative, as he comes to find himself part of a plot laid by others – one in which he does not marry the princess.

The effects of Mrs Joe's failure to embody the womanly ideal are also evident in the representation of Joe. His feminisation in the narrative is an indication of Mrs Joe's emasculating power, and Pip's need for a mother-surrogate. Pip's descriptions of his sister and Joe seem almost to reverse the traits typically associated with the masculine and feminine ideals in Victorian fiction. His appraisal of his sister at the opening of chapter II echoes his speculative account of his father's appearance taken from the tombstone in chapter I. He observes in her the 'black hair and eyes' attributed to Philip Pirrip, and adds that 'she was not a good-looking woman' (8). Her 'likeness' to the father is not only a sign of family resemblance, but also suggests her dominant position within the household. In contrast to his dark and aggressive wife, Joe, says Pip, 'was a fair man, with curls of flaxen hair on each side of his smooth face, and with eyes of such a very undecided blue that they seemed to have somehow got mixed with their own whites' (8). As in the case of Oliver Twist, physiognomy is regarded here as one of nature's signs, providing a clue to Joe's gentleness and deference to his more powerful wife.

This reversal in the attributes of gender is also evident in Pip's association of the husband and wife with their home, for while he admits that it had 'never been a very pleasant place to me, because of my sister's temper ... Joe had sanctified it' (104). In sanctifying the home, Joe fulfils the duty that devolved upon the domestic woman in Victorian middle-class ideology – that of the Angel in the House. When Joe refuses compensation from Jaggers for the loss of his apprentice, Pip remarks that he 'laid his hand upon my shoulder with the touch of a woman', and is prompted by his overwhelming guilt to cry: 'O dear good faithful tender Joe, I feel the loving tremble of your hand upon my arm, as solemnly this day as if it had been the rustle of an angel's wing!' (139). The sentimentality of Pip's apostrophes betrays the idealising imagination of the narrator, suggesting that more is being said here about *his* anxieties and obsessions than about the 'reality' of Joe's position. But this construction of a subjectivity burdened by guilt and a sense of exclusion distinguishes Pip's autobiographical narrative throughout. In his moral analyses of behaviour, Pip is desperately laying claim to a position within the discourse of middle-class domesticity, and the assumptions informing his representation of the family and female nature are one of the means by which he seeks to establish his own identity.

Like Joe, Pip is shown to be a victim of Mrs Joe's emasculating power. He blames his vulnerability to Estella's contempt upon his sister, whose 'bringing up', he says, 'had made me sensitive' (61). Spurned by Estella on his first visit to Satis House in chapter VIII, he muses upon the sense of 'injustice' bred within him by Mrs Joe using the imagery of nurture to highlight her inadequacy as a maternal substitute. The participles which describe the development of his sense of injury – 'sustained', 'cherished', 'nursed' – belong to an image of motherhood which is clearly missing in the portrait of Mrs Joe's brutal care. What is not immediately obvious from this account, however, is why Pip should want to blame his susceptibility to Estella's attacks upon his sister's 'bringing up' – why he should explain his reactions by drawing a parallel between these two women. They could hardly seem more unlike, and yet both women undermine the power and authority that the self-named male subject believes he should (naturally) possess. Pip casts himself as a victim of female dominance and scorn in an effort to create the effect of his own development here, and uses gender as the common ground from which to condemn class and generational differences as arbitrary and unfair. Focussing upon the essential similarity between the two women who threaten his masculinity, Pip's presentation of his thoughts here is an early example of the way in which representations of women are used to write the narrative of male development in *Great Expectations*.

Although it would seem that Estella has newly awakened the young Pip to a consciousness of class by her contempt for his 'coarse hands' and 'thick boots' (59), the earlier account of Mrs Joe's 'bringing up' is distinguished by his awareness of her social pretension. For example, Pip notes in a comic parenthesis Mrs Joe's monopoly of the family connection with Uncle Pumblechook: '(Joe's uncle, but Mrs Joe appropriated him), who was a well-to-do corn-chandler in the nearest town, and drove his own chaise-cart' (23). Pip is 'not allowed to call him uncle, under the severest penalties' (24). The 'chaise-cart' provides the occasion for further satire on the preoccupation with social position when it is subsequently referred to by Joe as a 'shay-cart'. The significance of the linguistic difference is comically highlighted in one of Dickens's *Sketches*, 'The Tuggses at Ramsgate', which describes the pretensions of a family who come into the unexpected possession of twenty thousand pounds. The daughter and son change their names to match their new sense of social superiority – Charlotte calling herself 'Charlotta', and Simon becoming 'Cymon'. But their father incorrigibly betrays his origins when transportation from Ramsgate to Pegwell is sought:

'A shay?' suggested Mr Joseph Tuggs.
'Chaise,' whispered Mr Cymon.
'I should think one would be enough,' said Mr Joseph Tuggs aloud, quite un-conscious of the meaning of the correction. 'However, two shays if you like.'[8]

Like Mr Joseph Tuggs's preference for a 'shay', Joe's language signifies a lack of concern for social prestige which the narrator views with approval alongside the absurd pretensions of Mrs Joe and Uncle Pumblechook.

The class consciousness exhibited in the behaviour of Mrs Joe links her with another significant embodiment of maternal dereliction described in Pip's narrative: Mrs Pocket. But while Mrs Joe's social pretension is shown in her appropriation of Uncle Pumblechook and the elaborate rituals of the Christmas dinner, Mrs Pocket's snobbery is manifested in her domestic incompetence. Pip is introduced to the Pockets in volume II, chapter III, and the ambivalence of the narrator's moral discourse is suggested in his disingenuous observation of the family: 'unless I deceive myself on a point where my interests or prepossessions are certainly not concerned, I saw that Mr and Mrs Pocket's children were not growing up or being brought up, but were tumbling up' (184). Pip may not be deceived about the upbringing of the young Pockets, but his 'interests' and 'prepossessions' strongly influence his representation of this family. Pip clearly perceives Mrs Pocket as yet another inadequate mother, and he continually criticises her domestic mismanagement and neglect of her children in the observations recorded in his narrative. Upon their first meeting, he describes her, with seeming neutrality, 'sitting on a garden chair under a tree, reading, with her legs upon another garden chair' (184), but the insinuation of her idleness is apparent in the detail of her languid posture and the following mention of the 'two nursemaids', Flopson and Millers, who are evidently required to supply her deficiency. Absorbed in her book, she is oblivious of the children tripping themselves up around her, and when given her baby to nurse, Pip notes that she 'inexpertly danced the infant a little in her lap' before ordering the children off for a nap.

The book proves to be 'all about titles' (190) and Mrs Pocket's aristocratic pretensions are thoroughly satirised in the next chapter, where Pip outlines her ancestry. There he emphasises the baselessness of her family's claim to entitlement in his ironic references to the 'invention' of a 'conviction' that a baronetcy was due to Mrs Pocket's grandfather, but for 'somebody's' determined opposition, and the dependence of her father's 'right' on 'this suppositious fact' (187). The loss of a distinction between fact and fabrication is also suggested in the vagueness characterising Pip's memory of the details of this history: he 'forgets' which individuals are involved, and cannot remember the particular 'occasion of the laying of the first stone of some building or other' when Mrs Pocket's father was knighted 'for handing some Royal Personage either the trowel or the mortar' (187).

Like Dora Copperfield, Mrs Pocket is said to have 'grown up highly ornamental, but perfectly helpless and useless' (187); but unlike David Copperfield, Pip has no illusions about the desirability of this upbringing. Mrs Pocket's aristocratic pretensions are signalled by her domestic incompetence: the servants control the household, cheating their employers and keeping 'a deal of company down stairs' (188), and Mrs Pocket becomes aware of their activities only by chance report – such as the note received from a neighbouring lady who 'wrote in to say that she had seen Millers slapping the baby' (188). The Pocket home is hardly Ruskin's 'temple of the hearth watched over by household gods', since it is vulnerable to public intrusions of this kind, and Pip's account of the dinner held on the day of his installation as pupil betrays his embarrassment at witnessing such transgressions of the boundary between public and private life: 'We all looked awkwardly at the table-cloth while this was going on' (192), he says, when Matthew Pocket's habitual attempt to lift himself up by his own hair in exasperation with his wife is repeated. Above all, however, Pip is a critical witness at this dinner of Mrs Pocket's maternal inadequacies. He is troubled to observe her extraordinary lack of vigilance with regard to her children at the dinner-table: 'I was made very uneasy in my mind by Mrs Pocket's falling into a discussion with Drummle respecting two baronetcies, while she ate a sliced orange steeped in sugar and wine, and forgetting all about the baby on her lap: who did most appalling things with the nutcrackers' (191). The comment joins together Mrs Pocket's neglect of her child, worship of rank and indulgence in the aristocratic style of living signified by the excessive sweetness and delicacy of her fragrant dessert. She is drawn towards Drummle as 'the next heir but one to a baronetcy' (189), and later defends the cook (who is discovered lying insensibly drunk on the kitchen floor in the evening), because she had acknowledged Mrs Pocket's aristocratic disposition: 'the cook has always been a very nice respectful woman, and said in the most natural manner when she came to look after the situation, that she felt I was born to be a Duchess' (194).

However, the most bizarre example of maternal deviance in the novel is provided by the figure of Miss Havisham. As the emblem of faded virginity, Miss Havisham forms the focus for a cluster of ideas associated with sterility, solitude, decay and death in the novel. She has reached the third biological stage of womanhood defined in Victorian medical discourse, the 'climacteric' or menopause, without ever having experienced the stage most crucial in the formation of female subjectivity: pregnancy. Her ageing female body, like the 'wilderness of empty casks' (62) scattered in the disused brewery-yard surrounding the house, suggests barrenness and senescence. Given the importance of reproductive activity in defining the 'nature' of women in the dominant discourses of the period, the surcease of menstruation in effect meant that womanhood itself was at an end.[9] Miss Havisham is represented as a decaying woman in white, a woman who has apparently failed to undergo the 'proper' female development from bride to mother. Pip's description of her ironically named home, Satis House, lays great emphasis upon the exclusion of 'nature' from the ghostly building. The rooms are lit by candles which burn 'with the steady dulness [*sic*] of artificial light in air that is seldom renewed'

(299), the fire kindled in the grate is 'more disposed to go out than to burn up' (82), and Miss Havisham herself looks 'as if the admission of the natural light of day would have struck her to dust' (59). This weird, artificial atmosphere provides the context for her 'unnatural' mothering of Estella, the child 'brought up in that strange house from a mere baby' (264).

Miss Havisham is Estella's mother by adoption. However, it is not the absence of a blood-tie that accounts for the abnormality perceived by Pip in their relationship, but rather the quality of Miss Havisham's affection and the deformation of Estella's female 'nature' as a result of her peculiar upbringing. In Pip's narrative, the fading white garments of Miss Havisham act as a reminder of her arrested development from bride to mother, a sign of female 'insufficiency' in the frozen anticipation of an ever-imminent wedding. Devoid of the prospect of motherhood, she adopts a daughter to rear upon her cold hearth, where she gives forth 'a burning love, inseparable from jealousy at all times, and from sharp pain' (300). The perversity of this mother–daughter bond is continually suggested in the references to the rapacity of Miss Havisham's affection for Estella: she has a 'miserly relish of Estella's moods' (93), she kisses her hand to the departing Estella 'with a ravenous intensity that was of its kind quite dreadful' (237), and as Estella grows older, Pip notes that 'there was something positively dreadful in the energy of [Miss Havisham's] looks and embraces. She hung upon Estella's beauty, hung upon her words, hung upon her gestures, and sat mumbling her own trembling fingers while she looked at her, as though she were devouring the beautiful creature she had reared' (298).

The ferocious affection evident in Miss Havisham's mothering has its inevitable effect upon Estella's 'nature'. Estella calmly warns Pip in volume II, chapter X that she has no heart, and in chapter XIX points out the unreasonableness of Miss Havisham's demand for love from her adopted daughter, likening it to the situation of a child kept in darkness and taught to abhor the light who is then, 'for a purpose', expected 'to take naturally to the daylight' (302). Estella's lack of feeling is held to be a product of her 'unnatural' upbringing: 'I am what you have made me' (300), she tells Miss Havisham, and 'I must be taken as I have been made' (302). Herbert Pocket explains to Pip that Estella 'has been brought up by Miss Havisham to wreak revenge on all the male sex' (175), her vindictive purpose forming a parallel with Magwitch's determination to make Pip a gentleman so as to revenge himself upon the moneyed social class he holds responsible for his victimisation. Unlike Magwitch, Miss Havisham is eventually brought to the realisation of her error by the example of Pip's sorrow, and admits the destructive effects of her teaching: 'I stole her heart away and put ice in its place' (395). 'Better', says Pip, 'to have left her a natural heart, even to be bruised or broken' (395). However, the very notion of female 'nature' involved in this account is put into question by the insistence upon the constructedness of identity in Pip's narrative, by the suggestion that women like Estella are not born but made. The distance between the moral discourse of the adult narrator, and the illusions associated with his younger self, is measured by the persistence with which Pip attempts to understand Estella in the light of Victorian middle-class assumptions about female 'nature'.

Pip's account of Miss Havisham, like his accounts of Mrs Joe and Mrs Pocket, implicitly invokes an absent ideal of motherhood, and situates the narrator within the discourse of domesticity. Through the depiction of female deviance, Pip assumes a shared image of maternity that is not only constitutive of his own identity, but of his readership as well. In articulating the values and assumptions of domestic ideology, Pip positions his readers as middle-class individuals and draws them together by basing his account upon a concept of family and female identity supposedly held in common. This construction of the universality of middle-class norms is also part of the narrative of personal development. These representations of female deviance function to produce the effect of Pip's moral growth and maturity, as he moves from the selfish pursuit of wealth and gentility to the fellowship and familial love of the 'true' gentleman in the course of the novel. They help to suggest his destination as a man who has come to perceive the value of home and family, one who appreciates the virtues of kindness, gentleness and loyalty, and who has no more illusions about the lures of wealth and social pretension. But the progress implied in this movement towards understanding and the eschewal of romance is by no means straightforward. Pip's autobiographical narrative rests upon a conception of the self as an autonomous subject that is gradually undermined by the very means used to chart his development. This radical self-questioning emerges in his representation of the two women he contemplates marrying – Estella and Biddy – as well as inhering in the confessional form of his first-person narrative.

The star imagery of Estella's name situates her as a glittering goal, an unattainable prize for the young Pip. She is the object of his desire, awakening in him that sense of a lack which motivates his narrative. She has no 'self'; she has only a role. She is not constructed as a psychologised, classed, developmental individual in the way that Pip is, notwithstanding the destabilisation of identity he is forced to undergo; and she therefore helps to sharpen the focus on the role of gender and autobiographical narrative in the construction of the 'self' in the novel. For Pip, she functions as a sign of the restless pursuit of gentility that characterises his un-reformed self (and she is contrasted with Biddy for this purpose). He returns from his first visit to Satis House with a new view of himself as a 'common labouring-boy' (64) obtained from Estella. The two words she uses to condemn him – 'coarse' and 'common' – are repeated in the narrative as a kind of mnemonic formula designed to connect Pip's discontent with its origin in her disdain. In chapter x, after meeting the stranger with the file at the Three Jolly Bargemen, Pip thinks of what a 'guiltily coarse and common thing it was, to be on secret terms of con-spiracy with convicts' (77); in chapter xiv, he rejects his earlier perception of the forge 'as the glowing road to manhood and independence' with the admission, 'Now, it was all coarse and common, and I would not have had Miss Havisham and Estella see it on any account' (104–5); and in chapter xviii, he declines showing his new clothes to the patrons of the Three Jolly Bargemen because they would make 'such a coarse and common business' (142) of the exhibition.

This linguistic connection between Pip's social ambition and his desire for Estella supplements the explicit link claimed when the adult narrator reflects upon the fantasies that beguiled his younger self. In volume ii, chapter x, Pip anticipates his reunion with Estella following her return from France by 'painting brilliant pictures' of Miss Havisham's plans for his future. He imagines that 'She reserved it for me to restore the desolate house, admit the sunshine into the dark rooms, set the clocks a going and the cold hearths a blazing, tear down the cobwebs, destroy the vermin – in short, do all the shining deeds of the young Knight of romance, and marry the Princess' (229). But despite his use of the language of romance, the narrator denies having held any illusions about Estella throughout their relationship: 'Once for all; I knew to my sorrow, often and often, if not always, that I loved her against reason, against promise, against peace, against hope, against happiness, against all discouragement that could be' (229). Instead, he casts himself as a victim of her 'all-powerful' influence, describing the strength of her 'irresistible' attraction, and emphasising his own passivity and powerlessness. But in assigning her the agency for his predicament, Pip also uses Estella to ground his own identity, to signify his own moral development. The most significant illusion held here is contained in the assertion of Estella's power and autonomy, for she can only be represented by Pip – whether it be as the princess who will marry the young knight, or as the object of his unsatisfied desire whose pursuit is an index to male psychology and moral growth in the novel.

The description of Pip's subsequent meeting with Estella in this chapter reiterates the claim of a connection between his pursuit of gentility and his desire for her. Estella's transformation into an 'elegant lady' (232) makes him conscious of his own lack of 'progress', leading to an explicit identification of his desire for her with his unregenerate self:

Truly it was impossible to dissociate her presence from all those wretched hankerings after money and gentility that had disturbed my boyhood – from all those ill-regulated aspirations that had first made me ashamed of home and Joe – from all those visions that had raised her face in the glowing fire, struck it out of the iron on the anvil, extracted it from the darkness of night to look in at the wooden window of the forge and flit away. In a word, it was impossible for me to separate her, in the past or in the present, from the innermost life of my life. (233)

The point is made again in volume II, chapter XV, when he reflects upon the influence of his expectations 'on my own character':

Yet Estella was so inseparable from all my restlessness and disquiet of mind, that I really fell into confusion as to the limits of my own part in its production. That is to say, supposing I had had no expectations, and yet had had Estella to think of, I could not make out to my satisfaction that I should have done much better. (268–9)

The inadequacy of this self-assessment is apparent in the spurious distinction he attempts to draw between Estella and his great expectations, since they are structurally equivalent in his narrative. Estella is the very image of those desires awakened by the promise of 'great expectations', and while Pip's yearning for all that is perceived as 'uncommon' is set in opposition to an alternative vision of life in the 'honest old forge' – 'many a time of the evening, when I sat alone looking at the fire, I thought, after all there was no fire like the forge fire and the kitchen fire at home' (268) – the clear-sightedness implied in the moral comment is undercut by the nostalgia with which 'home' is imagined.

Pip's pursuit of the fairy-tale world of wealth and gentility he identifies with Estella is also marked by his embrace of an aristocratic economy. This involves the redecoration of his chambers in Barnard's Inn with 'incongruous upholstery work', and the cultivation of 'lavish habits' which lead to the contraction of 'a quantity of debt' (269). He also starts 'a boy in boots – top boots', whom he clothes 'with a blue coat, canary waistcoat, white cravat, creamy breeches, and the boots already mentioned' (216), and facetiously nicknames the Avenger, in honour of Frankenstein's monster, who also haunted his maker's existence. In Pip's case, the Avenger seems to embody his guilt in seeking upward mobility. But he is also a double for Pip as a 'made' man, a clue to the 'imposture' of Pip's expectations and his making by Magwitch which will be explained when his convict origins are finally revealed.

As part of his new genteel lifestyle, Pip decides to join a club – the Finches of the Grove – an institution whose only achievements appear to be 'that the members should dine expensively once a fortnight, to quarrel among themselves as much as possible after dinner, and to cause six waiters to get drunk on the stairs' (269). Dickens himself enjoyed an active club life, having been a founding member of the short-lived Shakespeare Club in 1838; he joined the Parthenon Club, and later the Garrick and the Athenaeum. As George Augustus Sala, one of Dickens's circle of 'young men', observed in his account of the fashionable club in 1859, 'A man may, if he be so minded, make his club his home; living and lounging luxuriously, and grazing to his heart's content on the abundant club-house literature, and enjoying the conversation of club friends.'[10] The importance of club membership as a mark of social position is indicated in Sala's remark that 'hundreds of the superior middle-classes [*sic*], nay, even of the aristocracy ... would consider themselves social Pariahs now-a-days, if they did not belong to one or more clubs'.[11] They were places of elite male conviviality, and Pip's participation in club life is another sign of his aristocratic pretensions. Like a young rake, he frequents Covent Garden with the Finches and engages in a foolish dispute with another honourable member – Bentley Drummle – over the privilege of Estella's acquaintance. The ubiquitous club is set in opposition to the home in the advice manuals published throughout the Victorian period, and male profligacy is held to be the inevitable consequence of a woman's failure to create and maintain the sort of 'comfortable' home that would entice husbands and sons to forgo the homosocial pleasures of the club and remain indoors. The risk is satirically outlined in the introduction to Catherine Dickens's *What Shall We Have For Dinner?* Lady Maria Clutterbuck, the 'author' of this small volume, laments the unhappy domestic circumstances experienced by many of her 'female friends' whose 'daily life is embittered by the consciousness that a delicacy forgotten or misapplied; a surplusage of cold mutton or a redundancy of chops; are gradually making the Club more attractive than the Home, and rendering "business in the city" of more frequent occurrence than it used to be in the earlier days of their connubial experience'.[12] Pip's involvement with the Finches of the Grove is partly explained by his bachelorhood. But this is only another sign of his alienation from the values of domesticity. The Finches represent extravagance, indolence, dissipation and male homosociality, and as such they mark a repudiation of the virtues of the middle-class family.

In keeping with the bad habits cultivated by the Finches, Pip adopts a style of living that takes him further and further into debt, and his attitude towards this state of affairs, as much as his insolvency itself, signifies his embrace of an aristocratic economy. 'We spent as much money as we could, and got as little for it as people could make up their minds to give us' (270), he says of his housekeeping with Herbert in Barnard's Inn. Such wastefulness and lack of moderation are totally opposed to the practice of 'domestic economy' associated with the middle-class ideal of the family. Pip periodically and half-heartedly attempts to remedy the situation by making an appointment with Herbert to look into their affairs: 'I always thought this was business, this was the way to confront the thing, this was the way to take the foe by the throat' (272), says Pip. But the clichés expose the speciousness of the enterprise. Pip and Herbert play at being men of business, their vital attention to the pleasurable requirements of gentility undermining their efforts at self-discipline and industry. They order 'something rather special for dinner' and equip themselves with a copious supply of stationery for the occasion. The desire for excess which has led them into debt in the first place is in every way indulged in the effort to overcome its effects. Moreover, in making a memorandum of his debts, Pip finds it 'difficult to distinguish between this edifying business proceeding and actually paying the money' (272) – an attitude that recalls Mr Skimpole's view that his creditors should be content to accept his good intentions in lieu of payment – and he develops an expensive habit of 'leaving a Margin', which leads him to run 'into new debt immediately, to the full extent of the margin' (273). These dilettantish forays into business leave Pip 'soothed' and self-satisfied, and contrast with the habits of thrift and quiet domestic economy associated with the household management of Biddy, acknowledged earlier in the novel by the young Pip: 'She managed our whole domestic life, and wonderfully too' (123).

Biddy is made to stand for home and the forge, to represent the values of domesticity, in Pip's narrative. Christened with the generic name for an Irish servant-maid, she represents the antithesis of Pip's aristocratic aspirations. Her role in his narrative is most clearly delineated in chapter XVII, which opens with Pip's comment upon the 'regular routine of apprenticeship life' and his loathing for it under the influence of Satis House. With the admission that he 'continued at heart to hate [his] trade and to be ashamed of home' (122), Pip proceeds to examine his relationship with Biddy – the conspicuous shift in his focus, from work to woman, pointing to her narrative function: 'Imperceptibly I became conscious of a change in Biddy, however. Her shoes came up at the heel, her hair grew bright and neat, her hands were always clean. She was not beautiful – she was common, and could not be like Estella – but she was pleasant and wholesome and sweet-tempered' (123). Pip draws a distinction here between the charms of Biddy and Estella that is based upon a difference of class. 'Beauty' is made an attribute of gentility. Biddy's designation as 'common' refers at once to her rank and her physiognomy – the ambiguity marking a slippage from the social to the 'natural' in Pip's thinking. He notes that 'she had curiously thoughtful and attentive eyes; eyes that were very pretty and very good'. But while noting that her eyes are 'pretty', most of his appreciation is devoted to the moral virtues they seem to signify: her 'thoughtfulness' and 'attentiveness'. Her eyes suggest a capacity for kindness and self-sacrifice stereotypically associated with the middle-class feminine ideal. Watching her busily engaged in her needlework, Pip marvels at Biddy's ability to keep pace with him in his learning. His wonder draws attention to the invisibility of women's work, since Biddy's self-education is apparently pursued with the same quietness and undemonstrativeness that characterise her housekeeping. But while the young Pip acknowledges the domestic virtues of Biddy, he nevertheless discounts their value. Her 'wholesomeness' is no match for Estella's promise of glamour and exclusivity.

In analysing his feelings and motives, Pip constantly compares the two women, and his vacillation between them creates the effect of his self-division and psychological development. That Pip's dissatisfaction with his own lot should be registered in the form of a choice between two contrasting images of womanhood highlights the link between the family and female identity in middle-class ideology. The family played a vital role as an imaginary construct in mitigating the effects of the alienation of market relations under capitalism in the nineteenth century. The representation of gender as an apparently fixed system of differences between female and male 'nature' was used to determine social roles and to provide a grounding for the separation of the spheres in which the home could be ideologically preserved as a space where no one was alienated. This special sanctity of the home of course depended upon the conceptualisation of the woman who superintended it. Thus the domestic woman – 'naturally' self-sacrificing, pure and loving – occupied a vital place in the symbolic economy as the guarantor of, among other things, male identity. It comes as no surprise, then, that Pip's identity should depend upon his mobilisation of two contrasting images of womanhood. The adult narrator charts the young Pip's moral and psychological development by analysing his shifting relationships with, and attitudes towards, these two women. They signify his wavering between the worlds of gentility and domesticity. The narrative opposition between Biddy and Estella displays the shift in meaning associated with the idea of the 'gentleman' in the novel, as merit comes to dominate birth in the definition of the term.

The debate about the qualities distinguishing the 'gentleman' has been widely discussed in critical accounts of *Great Expectations*.[13] Derived from the chivalric ideal, the concept of gentlemanliness was redefined through-out the nineteenth century to accommodate the aspirations of rising men in the professions. The 'gentleman' became an important enabling metaphor in the representation of middle-class ascendancy. The appro-priation and redefinition of 'gentlemanliness' as a mark of character, rather than a sign of birth, enabled the upwardly mobile professional classes to be assimilated into the existing hierarchy through the middle-class discourse of morality. Dickens explores the complex dimensions of the concept of the 'gentleman' in the application of the term to the villainous Compeyson, in basing Pip's gentility upon the patronage of a transported convict, in the disclosure of the relation between Magwitch, Molly and Estella, and in Pip's prayer for Joe – 'O God bless him! O God bless this gentle Christian man!' (458) – which transfigures gentility into middle-class morality by splitting the term 'gentleman' into its supposedly classless elements. In its affirmation of Joe as the 'true gentleman' at this point, the novel would appear to mark a decisive shift in social relations from an earlier order, in which birth functioned as the primary criterion of gentlemanliness, to a new order distinguished by the ascendancy of middle-class values. But Pip's story has also shown middle-class self-making to be a myth. It has cast doubt upon the possibility of determining one's identity, of acquiring a social position irrespective of 'birth'. With the shattering discovery that Pip owes his status to crime and money, the novel indicates that origins *do* signify. The idea of the 'gentleman' con-tinues to be shaped by considerations of class, because its legitimising force depends upon the privilege of exclusivity associated with its aristocratic derivation.

The ambivalence with which Dickens regards the idea of the 'gentleman' adds to the equivocation inherent in the form of Pip's narrative. As a fictional autobiographer, Pip gives a shape to his past; he attempts to order the plot of his life; he is engaged in writing the self. But the novel displays a tension between the apparent assertion of autonomy and volition involved in this autobiographical stance, and the gradual discovery of Pip's social determination and emplotment: he is made a gentleman by Magwitch, tracked by Compeyson and used as an instrument of Miss Havisham's revenge. Moreover, this powerlessness is built into the very form of Pip's narrative. Its model is the confession and, as Foucault points out, the obligation to confess is 'the effect of a power that constrains us'.[14] The belief that confession frees is an illusion based upon the misconception that 'truth does not belong to the order of power'.[15] The situation in *Great Expectations* is complicated further by the fact that Pip's narration is retrospective – his destination everywhere informing the analysis of his younger self and of the women who help to create it. This has important implications for the representation of the family, because, while the narrator situates himself within the discourse of domesticity, and produces a narrative constitutive of a middle-class reading subject, he himself is clearly *not* part of a family. Pip's narrative is pervaded by a sense of displacement and dislocation, constructing a perspective for the pseudo-autobiographer that is distinguished by his awareness of exclusion from the families he describes. The narrator's preoccupation with deviations from the norm of domesticity, his eventual acknowledgment of Biddy's 'value', and his recognition of the 'true gentleman', all work to affirm the ideology of the middle-class family. But at the same time, Pip's sense of his own marginality insinuates the failure of this family to constitute itself properly. His story does not close with a vision of ever-lasting domestic bliss, thus leaving a question mark over the familial ideal supposedly endorsed throughout the narrative.

In an important way, *Great Expectations* rewrites the family plots of *Oliver Twist* and *David Copperfield*, finding both of them inadequate. *Oliver Twist* uses a notion of family as genealogy to plot Oliver's recovery of his middle-class birthright, the discovery of his familial origin. Born into the workhouse and forming an 'excellent example of the power of dress' – 'wrapped in the blanket which had hitherto formed his only covering, he might have been the child of a nobleman or a beggar; it would have been hard for the haughtiest stranger to have assigned him his proper station in society' (3) – Oliver's 'true' social identity is nevertheless apparent as soon as he speaks. The middle-class origin indicated by his accent is also signified by the familial ideals he upholds. Oliver's violent altercation with Noah Claypole in chapter VI depends upon a reverence for the sanctity of motherhood that is part of middle-class ideology. When Noah impugns the virtue of Oliver's dead mother, the orphan undergoes a complete transformation:

A minute ago, the boy had looked the quiet, mild, dejected creature that harsh treatment had made him. But his spirit was roused at last; the cruel insult to his dead mother had set his blood on fire. His breast heaved; his attitude was erect; his eye bright and vivid; his whole person changed, as he stood glaring over the cowardly tormentor who now lay crouching at his feet: and defied him with an energy he had never known before. (36)

Oliver is instantly transformed from workhouse drudge to middle-class hero, glowing with defiance and courage. The insult to his mother galvanises him to action, as the debilitating ignominy, victimisation and powerlessness of his orphanhood are temporarily shed in this vigorous display of filial piety. Similarly, Oliver's subscription to middle-class views of the family is also demonstrated as he speculates in chapter VIII upon the relationship between the Artful Dodger and the 'spectable old genelman' who is his 'Patron'. Oliver concludes that 'being of a dissipated and careless turn, the moral precepts of his benefactor had hitherto been thrown away upon [Mr Dawkins]' (49). Oliver's assumptions about the moral instruction accompanying paternal authority (together with his disapproval of wastage) define his middle-class perspective. Despite his orphanhood and the threat of his absorption into the criminal under-world, Oliver's middle-class birthright is never really in question.

In *David Copperfield*, the orphan must earn and secure his social identity by founding his own family. This novel uses the formation of an ideal domestic unit at the close of the narrative to signify the hero's maturation. David's middle-class self-making is exhibited and legitimised in his final union with Agnes, the quintessential Angel in the House. This union represents the culmination of David's search for a family. His efforts in this direction are first displayed in the visit to Yarmouth taken while his mother remarries. David is perplexed to find that the inhabitants of the boat-house do not fit the familial categories – father, mother, son and daughter – into which he automatically places them (26). But they manifest the close emotional ties identified with the middle-class family, and, most importantly, occupy the kind of domestic haven associated with this ideal:

After tea, when the door was shut and all was made snug (the nights being cold and misty now), it seemed to me the most delicious retreat that the imagination of man could conceive. To hear the wind getting up out at sea, to know that the fog was creeping over the desolate flat outside, and to look at the fire, and think that there was no house near but this one, and this one a boat, was like enchantment. (25)

After the magic of his Yarmouth idyll, David is introduced to a family with aristocratic pretensions in the Steerforths, and in their comic counterparts, the Micawbers. Having heard Steerforth's recommendation of Doctors' Commons as a genteel source of employment (281), David is articled to Mr Spenlow, whose home at Norwood is held in veneration by the stipendiary clerks amongst whom he works. One of these, Mr Tiffey, has had the honour of penetrating to Mr Spenlow's breakfast-parlour, and 'He described it as an apartment of the most sumptuous nature, and said that he had drunk brown East India sherry there, of a quality so precious as to make a man wink' (315). But these marks of gentility are soon overshadowed by the feminine charms of Mr Spenlow's daughter, Dora. As the all-consuming object of his desire, Dora represents all of David's 'undisciplined' longings and aspirations: 'She was a Fairy, a Sylph, I don't know what she was – anything that no one ever saw, and everything that everybody ever wanted' (317). David's pursuit of Dora is characterised by the same extravagance and dandyism that mark Pip's genteel aspirations. However, Dora's failure to comprehend domestic economy clearly makes her an inappropriate partner for the hero of middle-class self-making. When David transfers his affections from Dora to Agnes, he chooses domesticity over other family forms, and confirms his identity as a middle-class subject. He finds in Agnes his own best self: 'Clasped in my embrace, I held the source of every worthy aspiration I had ever had; the centre of myself, the circle of my life, my own, my wife; my love of whom was founded on a rock!' (707). As the last in a series of images of women helping to compose David's narrative, the representation of Agnes works to produce the effect of his maturation and moral discipline.[16]

At first sight, Pip's narrative would appear to employ a similar technique. In contrast with the hero of *Oliver Twist*, the orphan in *Great Expectations* attempts to escape his origins and make a new social identity for himself. Just as the various incarnations of woman in *David Copperfield* are used to create the effect of the hero's maturation, so Pip's development in *Great Expectations* is charted in terms of a choice between Estella and Biddy. Both David and Pip are introduced to exemplary home-makers who alert them to the unsuitability of the first choices they make. David is presented with the example of Sophy, Traddles's sweetheart, who can neither paint nor play the guitar (492), but who dutifully performs the housekeeping and mothering of her entire family. Pip's conversion to the values of domesticity is prompted by the example of Herbert's Clara, whose life is devoted to nursing her 'bedridden Pa' (367). Bearing a basket of provisions, she meets Pip for the first time in volume III, chapter VII, and he is impressed by her womanly charms:

There was something so natural and winning in Clara's resigned way of looking at these stores in detail, as Herbert pointed them out, – something so confiding, loving, and innocent, in her modest manner of yielding herself to Herbert's embracing arm – and something so gentle in her . . . that I would not have undone the engagement between her and Herbert, for all the money in the pocket-book I had never opened. (372)

Significantly, this meeting had been delayed by Clara's disapproval of Pip's extravagant, genteel lifestyle, and her view of him as 'an expensive companion who did Herbert no good' (367). While Herbert and Clara might seem to represent another version of Traddles and Sophy, however, David's eventual marriage with his better angel, Agnes, is not re-enacted in Pip's case, despite his final recognition of Biddy's worth.

Pip's rebirth into a new and better self after his illness is marked by his decision to return to the forge and marry Biddy. He casts himself as a prodigal son in describing his homecoming in volume III, chapter XIX: '[M]y heart was softened by my return, and such a change had come to pass, that I felt like one who was toiling home barefoot from distant travel, and whose wanderings had lasted many years' (471). Pip imagines 'the change for the better that would come over my character when I had a guiding spirit at my side whose simple faith and clear home-wisdom I had proved' (471). In finally choosing Biddy to be his 'guiding spirit', Pip would appear to demonstrate his moral growth. Abandoning the hopeless pursuit of gentility that has been signified by his desire for Estella, he seems to acknowledge the true value of domesticity. But Pip's story is a darker one than David Copperfield's, and this looked-for union with an Agnes-like home-maker does not eventuate. Biddy is discovered to be already married to Joe, and Pip is forced to attach himself as an adjunct to the family of Herbert and Clara. Pip's inability to marry Biddy disrupts the conventional closure towards which his narrative seemed to be moving. It destabilises the identity he has been desperately attempting to

construct and transforms the remaining pages of his autobiography into a
kind of postscript. Coming back to the forge after his sojourn in the East,
he looks into the old kitchen 'unseen': 'There, smoking his pipe in the old
place by the kitchen firelight, as hale and as strong as ever though a little
grey, sat Joe; and there, fenced into the corner with Joe's leg, and sitting on
my own little stool looking at the fire, was – I again!' (475). Pip finds himself
displaced from the family fireside by his namesake, just as he has been
displaced from the centre of his own narrative. He is not part of this cosy
family unit, and his marginality is further emphasised by his status as
voyeur, gazing in upon the hearth-side scene of domestic life.

But Pip's inability to marry Biddy is not the only way in which *Great
Expectations* revises the family plot of *David Copperfield*. For the strategy
through which Pip's development is presented in terms of a choice between
two contrasting images of womanhood relies upon an essentialist notion
of female identity that is itself destabilised in the narrative. While drawing
upon the ideology of domesticity in his critique of the novel's fractured
families, Dickens also subverts the ideological function of woman as the
guarantor of male identity through the figure of Estella, who lacks the self-
consistency and indivisibility upon which this function depends. She is a
profoundly unstable foundation for male identity, lacking her own 'self'
altogether. Miss Havisham's mothering leaves her adopted daughter without a heart, and for a long time Pip refuses to believe that Estella has been
thus 'denatured': 'Surely it is not in Nature', he responds, when she insists
again upon her lack of feeling in volume III, chapter V: '"It is in *my* nature,"
she returned. And then she added, with a stress upon the words, "It
is in the nature formed within me"' (358). Estella's comment discloses
the contradiction underlying the concept of female 'nature' in Pip's
narrative. She throws into question the Victorian middle-class ideology
of gendered subjectivity which assumed that female nature was internally
consistent, non-alienated and uniformly 'other' to male nature. Pip's futile
efforts to stabilise and aspire towards an image of Estella in the construction of his own identity only draw attention to the ideological work
involved here.

The failure of this narrative strategy starts to show when Pip is made
aware of similarities between his own situation and Estella's, because this
likeness undercuts the foundational difference held to define the relation
between the two sexes. In volume II, chapter XIV, he meets Estella at the
coach-office in Cheapside and learns of the arrangements to be made for
her travel and accommodation. Any deviation from these is out of the
question, as Estella informs him: 'We have no choice, you and I, but to

obey our instructions. We are not free to follow our own devices, you and I'
(261). At first, Pip interprets these references to their mutual obligation
favourably: he hopes for an 'inner meaning' that foretells of their eventual
marriage. But as Estella continues to emphasise and acquiesce in her
own subjection, he becomes anxious. 'Her reverting to this tone as if our
association were forced upon us and we were mere puppets, gave me pain;
but everything in our intercourse did give me pain', he laments (264).
While his pain is a sign of unassuaged desire, of his unresolved hankering
to be uncommon, it also reveals a more profound dilemma associated with
the way in which selfhood is represented in the novel. In lacking a stable,
feminine self that may be used to ground male identity, Estella exposes
the failure of middle-class ideology to resolve the alienation written into
male subjectivity. Far from constituting that ideal 'other' who might be
the partner of his dreams, Estella is eventually discovered to *resemble*
Pip almost as much as she differs from him: the novel encourages an
identification between Miss Havisham's making of *her* and Magwitch's
making of *him*.

The parallels between Miss Havisham and Magwitch as revengers in
the novel are highlighted by their victimisation at the hands of a common
malefactor: Compeyson. Deceived and jilted on her wedding-day, Miss
Havisham stops the clocks and confines herself for ever inside Satis House;
exploited and betrayed by the wily Compeyson, Magwitch is jailed and
transported for life. Miss Havisham becomes parent to Magwitch's child
in her adoption of Estella, while Magwitch is the origin of Pip's 'great
expectations' which seem, throughout the first half of the novel, to proceed
from her. The affinity between Miss Havisham and Magwitch, underlined
by their revenge plots, points to a similarity in the oppressed positions of
women and working-class men under the system of patriarchal capitalism,
for by adopting personal schemes of vengeance in response to the
experience of social injustice, Miss Havisham and Magwitch inevitably
embrace the ideology they struggle against and are defeated. And
it is out of their defeat that those who occupy positions legitimised by
the dominant order – powerful men like Jaggers – are able to make a
living.

Jaggers is the exemplary 'go-between' in the novel, connecting supposedly disparate areas of the plot with an apparent coincidence that
belies his symbolic function in representing the all-pervasive power of
the legal system. The moral neutrality associated with his status as
representative of the law is complicated by the ethical considerations
involved in his manipulation of evidence and bullying manner, and by

his complicity in profiting from the inequitable system. Jaggers is 'paid for his services' (137) to Magwitch (or else he would not render them), he makes his career out of the trial of Molly (388) and there is the vague suggestion that in 'taming' this murderess to be his housekeeper, Mr Jaggers has also fashioned a mistress for himself. In exploiting the legal system for personal gain, Jaggers demonstrates the way in which the discourse of 'truth' is not transcendent, but is implicated in maintaining the power of the law.

The ideological tensions exhibited in the treatment of the law, and in Pip's representations of Estella and Biddy, extend through to the opposition of home and workplace in the novel, since this division under-pins the middle-class definition of female and male identity. The problem of gender is inextricably involved with the problem of the separation of spheres illustrated in the representations of Joe and Wemmick. Joe is already feminised by the reversal of gender roles involved in his relation-ship with the aggressive Mrs Joe. This inversion is only reinforced by the contrast between Mrs Joe's resentment at the labour required of her as a home-maker, and Joe's love for his work at the forge. Far from performing her household duties and mothering of Pip as a labour of love, Mrs Joe constantly complains about the trouble involved, and at one point asks Joe 'why he hadn't married a Negress slave at once' (96). Her grudgingly performed domestic labour challenges the definition of female nature as selfless and the sequestration of the home as a place of peace and privacy where housekeeping is a ritual of female devotion. In contrast, Joe's work is an expression of his self. Belonging to a pre-industrial world of non-alienated labour, his experience approximates the situation of the Victorian domestic woman whose labour within the home was held to be self-consistent and 'natural' since it was supposedly determined by her reproductive capacity. Thus Joe is most 'at home' in his working dress: 'In his working clothes, Joe was a well-knit characteristic-looking blacksmith; in his holiday clothes, he was more like a scarecrow in good circumstances, than anything else. Nothing that he wore then, fitted him or seemed to belong to him; and everything that he wore then, grazed him' (22).

There is no separation between the forge and the kitchen fire for Joe. Wemmick's case, however, is altogether different. His characterisation in the novel is a parody of the extreme alienation of labour under capitalism. Dickens satirises the split between public and private life in the double identity assumed by Wemmick. When Pip enjoys his first visit to the Castle at Walworth in volume II, chapter VI, Wemmick explains that '[T]he office is one thing, and private life is another. When I go into the office, I leave the

Castle behind me, and when I come into the Castle, I leave the office behind me. If it's not in any way disagreeable to you, you'll oblige me by doing the same. I don't wish it to be professionally spoken about' (206). Try as he may to 'cut off the communication' (204) between his Castle and the rest of London, however, Wemmick's very reliance upon 'the idea of fortifications' (204) is itself an admission of the vulnerability of his home in the midst of the bustling life of the city. The success of his scheme depends upon the ingenuity of his contrivances as he tries to create the illusion of a medieval castle – the gothic windows are mostly sham, the vegetable garden is located at the back 'out of sight' and the drawbridge is a plank crossing 'a chasm about four feet wide and two deep' (204) – and this involvement in fabrication links him with all the other fiction-makers in the novel. While Wemmick insists that Walworth and Little Britain 'must not be confounded together' (288), they are nevertheless linked by their dependence upon fictions of various kinds. Wemmick's fiction is the more innocent – like the pastoral fiction associated with the cottage of the Plornishes in *Little Dorrit* – but it also makes visible the alienation written into male subjectivity, and the need to repair this self-division by preserving the home as a sanctuary.

As an autobiographical narrative apparently devoted to the faithful record of Pip's quest to establish his own identity, *Great Expectations* ultimately questions the assumptions about selfhood which underlie its form. Not surprisingly, the ideology of domesticity figures significantly in Pip's attempt to write the self, but the novel offers a profoundly ambiguous representation of the family. On the one hand, it invests heavily in the domestic ideal, for Pip's portraits of Mrs Joe, Mrs Pocket and Miss Havisham invoke a norm of maternal behaviour that would appear to situate him securely within the discourse of the middle-class family. Allied to this is his belated choice of Biddy as a proper partner for marriage. His eventual recognition of Biddy's true worth is meant to indicate his moral and emotional development, and to mark his adherence to the values of domesticity. On the other hand, however, these efforts to situate himself at the centre of things by appealing to the norms of the middle-class family prove to be mistaken. He is shown to have deluded himself about the plot of his own life, which turns out to be quite different from the tale of 'great expectations' he had imagined. The autonomy conventionally associated with autobiographical narration is gradually revealed to be an illusion. The very process by which conceptualisations of the family and female identity are used to write the narrative of Pip's development is undermined by its exposure as a symbolic operation that is fraught with contradiction. The representation of Estella unsettles the illusion of autobiographical achievement, making visible her imaginary function within the novel. Instead of closing securely with the formation of a new family, *Great Expectations* ends in indeterminacy, with a narrator who remains vulnerable and radically displaced.

CHAPTER 7

Our Mutual Friend

According to J. Hillis Miller, 'Our Mutual Friend is about "money, money, money, and what money can make of life".'[1] This critical view of the novel's dominant concern with commercialism is a long-established one which has, in more recent years, been given a fresh direction by theoretical developments which have led to a new focus upon the complex relationship between money and language as systems of signification in the narrative. As a novel pervasively concerned with the force of capitalism and framed by an inheritance plot in the story of the Harmon patrimony, Our Mutual Friend suggests itself for discussion in terms of the politics of the family in some obvious ways. The relationship between the family and the economy has always been a focus in Marxist studies, and Our Mutual Friend would seem to document the split between productive and reproductive relations held to be characteristic of capitalist social organisation, providing in the process a devastating critique of the morality of individualism associated with laissez-faire economics. The commercial ethos is satirised, for example, in the portrait of the Lammles, whose marriage exposes the extraordinary signifying power of money – a power that resides in its circulation as a collective fiction. Discussion of this function of the family as part of Dickens's attack upon the 'uniform principle' of 'bargain and sale' (196) is familiar in criticism of the novel. However, like Great Expectations, Our Mutual Friend offers a representation of the family that is more ambiguous than the sort of Marxist reading alluded to here would suggest.

On the one hand, Our Mutual Friend appears to invest heavily in the ideology of domesticity. The satiric portrayal of the Wilfer family works to define a middle-class familial ideal; the peculiar power of 'womanly influence', deriving from the sanctity of the hearth, is allowed to prevail in Lizzie Hexam's eventual redemption of Eugene Wrayburn; the Harmon patrimony arrives at its 'proper' destination only after passing through the hands of the servants, Mr and Mrs Boffin, thereby disrupting the notion of the family based upon blood; and, above all, the novel plots moral transformation as a process of domestication – most notably in the depiction of Bella Wilfer – inscribing the middle-class familial ideal as a resolution in which love is held to transcend financial and social status.

On the other hand, however, there seems to be a new self-consciousness informing Dickens's use of the rhetoric of domesticity in the novel that is part of the book's pervasive doubt about the efficacy of language and signification – its exposure of the gap between words and intentions. The reassuring triumph of the middle-class family is put into question by the very narrative methods used to secure it, for the novel relies upon the representation of gender difference to overcome the problems seen to be generated by economic and social inequalities. By apparently grounding other forms of difference in a binary organisation of sex, the novel seeks to manage the social conflicts associated with the capitalist system. However, the conceptualisation of sexual difference as ahistorical and 'given' is itself an unstable construction enabling a range of ideological effects which become visible in the tensions pervading Dickens's narrative technique. Formal properties of the text help to expose ambivalences in the very ideology of the family the novel would seek to promulgate. The implications of narrative omniscience are questioned, as the opposition between private and public, so fundamental to the ideology of domesticity, is subverted by John Harmon in his capacities as lodger and private secretary. The novel betrays a disjunction between form and ideology, ultimately suggesting Dickens's ambivalence about his own novelistic activity.

Modern discussion of the relationship between capitalism and the family is heavily indebted to the work of Engels. According to his formulation, capitalism involves a split between the realms of production and reproduction, work and home, in the organisation of society.[2] Within this dichotomous model, the family performs two crucial functions. Economically, it provides a certain type of productive labour force and an arena for massive consumption. Ideologically, it becomes the source of identity for the alienated labourer, reproducing some of the lost ideals of peasant, feudal society. Situated away from the arena of material production, the family is conceptualised as the centre of personal life, removed from the vicissitudes of political and economic activity.

Our Mutual Friend would seem to thematise some of these issues in the variety of family structures and financial ventures it represents. The juxtaposition of the first two chapters highlights the dominant impulse of rapacity governing a materialistic world in which the traditional image of wealth as dust is used to insist upon the filth of money. The livelihood of the river scavenger, Gaffer Hexam, who bears 'a certain likeness to a roused bird of prey' (3), is suggestively set against the conspicuous consumption displayed by the Veneerings, who host a characteristically ostentatious dinner-party in chapter II. The Veneerings are 'bran-new people in a bran-new house in a bran-new quarter of London' (6), and the emphasis given to their sticky 'surface' in the narrative implies a distinction between substance and façade that betrays the false consciousness supporting their social and economic position. The Veneerings have money – apparently – but have no past, and thus they plague the feeble soul of Twemlow, first cousin to Lord Snigsworth, with 'the insoluble question whether he was Veneering's oldest friend, or newest friend' (7). The blood ties which distinguish aristocratic families, like the Dedlocks in *Bleak House,* are here replaced by the bonds of the cash-nexus which enable Veneering to evade the question of his origins. The successful bourgeois merchant buys a set of 'family friends' whom he assembles to discuss 'an interesting family topic' (115) in chapter x: namely, the marriage of the Lammles. Included in this 'little family consultation' (116) is Mr Podsnap, whose establishment, like Veneering's, is also formidable as a site of conspicuous consumption. Not a 'mushroom man' himself, however, Mr Podsnap's display of riches is more substantial. The 'hideous solidity' of his plate flaunts his social and commercial success, which has been secured through a 'good inheritance', prudent marriage and thriving business in 'the Marine Insurance way' (128). His home is the product of an advertising society, a venue for self-publicity which everywhere displays signs of the demands of consumption and exchange.[3]

While the satirical portraits of the Veneerings and the Podsnaps suggestively link the representation of the family to the success of commodity capitalism, the second aspect of the economic role served by the family under capitalism – the provision of a certain type of productive labour-force – is broached in the depiction of the Wilfer family. The Wilfers are supported by the exertions of R. W. in his capacity as clerk in the drug-house of Chicksey, Veneering, and Stobbles. R. W.'s life is divided between his place of employment and his tempestuous home, to which he returns every evening according to the pattern of capitalist social organisation. However, the ideological function of the family as a centre of stable subjectivity and emotional fulfilment for the alienated worker is obviously put into question here. The satiric treatment of the R. Wilfer family in the novel depends for its effect upon a perceived discrepancy between the domestic ideal and the actual disharmony of an impoverished lower-middle-class home. While the comic representation of the unhappy

Wilfers would seem to subvert the ideology of domesticity, exploding its most cherished myths of love and harmony with laughter, their deviant example helps to formulate a normative definition of the Victorian middle-class family.

According to the narrator, R. Wilfer signs himself thus – using only the initial R. in his signature – to conceal the aspiration and self-assertion he feels to be implicit in the illustrious name of 'Reginald'. This evidence of his shyness and modesty is one of the first indications of the reversal of gender involved in the portrayal of the Wilfers, husband and wife. R. Wilfer is likened to 'the conventional cherub' – 'So boyish was he in his curves and proportions, that his old schoolmaster meeting him in Cheapside, might have been unable to withstand the temptation of caning him on the spot' (32) – and his soft and succulently plump physique under-lines the emasculating power of Mrs Wilfer, whose tallness and angularity immediately set her in opposition to the feminine ideal. She is character-ised by the 'majesty' of her presence, and by a rigidity and coldness of demeanour that are perfectly repellent. The austerity and gloom of her aspect are designed to express her sense of social humiliation in having condescended to marry a humble clerk, and her portrayal is part of the analysis of class resentment in the novel. The clearest indication of this is given in the oration delivered upon the occasion of her wedding anniversary in Book the Third, chapter IV, in which she recalls the aspira-tions and opportunities of her youth, and the 'dark coincidences' which led to her marriage. Here, Dickens's satire emerges in the timorous presence of the ironically named Mr George Sampson, who is typically confined to a parenthetical existence within Mrs Wilfer's text, and further disempowered in having his nervous speech reported by the narrator in free indirect discourse: recalling the presence of the 'wits of the day' in her parents' house, Mrs Wilfer reports, '"I have known as many as three copper-plate engravers exchanging the most exquisite sallies and retorts there, at one time." (Here Mr Sampson delivered himself captive, and said, with an uneasy movement on his chair, that three was a large number, and it must have been highly entertaining.)' (456). The relationship between Mrs Wilfer and her prospective son-in-law is expressed in the language of warfare, with Mrs Wilfer sternly pursuing the cowardly Mr Sampson, 'who had not the courage to come out for single combat', in order to 'force that skulker to give himself up' (456).

Mrs Wilfer is an important part of the novel's analysis of social dis-satisfaction. However, this class discontent is translated into the terms of a gender conflict in her characterisation. In articulating difference upon the basis of sex, and in the form of a binary opposition between an 'unwomanly' wife and an 'unmanly' husband, Dickens's fiction helps to produce a norm of female identity founded upon woman's 'proper' domestic role. Mrs Wilfer's failure to embody the womanly ideal is emphasised in the self-consciousness with which she exploits its rhetoric. In Book the Third, chapter IV, she refers, with assumed modesty, to her position as 'a mere woman, in every-day domestic life' (456). In Book the First, chapter IV, she parades her own 'self-sacrifice' in praising the female heroism of her daughters, as she addresses Lavinia:

The self-sacrifice of Cecilia reveals a pure and womanly character, very seldom equalled, never surpassed. I have now in my pocket a letter from your sister Cecilia, received this morning – received three months after her marriage, poor child! – in which she tells me that her husband must unexpectedly shelter under their roof his reduced aunt. 'But I will be true to him, mamma,' she touchingly writes, 'I will not leave him, I must not forget that he is my husband. Let his aunt come!' If this is not pathetic, if this is not woman's devotion –! (36)

Mrs Wilfer's investment in the rhetoric of domesticity is conspicuous: 'devotion', 'self-sacrifice', 'purity', and 'truth', are terms that define the 'womanly' woman, and their comical misapplication here points to a discrepancy between ideal and actuality that helps to produce a normative conceptualisation of female identity.

These examples of deviation from the middle-class feminine ideal frame other representations of the Wilfers' family life. In Book the First, chapter IV, the Wilfers' dining ritual is described with a narrative delight reminiscent of the cosy meals enjoyed in the Christmas Books. Mr Rokesmith's payment of his rent enables the Wilfers to agree upon the purchase of a 'treat' for their supper. 'Veal-cutlet' is the favoured article, and its preparation is reported in typical Dickensian style with lip-smacking relish:

R. W. himself went out to purchase the viand. He soon returned, bearing the same in a fresh cabbage-leaf, where it coyly embraced a rasher of ham. Melodious sounds were not long in rising from the frying-pan on the fire, or in seeming, as the firelight danced in the mellow halls of a couple of full bottles on the table, to play appropriate dance-music. (40–1)

The comical description of the cutlet's affectation of modesty, as it lovingly clings to the virile rasher of ham, recalls the sexualised accounts of food in the Christmas Books. As in their convivial descriptions of homely meals, the fire is a focus of attention here, radiating warmth and comfort as it cooks the supper and produces 'melodious sounds' suggestive of social harmony. The two bottles on the table hold Scotch ale and rum, and the second of these is mixed to form a heart-warming beverage that completes the transformation of the Wilfer battlefield into a Home: 'The latter perfume, with the fostering aid of boiling water and lemon-peel, diffused itself throughout the room, and became so highly concentrated around the warm fireside, that the wind passing over the house-roof must have rushed off charged with a delicious whiff of it, after buzzing like a great bee at that particular chimney-pot' (41–2). The scent of the steaming mixture is an image of familial feeling, centring upon the hearth and emphasising an opposition between snug interior and cold, blustery exterior. It exerts a moral influence upon Bella, who is made thoughtful. She questions her father about the motives of old Harmon while 'sipping the fragrant mixture and warming her favourite ankle' – a narrative comment that links female desirability with vanity and the pleasures of food in such a way as to suggest the potential for domestication embodied in the unreformed Bella.

The ideological value of food and drink in the novel is made apparent in the contrast between the description of the Wilfers' homely repast and the Veneering banquet in chapter II. The invigorating warmth of the 'fragrant mixture' enjoyed by Bella carries a moral and social significance missing in the chilled wines served by the Analytical Chemist. The 'Chablis', 'Champagne' and 'claret' introduce a foreign element which contrasts with the cosy Englishness of the Wilfers' punch, and indicates the Veneerings' emphasis upon refinement, luxury and *haute cuisine*. The progress of the evening is marked by an elaborate succession of courses, moving from 'soup' through to 'the fish stage of the banquet' and finally on to the removal of the 'ice-plates' and dessert, and includes a variety of exotic delights 'from all parts of the world' (11). Such fare is ostentatious evidence of wealth and social pretension, and it contrasts with the homely but special treat enjoyed by the Wilfers in chapter IV, and with the veal and ham pie hospitably provided for the supper of Silas Wegg by Mr Boffin.

Like the tripe savoured as a New Year's treat by Trotty Veck in *The Chimes*, these humble meals are a significant part of the discourse of domesticity in Dickens's fiction, contributing to the ideological separation of home and workplace associated with the development of capitalism. However, while *Our Mutual Friend* would seem to document this split between productive and reproductive realms in its representation of the

Wilfers, such an account of the relationship between capitalism and the family is complicated by the ideological function of this division in the novel. Dickens's representation of the family suggests that the assumption of a split between production and reproduction is an ideological formation which is not so much the result of a capitalist system as a way of affirming the ascendancy of middle-class values.

One of the ways in which the novel begins to undermine the sphere ideology it also purveys is through the figure of the lodger. Since R. W. has a 'limited salary and an unlimited family' (32), the straitened circumstances of the Wilfers necessitate the accommodation of a lodger. The meagre dimensions of their home in Holloway are described in Book the First, chapter IV, as the heroic Mrs Wilfer herself proceeds through the 'little hall' and 'little front court' to open the gate for her returning husband, and they enter and pass 'down a few stairs to a little basement front room, half kitchen, half parlour' (34). The point is made again in chapter IX, where the genteel fictions used to conceal the realities of lower-middle-class impoverishment are satirised. When Mr and Mrs Boffin visit the Wilfers, Lavinia feigns surprise at finding them waiting on the doorstep to conceal the family's lack of a servant, and upon entering the house, the Boffins perceive 'three pairs of listening legs upon the stairs above. Mrs Wilfer's legs, Miss Bella's legs, Mr George Sampson's legs' (106–7), suggesting not only the comical curiosity of the family members, but also the absence of those housing arrangements which would regulate the introduction of a visitor into a home, and help to determine the social interactions involved in their entry. Other tell-tale signs of the fictions at work are apparent in the family sitting-room, 'which presented traces of having been so hastily arranged after a meal, that one might have doubted whether it was made tidy for visitors, or cleared for blindman's buff' (107), and when Mrs Wilfer decides to call Bella into the presence of the Boffins, the narrator takes great delight in exposing the elaborate manœuvres required to maintain the pretence of a genteel lifestyle, since the proclamation is delivered 'with her maternal eyes reproachfully glaring on that young lady in the flesh – and so much of it that she was retiring with difficulty into the small closet under the stairs, apprehensive of the emergence of Mr and Mrs Boffin' (108). Despite the efforts made to conceal their impoverishment, there is no evading the fact that the Wilfers have been obliged to take in a lodger, and when Mr Boffin seeks a confirmation of Rokesmith's residence, Mrs Wilfer is forced to admit it: ' "A gentleman," Mrs Wilfer answered, qualifying the low expression, "undoubtedly occupies our first floor" ' (111).

Leonore Davidoff has discussed the significance of lodging as a common housing arrangement in Victorian society that questions the separation of home and work so crucial to capitalist social organisation and middle-class ideology.[4] Clearly, the provision of lodging as a profit-making exercise blurs the distinction between market and domestic activities, making it impossible to locate the economy firmly outside the home. The introduction of a lodger into the Wilfer home is thus another indication of the pervasive economic imperative in the social world of *Our Mutual Friend*, where 'bargain and sale' represent the 'uniform principle' (196) of daily life. But of particular significance for the politics of the family is the threat posed to the requirements of the domestic ideal by such a practice. Davidoff notes the moral and social opprobrium that was attached to the taking-in of lodgers from the late eighteenth century onwards. This can be explained in part by a shift in authority patterns within the household, as the paternalistic practice whereby apprentices lived in their masters' houses began to break down in the eighteenth century with the substitution of cash payments for labour, instead of training. This meant an increase in the number of lodgers living in a household but not subject to the control of its head.[5] However, the new demand for privacy most crucially accounts for Victorian middle-class attitudes towards lodging, for, as Davidoff explains, 'Living in lodgings . . . with its sharing of part of someone else's house, was a sign that the family could no longer be kept private and implied a loss of caste.'[6] For Mrs Wilfer, the plan to devote their first floor to the tuition of 'two young ladies of the highest respectability' would have been a much more reputable alternative than the ignominious resort to taking in lodgers. She deplores the loss of caste, and enjoys considerable satisfaction later when she is able to convert the patronage bestowed upon Bella by Mr and Mrs Boffin into disdain for Mr Rokesmith, urging her daughter,

'I trust that as a child of mine you will ever be sensible that it will be graceful in you, when associating with Mr and Mrs Boffin upon equal terms, to remember that the Secretary, Mr Rokesmith, as your father's lodger, has a claim on your good word.'

The condescension with which Mrs Wilfer delivered this proclamation of patronage, was as wonderful as the swiftness with which the lodger had lost caste in the Secretary. (208)

But as well as the descent in social standing caused by the lodger's entry into the home, the loss of privacy also carried implications for gender and generational hierarchies within the household, since the home was no longer clearly to be regarded as a separate sphere, removed from the marketplace. The disruptive effect produced by John Rokesmith in his capacity as lodger is emphasised in Book the First, chapter IV, when his sudden appearance 'knocking at the half-open door of the room' in which the family are assembled startles Bella, who utters 'a short and sharp exclamation', scrambles off the hearth-rug and 'masse[s] the bitten curls together in their right place on her neck' (38). The sexual implications of the lodger's admission are immediately set in focus, and the narrator's comment upon his appearance is highly suggestive: 'A dark gentleman. Thirty at the utmost. An expressive, one might say handsome, face. A very bad manner. In the last degree constrained, reserved, diffident, troubled. His eyes were on Miss Bella for an instant, and then looked at the ground as he addressed the master of the house' (38). The description is conspicuously designed to awaken the suspicions of its readers, forming one of the clues laid by Dickens to disclose the 'mystery' of the hero's identity. But he is also exploiting the fears and anxieties associated with the practice of lodging here, and it is ultimately impossible to distinguish between the tension attributable to John Rokesmith's presence as lodger, and that produced by his double identity as John Harmon – between the ideological implications of this situation, and the suspenseful effects generated by the 'hidden' design of the plot.

This particular conjunction helps to reveal some important assumptions about personal and social identity in Victorian culture, joining together the invasion of privacy involved in the practice of lodging with the use of an alias, the assumption of a false identity. In general terms, this suggests the extent to which concepts of selfhood are bound up with representations of the family in the dominant discourses of the period. More specifically (and not surprisingly), it means that the ideology of domesticity is associated with an essentialist view of the 'self'. Disclosure of the lodger's 'true' self is precluded – explicitly by his plot, but implicitly, by his ambiguous status as an interloper. He is both an insider and an outsider in relation to the family with whom he lodges, and this equivocal position is a source of instability in the narrative. No one seems to be very clear about how he is to be regarded. In establishing the terms of the agreement for occupation of the rooms in chapter IV, Mr Wilfer expects his lodger to receive the request for a reference 'as a matter of course' (39), and is perplexed to find himself put off by the prospect of a reciprocal demand from Mr Rokesmith, who explains, 'I require no reference from you, and perhaps, therefore, you will require none from me' (39). Mr

Wilfer's authority as landlord is subverted by Rokesmith's allusion to the 'embarrassed circumstances' which have led to his taking in a lodger in the first place.

This confusion over status accords with the difficulty in defining lodging experienced by the Special Commissioners of the Metropolitan Police, who were charged with the inspection and regulation of lodging under the Common Lodging Houses Act of the early 1850s. In the absence of any definite idea as to what constituted a 'common lodging house', they had great difficulty in determining where to intervene.[7] The problem was also encountered by the census enumerators of the Registrar General's Office, who had trouble deciding whether lodgers were to be regarded as part of the family of the occupier (i.e. as 'boarders') or were to be counted as single families.[8] These difficulties of definition expose the normative function of the middle-class family in defining other forms of living arrangement as, indeed, 'other'. They also register an extraordinary wish to respect the imaginary boundaries held to separate one family from another – a wish to believe in the solidity of walls that were, in practice, highly permeable. The lodger's ability to transgress these boundaries was clearly a source of threat. Even while gaining the privilege of access to the family, the lodger was also beyond the supervisory control of the head of the household and this placed him (and single lodgers were mostly male) in a position of peculiar power.

The unease with which the Wilfers' lodger is regarded becomes apparent in Book the First, chapter xvi, when Rokesmith and Bella pretend to meet by chance in the fields near their mutual home. Bella makes the discovery of Rokesmith's 'admiration' for her early in the novel, but according to the narrator, is unsure of 'her own heart' in the matter (112). The conversation in chapter xvi establishes her vulnerability as well as the power of the lodger's admiring gaze, for there is a fundamental imbalance in the presentation of point of view in this dialogue which works to represent gender difference. The direct speech of the lodger is generally presented as free direct speech – without the contextualisation of a reporting clause. In contrast, Bella's speech is typically mediated by the third-person narrator, whose report of her words frequently includes evaluative commentary upon their delivery:

'I am charged with a message for you, Miss Wilfer.'
'Impossible, I think!' said Bella, with another drawl.
'From Mrs Boffin. She desired me to assure you of the pleasure she has in find-ing that she will be ready to receive you in another week or two at furthest.'

Bella turned her head towards him, with her prettily-insolent eyebrows raised, and her eyelids drooping. As much as to say, 'How did you come by the message, pray?'

'I have been waiting for an opportunity of telling you that I am Mr Boffin's Secretary.'

'I am as wise as ever,' said Miss Bella, loftily, 'for I don't know what a Secretary is. Not that it signifies.'

'Not at all.'

A covert glance at her face, as he walked beside her, showed him that she had not expected his ready assent to that proposition. (205)

As this last sentence suggests, the narrator's comments upon the behaviour of the lodger serve only to 'reveal' his skill in reading the character of Bella, the quotation marks indicating that the process of disclosure cannot be assumed, because it is an effect of speech presentation and is part of the formation of sexual difference in the narrative. Gender is encoded in the narrative rendering of Bella's body as a site for character analysis, for textual interpretation. An opposition is set up between the descriptions of her appearance – together with the transparency of meaning apparent in the details of her dress, drawling speech, head movements, 'prettily-insolent eyebrows' and drooping eyelids – and the invisibility of Rokesmith, whose physical presence is downplayed at the same time as the assumption of his perspective explains the nature of the focus on Bella. His gaze determines narrative point of view here, and the spectator himself remains hidden from the reader's sight. The asymmetry evident in the presentation of this dialogue privileges Rokesmith in a way that suggests a significant correspondence between the lodger's access to the family, and male narratorial access to female identity. A curious connection, between novelistic form and domestic ideology, begins to emerge here.

A number of feminist theorists have drawn attention, in recent years, to the links forged between woman and the specular in the maintenance of a phallocentric order. Since Freud analysed the role played by the sight of the penis in the discovery of sexual difference, visual prominence has frequently been used to secure male authority through the positioning of woman as the object of the gaze. Thus, given their mutual involvement in the logic of the specular economy, it is hardly surprising that *Our Mutual Friend* suggests a connection between narrative technique and domestic ideology which depends upon the phallocentrism of the visual.[9]

The prospect of Bella's removal to the Boffin mansion would seem to promise her freedom from the lodger's scrutiny. However, Rokesmith insinuates himself into that home as private Secretary, and continues to haunt her existence. While his surveillance of Bella might be undertaken with a benevolent purpose, it becomes morally ambiguous in the context of Eugene Wrayburn's pursuit of Lizzie. The voyeurism implicit in Harmon's stance resembles the surreptitious gaze of Eugene as he watches at Lizzie's window in Book the First, chapter XIII: looking 'long and steadily at her', he sees 'A deep rich piece of colour, with the brown flush of her cheek and the shining lustre of her hair, though sad and solitary, weeping by the rising and falling of the fire' (164). The emphasis given to sensory appeal, the references to Lizzie's 'cheek' and 'hair' and her objectification as a 'piece of colour' obviously establish her as the object of Eugene's desire. The narrative suggests a conjunction here between the violation of the private home by a hidden outsider, and the penetration of Eugene's gaze at Lizzie, affirming a connection between the family and female identity. The fire by which Lizzie sits serves to externalise her passion, making the 'inner depths' of her emotional being visible to the unseen spectator.[10] Eugene returns to Mortimer with a confession of the 'guilty' feelings he cannot repress and stops his friend taking a 'peep through the window' with the admonition, 'Best not make a show of her' (166). But he mysteriously disappears when Gaffer's body is recovered from the river, and afterwards, when questioned by Mortimer about his absence, disingenuously explains that having felt he 'had committed every crime in the Newgate Calendar', he 'took a walk' (177). Unlike the legendary Actaeon or Tiresias, Eugene is not punished for his unauthorised look at Lizzie. But such myths concerning the gaze at the naked woman underlie the suggestion of erotic theft involved in his desire to watch her. His voyeurism establishes the perspective of the male subject in a way that resembles the effects of Harmon's surveillance of Bella, and in both cases the specular position of the male is associated with questions of narrative omniscience.

In her analysis of the use of omniscient narration in Dickens's fiction, Audrey Jaffe defines omniscience as a fantasy 'of unlimited knowledge and mobility; of transcending the boundaries imposed by physical being and by an ideology of unitary identity':[11] 'At once refusing the boundaries of character but defining itself by manufacturing those boundaries, omniscient narration reflects a concern about character's limitations and represents an attempt to transcend these limitations by becoming a non-character, a presence but not an objectifiable participant.'[12] She describes John Harmon as the 'unproblematic, unquestioned embodiment' of the omniscient fantasy in *Our Mutual Friend*, because in the invention and survival of his own death, he contrasts with other characters, like Silas Wegg, who pretend to a knowledge they do not have.[13] To be sure, John Harmon assumes a unique position in the fashioning of his own identity. But his proximity to the omniscient narrator can hardly be described as 'unproblematic'.

Rokesmith temporarily takes over the narration in Book the Second, chapter XIII, as he recounts the story of John Harmon. His account of his own traumatic experience is written in the first person, but the issue of subjectivity is explicitly questioned in the text, as he struggles to formulate references to himself in describing his own 'death': 'But it was not I. There was no such thing as I, within my knowledge' (369). Harmon attempts to imagine a loss of self, but is unable to escape the position of the subject within language. Posing these questions about identity within the form of a first-person narrative suggests something of the self-division held to define the male subject under capitalism. But further evidence of a destabilisation of identity, and of John Harmon's problematic relation to the omniscient narrator, becomes apparent in the representation of Bella at the end of this chapter. The narrator's commentary gives way to the free indirect thought of Rokesmith/Harmon as he admires the beautiful daughter of his landlord:

Oh, she looked very pretty, she looked very, very pretty! If the father of the late John Harmon had but left his money unconditionally to his son, and if his son had but lighted on this lovable girl for himself, and had the happiness to make her loving as well as lovable! . . .

She was on a low ottoman before the fire, with a little shining jewel of a table, and her book and her work, beside her. Ah! what a different life the late John Harmon's, if it had been his happy privilege to take his place upon that ottoman, and draw his arm about that waist, and say, 'I hope the time has been long without me? What a Home Goddess you look, my darling!' (374)

The thoughts of the third-person narrator and the character merge imperceptibly here. The backshift in tense indicates indirectness, thereby corresponding with the form of narrative report. But the use of the third person is no guarantee that the views of the narrator are being presented here, because the character has a double identity in the narrative, and can be read as referring to his 'other self'. The tense and pronoun selection are appropriate to either character or narrator, making it impossible to use syntactic criteria to distinguish between them.

This alignment of narrator and character has ambiguous implications, privileging John Harmon as hero while at the same time raising questions about the ideological effects of Dickens's narrative technique. On the one hand, Harmon's erotic gaze is authorised by its blending with the perspective of the omniscient narrator here. The narrative establishes a kind of league between two male observers, constructing a position of masculine subjectivity for the reader. Rokesmith/Harmon's look of desire shades into the narrator's admiring description of Bella: 'The late John Harmon, looking at the proud face with the downcast eyes, and at the quick breathing as it stirred the fall of bright brown hair over the beautiful neck, would probably have remained silent' (375). The narrator's perspective is distinguished here in the report of the 'late John Harmon['s]' stance as onlooker, but the shift only serves to express a shared male desire. It is yet another instance of the practice, noted elsewhere by Kate Flint, in which Dickens's 'narrator, as well as his male protagonists, ogles his females'.[14] On the other hand, insofar as the issue of perspective remains indeterminate, and male narrator and protagonist cannot be distinguished, the ambiguity highlights the ideological implications of narrative omniscience, for if the private is made public by the presence of the lodger, this is also the transgressive activity practised by the narrator and author. Resemblance shades into identity as Dickens fails to insist upon the boundaries of character referred to by Jaffe, and the association established between male protagonist and narrator raises questions about the role of the novel in Victorian society as a form of discourse ambiguously implicated in the reproduction of the distinction between public and private life.

The link forged between the lodger and the narrator invites a critique of novelistic omniscience as a practice which depends upon privileged access to the private sphere. The type of narrative overview characteristically adopted by Dickens is summarised in *Barnaby Rudge*: 'Chroniclers are privileged to enter where they list, to come and go through keyholes, to ride upon the wind, to overcome, in their soarings up and down, all obstacles of distance, time and place' (69). The prototype of this narratorial agent was Asmodeus, the invisible demon of Le Sage's *Le Diable Boiteux*, who could fly above houses and see through their rooftops, or enter them while remaining invisible to their inhabitants. Dickens invokes him again in *Dombey and Son*, calling for 'a good spirit who would take the house-tops off, with a more potent and benignant hand than the lame demon in the tale, and show a Christian people what dark shapes issue from amidst their homes' (540). While such a roof-removing role is dictated by Dickens's social conscience, it also conflicts with the domestic ideal he would seek to promulgate. If the sanctity of the family depends upon a preservation of the private sphere, how is this to be reconciled with such intervention and exposure?

The model generally favoured by Foucault-inspired critics to describe Dickens's method of narrative overview is the panopticon.[15] The omniscient narrator in *Our Mutual Friend* can thus be held to exemplify the model of surveillance identified by Foucault as characteristic of the formation of disciplinary power in the eighteenth and nineteenth centuries. However, the application of this model would appear to invest the omniscient narrator with a totalising power that the surveillance also exercised by the lodger and private secretary, John Rokesmith, seems to challenge. The tension involved in the practice of omniscient narration and its relation to the representation of the family in *Our Mutual Friend* may be more usefully explained by another analogy capable of registering the ambivalences within the ideology of narrative form. For example, Jacques Donzelot's model of the development of the family as a 'mechanism' in the nineteenth century, described in the Introduction, provides a paradigm for a more nuanced reading of the regulatory effects of narrative omniscience in the novel.

Following upon the work of Foucault, Donzelot sees the family developing during the nineteenth century within two registers which he calls 'contract' and 'tutelage'. 'Contract' refers to an 'internal' mechanism of control within the family, exercised through 'the observance of norms that guarantee the social usefulness of ... [its] members'.[16] Insofar as the family successfully polices itself, and thereby performs its social function, it ensures its own autonomy; or, as D. A. Miller neatly puts it, the family 'remain[s] free by becoming its own house of correction'.[17] 'Tutelage' refers to an 'external' mechanism of control by which the family is subjected to intervention from without. This system of 'external penetration' of the family is enacted through state institutions like workhouses, schools, and prisons, which are designed to remedy its failures.

According to Donzelot, contract and tutelage form positive and negative incentives, respectively, towards the formation of the institution of the nineteenth-century family: the former was applied to the bourgeois family and the latter to the working classes to produce the family as a mechanism of social control. This structuring of relations between the family and the state that the systems of contract and tutelage regulate suggests a model for explaining the ambivalence which characterises the representation of omniscience in *Our Mutual Friend*. The narrator's assumption of omniscience would seem to resemble the system of tutelage, for he is able to penetrate behind surfaces, to enter the private sphere and reveal sights hidden from other eyes: 'Charming to see Mr and Mrs Lammle taking leave so gracefully, and going down the stairs so lovingly and sweetly. Not quite so charming to see their smiling faces fall and brood as they dropped moodily into separate corners of their little carriage' (142). He is privy to the 'truth' of identity, commenting on Bella's objection to the presence of suspicious lodgers, that her sense of grievance might have been greater, 'had she known, that if Mr Julius Handford had a twin brother upon earth, Mr John Rokesmith was the man' (43). The omniscient narrator is also able to see into the hearts and minds of the characters, noting, for example, that despite the quick perception that leads her to mistrust Mrs Lammle, Bella is led by her 'giddy vanity and wilfulness' to squeeze the mistrust 'away into a corner of her mind' (468). Narrative omniscience is a form of 'intervention' designed to expose the shadowy secrets of character. The use of the omniscient narrator to police the text thus works in a way similar to the operation of tutelage in the development of the nineteenth-century family.

However, less clearly 'mediated' forms of representation in the novel produce a normative effect resembling that entailed in the system of contract as outlined by Donzelot. These forms include the 'self-exposure' of character in dialogue, where the representation of deviance involves appeal to an unfulfilled ideal, and structural patterns, such as the unfolding of family plots which issue in domestic resolutions. Like the humanist illusions of identity produced by the strategic withdrawal from narrative omniscience, contract is an 'internal' regulatory system that ostensibly permits the family to preserve its autonomy 'by utilizing its economic capacity, controlling its needs in order to solve, in the private sphere of contractual exchanges, the problems that might arise with regard to the normality of its members'.[18] In a similar way, those forms of representation which do not *appear* to depend upon the intervention of the omniscient narrator work through the power of the norm as they deploy literary convention and appeal to dominant definitions of 'reality'.

The ideological resemblances between Dickens's narrative method in *Our Mutual Friend*, and the disciplinary techniques identified by Donzelot in the development of the nineteenth-century family, suggest the pervasiveness of the distinction between public and private spheres in the formation of modern culture. As a model for the emergence of the principles of social organisation associated with the development of capitalism, Donzelot's account of the nineteenth-century family also helps to explain something of the novel's ambivalence. In suggesting a likeness between fiction and other forms of social practice that is grounded in representations of the family, it displays the cultural significance of this institution, and indicates the way in which the structure of Dickens's novel is crucially bound up with the regulation and legitimation of power in Victorian culture.

These effects can also be detected in the operation of the plot, as Dickens uses a private narrative of female development to reinscribe the domestic ideal as a resolution to the novel. In Book the Second, chapter XIII, Bella's indignant comment to Rokesmith upon narratives as a form of currency used in the commodification of individuals highlights the nature of Dickens's investment in her story:

And was it not enough that I should have been willed away, like a horse, or a dog, or a bird; but must you too begin to dispose of me in your mind, and speculate in me, as soon as I had ceased to be the talk and the laugh of the town? Am I for ever to be made the property of strangers? (377)

Of course, Bella is not the only character in the novel to discover that her selfhood is made the 'property of strangers' in this way. Mr Veneering is said to have 'prospered exceedingly upon the Harmon murder', using 'the social distinction it conferred upon him' to make 'several dozen of bran-new bosom-friends' (134). Seeking to capitalise upon these successes at Mr Podsnap's dinner-party, 'he plunged into the case, and emerged from it twenty minutes afterwards with a Bank Director in his arms. In the mean time, Mrs Veneering had dived into the same waters for a wealthy Ship-Broker, and had brought him up, safe and sound, by the hair' (134). Dickens's imagery links the telling of the Harmon story with the unsavoury business of the river scavengers who traffic in drowned bodies. However, while he is made the 'property of strangers' at the Podsnap and Veneering dinner-tables in this way, John Harmon is also allowed to offer a personal account of his own history and to assume a share of narrative omniscience in Book the Second, chapter XIII, and these opportunities give him an autobiographical authority that is denied to Bella.

The story of Bella's transformation from a selfish and materialistic young girl into a selfless wife and mother is the first of the two plots of moral conversion offered in the novel. Her development from 'mercenary wretch' into 'mendicant's bride' is set in parallel with Eugene Wrayburn's conversion from an aimless and cynical 'gentleman' to an acceptance of the virtues of the middle-class family. Each story plots moral transformation as a solution to social conflicts, and as a process that depends upon changes in the conceptualisation of the family and female identity. The moral transformations of Bella and Eugene involve a conversion to the values of domesticity, and Dickens rewards them both with a fairy-tale ending that supposedly transcends the implications of his own social critique.

Bella, we learn, was once seen by old Harmon stamping her little feet, screaming with her little voice, and laying into her Pa with her little bonnet (42). This exhibition of wilfulness apparently prompted the tyrannical dust contractor to make his son's inheritance conditional upon marriage to Bella, as a wife likely to try his temper. While she is wilful and aggressive, however, Bella is also very pretty and shows a fondness for her father that functions as a redeeming trait, signifying her underlying moral worth throughout the novel. Her transformation into the perfect middle-class housewife and mother is foreshadowed in the anarchic escape of father and daughter from the battleground of the Wilfer family home (as if Dickens's enthusiasm for the happy hearth demanded a fictional outlet and led him to project the domestic fantasy into another context). But while the implied criticism of Mrs Wilfer's capacity as a home-maker is evident, there is no radical critique of the ideology of the family provided here. On the contrary, this excursion only reinscribes the requirement for privacy associated with the domestic ideal elsewhere. It is very like the domesticated version of Saturnalian ritual involved in Dickens's celebration of the Victorian middle-class Christmas. The apparent escape from the constraints of the Wilfer home provides Bella and Pa with an extraordinary opportunity to play with their familial roles. Bella makes a confession of her mercenary impulses to her father at the end of the day, because, she says, 'you are not like a Pa, but more like a sort of a younger brother with a dear venerable chubbiness on him' (320). But Bella and her father also play at being lovers during their 'innocent elopement', as well as pretending to be sister and brother. She laughs at her father's delicate hint 'that perhaps it might be calculated to attract attention, having one's hair publicly done by a lovely woman in an elegant turn-out in Fenchurch Street?' (315), and this propensity to arrange her father's hair 'innocently' sexualises their role-playing. Immediately after this, however, Bella sends her father off to purchase a new outfit with a maternal admonition: 'Now, Pa, attend to what I am going to say, and promise and vow to be obedient' (316). She later gives her father what remains of the fifty pounds, 'cramming it into one of the pockets of his new waistcoat' (321) as if it were indeed his 'pocket-money'.

This temporary escape from the familial battlefield, in which Bella and Pa can play at being lovers, or sister and brother, or mother and child, is like a period of misrule that ultimately conserves the power of the institution so gleefully subverted. Just as the authority of the lord of the manor is shored up by its ritualised breaching at Christmas, so too the institutional authority of the family is affirmed by its temporary overthrow. The retreat of Bella and Pa is contained within a structure of oppositions which sets the apparent freedom and happiness of the expedition to Greenwich against the bondage and turmoil of the home in Holloway, and this pattern is repeated in Book the Third, chapter XVI, when Bella joins her father in the City again after running away from Mr Boffin's. She finds Pa 'preparing to take a slight refection' in the window of the counting-house because, he explains, 'the occupations of the day are sometimes a little wearing; and if there's nothing interposed between the day and your mother, why *she* is sometimes a little wearing, too' (605). The 'quiet tea' he enjoys in the counting-house inverts the opposition between public and private spheres underpinning the ideal of domesticity. Pa finds the office after hours to be the place of peace he ought to find at home in Holloway, and identifies the temperament of his wife with the 'wearing' effect of his daily work. When John Rokesmith enters this peculiar haven immediately afterwards, his engagement to Bella is secured, and all three join in 'The Feast of the Three Hobgoblins'. The fairy-tale characterisation of their meal in the midst of a satiric narrative that also insists upon the reality of lower-middle-class impoverishment, emphasises the oddity, the singularity, of the occasion – 'To think . . . that anything of a tender nature should come off here, is what tickles me', (609) says the cherub – and this delight in eccentricity recuperates the middle-class family, as the exceptional and the irregular help to produce a definition of the normative and conventional.

That Bella's 'innocent elopements' with her father entail a reinscription of the domestic ideal in a place other than the Wilfer home is finally demonstrated in the management of her marriage in Book the Fourth, chapter IV. A more genuine 'runaway match', the secrecy which surrounds it is facetiously extended into the narrative method itself, as the chapter begins with thinly veiled hints about 'a rather particular appointment' to be kept by 'Pa and the lovely woman' (662), and the narrator fails to disclose the source of 'a mysterious rustling and a stealthy movement somewhere in the remote neighbourhood of the organ' (665) heard by the wedding party in the church. The stealth required to accomplish this marriage causes Pa to feel 'like a housebreaker new to the business . . . who can't make himself quite comfortable till he is off the premises' (662). The narrator's potentially subversive delight in this mixture of secrecy and guilt soon gives way to the moral vision of domestic bliss that is shown to be the outcome of the proceedings. Once married and given the opportunity to demonstrate her virtues, Bella emerges as the thoroughly domesticated little housewife celebrated in the Christmas Books:

She always walked with her husband to the railroad, and was always there again to meet him; her old coquettish ways a little sobered down (but not much), and her dress as daintily managed as if she managed nothing else. But, John gone to business and Bella returned home, the dress would be laid aside, trim little wrappers and aprons would be substituted, and Bella, putting back her hair with both hands, as if she were making the most business-like arrangements for going dramatically distracted, would enter on the household affairs of the day. (681)

Bella's fitness for this kind of work comes as no surprise. Her manifestation of a 'genius for home' is only the culmination of a process of domestication that is evident throughout the novel. In Book the First, chapter IV, she is characterised by her refusal to engage in the duties of the domestic woman, for as 'the acknowledged ornament of the family', her hands are employed 'in giving her hair an additional wave while sitting in the easiest chair' (41), rather than setting the table for supper. Bella's removal to the Boffin mansion promises her the genteel lifestyle of a lady. As Rokesmith tells her, 'you will have nothing to do but to enjoy and attract' (205), and Mrs Wilfer is quick to interpret the generosity of Mrs Boffin as an attempt 'to illuminate her new residence in town with the attractions of a child of mine' (207). Bella's installation in the 'eminently aristocratic family mansion' (209) brings her into contact with Mrs Lammle, who takes a great interest in her 'making a good match' and produces a selection of 'loose gentlemen' for Bella to choose from, 'Who in their agreeable manner did homage to Bella as if she were a compound of fine girl, thorough-bred horse, well-built drag, and remarkable pipe' (469). Like Mrs Merdle and Mrs Gowan in *Little Dorrit*, Bella and Sophronia discuss courtship and marriage as economic ventures, for as the prospective bride 'coolly' explains, 'The question is not a man, my dear . . . but an establishment' (469). Bella is made desirable by her wealth and beauty, and this notion of female value belongs to the world-view of the Veneerings and Lammles, who use money to buy the privileges of rank. Mr Podsnap holds a similar view of marriage in regarding Georgiana as 'safe within the Temple of Podsnappery, biding the fulness of time when she, Georgiana, should take him, Fitz-Podsnap, who with all his worldly goods should her endow' (274–5), and in his rebuke of Rokesmith, Mr Boffin speaks of the matrimonial market as an auction with a bluntness that makes Bella wince: 'This young lady was looking about the market for a good bid; she wasn't in it to be snapped up by fellows that had no money to lay out; nothing to buy with' (590). Mr Boffin's insistence upon the mercenary business of marriage drives Bella out of the 'eminently aristocratic family mansion' into the arms of John Rokesmith in a gesture which redefines marriage and female value according to the ideal of domesticity: as Pa tells Rokesmith,

she brings you a good fortune when she brings you the poverty she has accepted for your sake and the honest truth's! (608)

Rokesmith assures his new wife, 'I am rich beyond all wealth in having you' (680), and his sentiments form a rather disturbing variation upon the declaration of Little Dorrit to Arthur Clennam, 'I am rich in being taken by you' (681), for his words (*holding* rather than conferring riches) are in keeping with the imperative of possession which governs the world of bourgeois mercantilism. Bella's transformation, from 'mercenary wretch' into domesticated woman, does not enable her to evade commodification. While her value is now seen to lie in her embodiment of domestic virtue, rather than her wealth, she is no less an object of male desire.

These latent depths of moral value are signalled throughout the novel in Bella's relationships with moral touchstones like Pa, Mrs Boffin and Lizzie Hexam, and in episodes of return to the home in Holloway which mark out stages in her development. A significant movement towards the acquisition of that domestic proficiency which is to replace her wealth as a source of value is made on the occasion of the Wilfer wedding anniversary, when Bella insists upon being 'Cook' for the day. Her keenness to assume the duties of an industrious housewife is coyly relished by the narrator in his description of her apron 'coming close and tight under her chin, as if it had caught her round the neck to kiss her' (451). But his erotic interest is held in check by the comedy which informs the description of Bella's culinary inexperience (452). Dickens delights in subverting the rhetoric of the domestic ideal by literalising the figure of the home as a temple in his satirisation of the Wilfer wedding anniversary: 'It was the family custom when the day recurred, to sacrifice a pair of fowls on the altar of Hymen; and Bella had sent a note beforehand, to intimate that she would bring the votive offering with her' (449–50). This sort of satire echoes Eugene Wrayburn's exploitation of the rhetoric of the domestic ideal in Book the Second, chapter VI, when he fits out the fourth room in the legal chambers he shares with Lightwood as a kitchen, and explains to his friend the merits of the 'miniature flour-barrel, rolling-pin, spice-box . . .' and so on: 'The moral influence of these objects, in forming the domestic virtues, may have an immense influence upon me; not upon you, for you are a hopeless case, but upon me. In fact, I have an idea that I feel the domestic virtues already forming' (284).

The similarity between the omniscient narrator's satiric exposure of the rhetoric of domestic ideology, and Eugene's comic exploitation of the same discourse, again raises the question of narrative point of view. Eugene's moral transformation is made a parallel for Bella's change of heart in the novel. But the apparent symmetry of this parallel plotting is disrupted by differences which emerge in the position of the narrator with respect to each. Critics have often pointed out connections between the characterisation of Eugene Wrayburn, and the restlessness experienced by Dickens himself in his later life. Whether or not Eugene's sexual hunger and lack of mooring register the anxieties of his author, it is significant that Dickens appears to respect the 'autonomy' of this character, so to speak, in a way that distinguishes him from the other example of conversion in the novel, Bella Wilfer. Like Bella, Eugene is subject to an internal struggle which foreshadows the possibility of his transformation. Where Bella's inner conflict is expressed in contradictory feelings that register her painful sense of the contrast between the eminently aristocratic mansion and the home in Holloway – she wishes 'now that the deceased old John Harmon had never made a will about her, now that the deceased young John Harmon had lived to marry her' (322) – Eugene's struggle is to find a purpose. He casts himself as a riddle without an answer, a 'troublesome conundrum' (295). He is unable to fathom his own motives, and 'gives up' the question when pressed by Mortimer for an account of his relationship with Lizzie (295). This failure to account for his own intentions creates an area of obscurity in his characterisation that the omniscient narrator refrains from clearing away. It is as if the narrator colludes with Eugene in his failure to penetrate the meaning of his own heart and mind, despite the criticism of his psychological prevarication that is also implied, for occasional gaps exist in the description of Eugene's activities where the narrator forgoes a demonstration of his omniscience.

For example, Eugene's disappearance after the recovery of Gaffer Hexam's body is accounted for with the rather deceptive explanation in Book the First, chapter XIV, that he 'took a walk' (177). It is not until five chapters later, in Book the Second, chapter II, that we learn, through Eugene's retrospective account of his relationship with Lizzie, of what took place that night. He admits having been 'originally brought into contact' with her on 'two occasions' (237), but it is only the first of these that has hitherto been disclosed to the reader, and the contents of the exchange that took place on the night of Gaffer Hexam's death are only sketched in here. A potentially fascinating dialogue seems to have been left out of the text, while the narrator was busy following the drunken movements of Lightwood on his return to the Temple. Again, in Book the Third, chapter XVII, when Mortimer's clerk comes in search of his master's friend at another Veneering dinner-party, Young Blight's disclosure of the secret efforts being made by Eugene to pursue Lizzie – '"You told me to bring him [i.e. Mr Dolls], sir, to wherever you was, if he come while you was out and I was in," says that discreet young gentleman, standing on tiptoe to whisper; "and I've brought him"' (628) – comes as something of a surprise, despite the earlier revelation of Eugene's willingness to employ Dolls as a scout in Book the Third, chapter X. Apparently, Eugene has acted with a determination hitherto unknown of him. But chapter XVII concludes with a characteristic gesture of irresolution on his part – '"A stroll and a cigar, and I can think this over." . . . Thus, with a thoughtful face, he finds his hat and cloak, unseen of the Analytical, and goes his way' (628) – and here ended the fifteenth number of the original part-issue of the novel. The narrator does not explore the 'thoughts' of Eugene and makes no comment upon the direction of 'his way', but the opening chapter of Book the Fourth discovers him rowing towards Plashwater Weir Mill Lock, 'five-and-twenty mile and odd' (551) up stream from London.

As he abstains from exercising the privileges of his omniscience in this way, the narrator assumes a position of withdrawal that contrasts markedly with his perspective upon Bella. We are rarely denied access to the consciousness of Dickens's heroine. A comparison of the manipulation of point of view in two passages dealing with the relationships between Bella and John and Eugene and Lizzie respectively, reveals the asymmetry. In Book the Second, chapter VIII, Bella's objection to the ubiquity of Rokesmith is expressed in this way:

In spite of his seemingly retiring manners a very intrusive person, this Secretary and lodger, in Miss Bella's opinion. Always a light in his office-room when we came home from the play or Opera, and he always at the carriage-door to hand us out. Always a provoking radiance too on Mrs Boffin's face, and an abominably cheerful reception of him, as if it were possible seriously to approve what the man had in his mind! (309)

The use of free indirect thought presentation conveys the narrator's satire here. There is no question of a merging together of character and narrator, because irony establishes the distinction between them, creating instead a communion with the reader who 'shares the joke'. In his penetration of Bella's thoughts, the narrator repeats the very intrusion she complains of. In contrast, the narrator's presentation of Eugene's thoughts about his relationship with Lizzie, at the end of Book the Second, chapter xv, is much less invasive:

He knew his power over her. He knew that she would not insist upon his leaving her. He knew that, her fears for him being aroused, she would be uneasy if he were out of her sight. For all his seeming levity and carelessness, he knew whatever he chose to know of the thoughts of her heart.

And going on at her side so gaily, regardless of all that had been urged against him; so superior in his sallies and self-possession to the gloomy constraint of her suitor, and the selfish petulance of her brother; so faithful to her, as it seemed, when her own stock was faithless; what an immense advantage, what an overpowering influence were his that night! (406)

The pronoun selection marks the report of Eugene's 'knowledge' from a position 'outside' the consciousness of the character, and this external perspective is confirmed in the narrator's evaluative comments. While the narrator opens up 'direct' access to the consciousness of Bella in the use of free indirect narration to present her thoughts, Eugene appears to resist such narrative appropriation of his point of view – at least until the final clause in the passage quoted. The narrator's exclamation seems to betray a vicarious thrill in emphasising Eugene's power over Lizzie. But the shared perspective of masculine advantage is only further evidence of the narrative inscription of gender difference.

Eugene's moral transformation is brought about by the redeeming influence of Lizzie Hexam. His change of heart records a middle-class myth in which the virtues of the domestic woman are seen to exercise a saving moral power, and love is held to overcome class difference. A number of critics have remarked upon a tendency to de-sexualise Lizzie in the narrative, Deirdre David, for example, attributing her lack of 'sexual vitality' to 'Dickens's implicit distaste for a class structure which endorsed the sexual exploitation of working-class women'.[19] While Dickens's objection to this sort of abuse is evident, the insistence upon Lizzie's sexual purity is a kind of overcompensation for her working-class origin, as she is endowed with a middle-class subjectivity that does away with the class difference she is meant to illustrate. Dickens's effort to accommodate bourgeois sensibilities has been noted by many critics. But the political consequences of this narrative behaviour have not been considered. Lizzie's portrayal is an important part of the way in which the novel appears to neutralise class struggle by replacing this struggle with gender conflict. Social inequalities are made to seem temporary and relatively insignificant in comparison with the supposedly permanent and 'natural' differences of sex which are defined by the middle-class ideology of separate spheres.

Lizzie is characterised by her self-sacrificing devotion to her father and brother, her genteel manners and speech, and her moral superiority. In commenting upon Charley's relationship with Lizzie in Book the Second, chapter v, the narrator describes her as 'his patient little nurse in infancy, his patient friend, adviser, and reclaimer in boyhood, the self-forgetting sister who had done everything for him' (401). Lizzie works to get Charley placed as a pupil-teacher under Bradley Headstone at the National School; she denies herself an education in order to preserve the tie with her illiterate father; she defends him against the accusations of Rogue Riderhood; she takes off for the countryside to save her honour from the man she loves and because of Bradley Headstone's threats to harm him; she risks her life to save Eugene, and then nurses him back to health. Her selflessness, purity and devotion mark her as an embodiment of the middle-class feminine ideal, despite the physical strength, illiteracy and employment in the paper-mill which establish her tenuous connection with the working classes.

However, while Lizzie may represent the de-sexualised embodiment of the womanly ideal, it is by no means clear that her appeal for Eugene Wrayburn is so innocent. The issue of sexual attraction is implied in the offer of education, as Eugene and Bradley vie with one another for the 'right' to 'teach' Lizzie. Their fierce rivalry for sexual involvement with Lizzie is ambiguously suggested in the narrator's observation of 'some secret, sure perception between them, which set them against one another in all ways' (288). Sexual innuendo underlies Eugene's taunting inquiry,

'Are you her schoolmaster as well as her brother's? – Or perhaps you would like to be?' said Eugene.

It was a stab that the blood followed, in its rush to Bradley Headstone's face, as swiftly as if it had been dealt with a dagger. 'What do you mean by that?' was as much as he could utter. (292–3)

Like the maiming of Rochester or the blinding of Romney Leigh, Eugene's wounding by Bradley helps to defuse the sexual threat he has posed, and provides a situation in which Lizzie can safely demonstrate the domestic virtues she enshrines in her role as nurse. Significantly, it is the influence of this kind of woman, whose identity is conceived in terms of the middle-class ideal of domesticity, that saves Eugene morally as well as physically. This validation of the domestic ideal is a counterpart to the reaffirmation of the middle-class family in the marriage of Bella and John Harmon. While commentators have pointed to the ideological conservatism implied in the fact that Eugene's marriage to Lizzie is effected in the face of what seems to be his approaching death and does not produce any structural change in social relations, this conservatism is already present in the conceptualisation of the family and of female identity which underlies the development of their relationship.

Eugene's father acquiesces in the unorthodox marriage made by his son, but the union between the barrister and the 'female waterman' nevertheless represents a defiance of paternal authority. Eugene's 'Respected Father' has prearranged the destinies of all his children 'from the hour of the birth of each, and sometimes from an earlier period' (146), and the son's cynical attitude to this exercise of paternal control is expressed in his irreverent decision to 'shorten the dutiful tautology by substituting in future M.R.F., which sounds military, and rather like the Duke of Wellington' (146). Informing Mortimer in Book the First, chapter XII, that 'M.R.F.' has found a wife for his son, Eugene also announces that he will refuse to oblige him, and this filial opposition is a parallel for the reluctance to fulfil his father's scheme shown by John Harmon.

The analogy between these two sons is part of Dickens's exploration of the burden of inheriting in the novel. The distribution of Harmon's money in accordance with the provisions of his first will, and John Harmon's eventual marriage to Bella in fulfilment of the malicious condition imposed upon his inheritance, would seem to reaffirm the authority of the father. Similarly, paternal power is renewed in the Podsnap family, since by choosing to give back the money Georgiana Podsnap had intended for the Lammles, but not to disillusion her about their treachery, Mr Boffin supports the infantilisation of the daughter promoted by the domineering rule of Mr Podsnap. His well-meaning gesture – 'I may try to give a hint at her home that she is in want of kind and careful protection, but I shall say no more than that to her parents, and I shall say nothing to the young lady herself' (649) – provides no solution to the damaging effects of Mr Podsnap's paternalism.

However, while these outcomes might appear to qualify the critique of paternal authority in the novel, they are consistent with the reconceptualisation of the family demanded by the narrative. Indeed, as ambivalently resolved challenges to the authority of the father, these plots of inheritance and courtship reinscribe the domestic ideal. The crucial point about John Harmon's eventual acquiescence in the will of his father is that this outcome is effected through the mediation of Mr and Mrs Boffin. The Harmon patrimony is inherited by the son only after it has passed through the hands of the servants. As John Harmon explains to the newly exposed 'scoundrel', Wegg,

You supposed me just now, to be the possessor of my father's property. – So I am. But through any act of my father's, or by any right I have? No. Through the munificence of Mr Boffin. The conditions that he made with me, before parting with the secret of the Dutch bottle, were, that I should take the fortune, and that he should take his Mound and no more. I owe everything I possess, solely to the disinterestedness, uprightness, tenderness, goodness (there are no words to satisfy me) of Mr and Mrs Boffin. (788)

This diversion of the Harmon patrimony cuts across the lineage that forms the basis for the conceptualisation of the aristocratic family. While appearing to transcend class differences, however, this gesture reaffirms the middle-class ideal of domesticity as a surrogate father is shown to displace the biological father in setting the terms of the bequest. Mr and Mrs Boffin have stood as surrogate parents to John Harmon according to the requirements of the domestic ideal, and their power to transfer the Harmon patrimony legitimises the notion of family they represent. The original value of the estate bequeathed by old Harmon is now significantly increased by the worthiness of those who pass it on to the son. John Harmon may end up fulfilling the letter of his father's law, but the complications of the inheritance plot undermine the significance of genealogical ties, and affirm instead the affective bonds of the middle-class family. In terms of family identity and property relationships, the inheritance plot permits John Harmon to make a fresh start (a point made symbolically by his immersion in the Thames). Adhering to the values of the domestic ideal, as Eugene Wrayburn learns to do, he is enabled to form a family of his own choosing, and to re-establish his identity.

The tensions generated by poverty, greed, violence, and class discontent throughout the novel are ostensibly overcome with the founding of a new social order in the penultimate chapter. Mr and Mrs John Harmon preside over this counter-community, executing a system of reward and punishment that parallels the omniscience with which the narrator 'resolves' the novel and attempts to dispel its darkness: 'Mr and Mrs John Harmon's first delightful occupation was to set all matters right that had strayed in any way wrong, or that might, could, would, or should have strayed in any way wrong, while their name was in abeyance' (803). In addition to sharing the Harmon fortune with such generosity, the new abode of mendicancy permits Bella and John to welcome guests and visitors in a gesture of social expansiveness that resembles Dickens's renowned enthusiasm for entertaining: 'It was a grand event, indeed, when Mr and Mrs Eugene Wrayburn came to stay at Mr and Mrs John Harmon's house: where, by the way, Mr and Mrs Boffin (exquisitely happy, and daily cruising about, to look at shops) were likewise staying indefinitely' (811). Dickens links the family groups that emerge from the novel's reaffirmation of the domestic ideal in a spirit of conviviality. His fictional resolution is a vision of mutuality that is underlined by the gratitude expressed for the 'company' of his readers in the Postscript to the novel.

However, the consolation provided by such fictional closure is tenuously sustained in the face of the challenges to domestic ideology that emerge in the novel's representation of narrative omniscience. Through his ubiquitous presence as lodger and private secretary, for example, John Harmon would appear to throw the privacy of the family into question. Indeed, the very split between productive and reproductive realms, supposedly determined by the development of capitalism, becomes visible as an ideological formation that is already shaped by gender and class differences. A more trenchant examination of the relationship between capitalism and the family in *Our Mutual Friend* demonstrates some of the ways in which Dickens's representation of the family enabled the construction of the very ideology that the form of this novel would seem to subvert.

Postscript

Dickens's 'Postscript – In lieu of Preface' to *Our Mutual Friend* concludes with a remembrance of the Staplehurst railway accident in which he was involved while travelling from Folkestone to London following a ten-day holiday in France.[1] The express train leapt a 42-foot gap in the rails, where worn timbers were being replaced at the Staplehurst viaduct, and plunged into a ravine. Ten people were killed and forty were seriously injured. Not only did Dickens and his travelling companions survive, but so did the manuscript of his novel, which Dickens managed to retrieve from the wreckage:

On Friday the Ninth of June in the present year, Mr and Mrs Boffin (in their manuscript dress of receiving Mr and Mrs Lammle at breakfast) were in the South-Eastern Railway with me, in a terribly destructive accident. When I had done what I could to help others, I climbed back into my carriage – nearly turned over a viaduct, and caught aslant upon the turn – to extricate the worthy couple. They were much soiled, but otherwise unhurt. The same happy result attended Miss Bella Wilfer on her wedding day, and Mr Riderhood inspecting Bradley Headstone's red neckerchief as he lay asleep. I remember with devout thankfulness that I can never be much nearer parting company with my readers for ever than I was then, until there shall be written against my life, the two words with which I have this day closed this book: – THE END.

September 2, 1865 (822)

This closing address to his readers is thoroughly characteristic in its playful blurring of the boundaries between fiction and lived experience. Dickens's characters are held to inhabit the same discursive order as their creator in a rhetorical gesture which uses the staving off of a final farewell to distinguish the temporary parting with his readers necessitated by the end of his latest narrative. The passage shows his recurrent desire to override the separation between public and private spheres – a distinction nonetheless upheld elsewhere in his fictional representations of the family – by finding a way for his work to enter into the homes of his readers.

Dickens's novels seek to cast themselves as essentially private affairs, narratives to be read or listened to within the confines of the family home.[2] His prefaces, written at the end of each serial publication, often conclude with an implied construction of the mythological Victorian family, gathered around the hearth to read the novel he has just completed, from which the novelist sorrowfully takes his leave. In his Preface to the original edition of *Nicholas Nickleby*, for example, Dickens writes: 'As he has delivered himself with the freedom of intimacy and the cordiality of friendship, [the author] will naturally look for the indulgence which those relations may claim; and when he bids his readers adieu, will hope, as well as feel, the regrets of an acquaintance, and the tenderness of a friend.'[3] Dickens's eagerness to associate his work with the dissemination of the ideal of domesticity is indicated in the 'Preliminary Word' with which he began the first issue of *Household Words*,[4] as well as in the kind of exhortation with which he concluded his *Sketches of Young Couples* in 1840:

Before marriage and afterwards, let them learn to centre all their hopes of real and lasting happiness in their own fireside; let them cherish the faith that in home, and all the English virtues which the love of home engenders, lies the only true source of domestic felicity; let them believe that round the household gods, contentment and tranquillity cluster in their gentlest and most graceful forms; and that many weary hunters of happiness through the noisy world, have learnt this truth too late, and found a cheerful spirit and a quiet mind only at home at last.[5]

His success in identifying himself with the values of the hearth is evident in Margaret Oliphant's assessment that 'Mr Dickens has won for himself what is more to the purpose than the approbation of criticism, an affectionate welcome in the households and homes of his country.'[6]

Given the power of language and writing to materialise ways of being in the world, Dickens's representation of the family played a significant role in uniting individuals from different social groups according to a set of universal values, centring upon the home, and apparently common to them all. His fiction not only portrays, but *identifies* with, the family, as domestic ideology informs his narrative practice throughout. His novels speak not just for but from the hearth, creating the occasion for their own consumption in the domestic sphere. In the mutually authorising relationship thus established between fictional representation and social practice, his writing displays, in an exemplary form, the role of the nineteenth-century novel in the formation of cultural knowledge.

However, in spite of his efforts to associate his work with the sanctified space of the family home, Dickens found himself inevitably crossing the threshold between public and private domains in a number of ways which put the division itself under threat. The controversy surrounding the break-up of his marriage and its publicity in the pages of *Household Words* is a good example. Significantly, the Postscript to *Our Mutual Friend* fails to disclose the identity of the two companions travelling with Dickens in the train from Folkestone – Ellen Ternan and her mother – displacing their mention with comment upon his rescue of the Boffins and Lammles. In his novels, the provision of private, familial solutions for public problems is a fictional strategy which is frequently thrown into question by other elements in the narrative. While *Dombey and Son* ends with the founding of a new family and the eventual reconciliation of father and daughter, it also contains the germ of a new story in the mention of 'Another Wedding' celebrated on the same day Florence and Walter join hands. Chapter LVII opens with a description of preparations being made in the 'fine church where Mr Dombey was married' for the wedding of a 'yellow-faced old gentleman from India' to 'a young wife' who is 'to be given away, as an extraordinary present, by somebody who comes express from the Horse Guards' (673). The novel opens out here to suggest another tale of marital tension and exploitation (based upon the project of empire), belying the apparent closure effected by the vision of domestic bliss that Florence and Walter share. In *Great Expectations*, closure is undermined in both the printed versions of the ending Dickens wrote, for whether Pip and Estella are to be united is never clearly established, although, as Margaret Cardwell notes, any story of achievement for Pip 'could only be a post-script'.[7] The products of a unique and powerful poetic imagination, Dickens's endings have an uncanny ability to suggest the beginnings of other narratives that might modify the conclusions to be drawn about the one he has just completed. In turn, his prefaces take the retrospective form of postscripts, while also looking forward to the next narrative adventure with his readers: 'Deeply sensible of the affection and confidence that have grown up between us,' he writes at the end of the Preface to *Little Dorrit*, 'May we meet again!' (xxii). This amazing capacity for invention is not unrelated to the facility with which Dickens's fictions often subvert the familial ideology upon which they are nevertheless based. The Report of the 1851 Census identified a 'natural' and 'universal' desire held by 'every Englishman' to draw a 'sharp, well-defined circle' around his hearth.[8] But even as they gesture towards new narrative possibilities, Dickens's novels resist the closure of the middle-class family.

Notes

1 INTRODUCTION: THE MAKING AND BREAKING OF THE FAMILY

1 John Forster, *The Life of Charles Dickens*, ed. A. J. Hoppé, Everyman's Library, 2 vols. (1872–4; London: Dent, 1969), vol. II, p. 198.

2 Percy Fitzgerald, *Memories of Charles Dickens* (Bristol: J. W. Arrowsmith, 1913), p. 189.

3 Charles Dickens, 'PERSONAL', *Household Words*, 12 June 1858, 601.

4 Fitzgerald, *Memories*, p. 190.

5 Review of *The Battle of Life*, by Charles Dickens, *Morning Chronicle*, 24 December 1846. Quoted in Margaret Lane, 'Dickens on the Hearth', in *Dickens 1970: Centenary Essays*, ed. Michael Slater (New York: Stein and Day, 1970), p. 171.

6 Edgar Johnson, *Charles Dickens: His Tragedy and Triumph*, revised and abridged edn (London: Allen Lane, 1977), p. 461.

7 Norman and Jeanne Mackenzie, *Dickens: A Life* (Oxford University Press, 1979), p. 304.

8 Fred Kaplan, *Dickens: A Biography* (London: Hodder and Stoughton, 1988), p. 394.

9 Forster, *Life*, vol. II, p. 206.

10 Edmund Yates, *Edmund Yates: His Recollections and Experiences*, 4th edn (London: Bentley, 1885), pp. 300–1.

11 *Ibid.*, p. 300. It is a significant comment upon the formation of a division between public and private life in Victorian culture that the Oxford English Dictionary records the first usage of this expression in 1867 in Trollope's *The Last Chronicle of Barset*: 'I do not like to trouble you with my private affairs; – there is nothing, I think, so bad as washing one's dirty linen in public' (p. xliv).

12 Dickens, 'PERSONAL', 601.

13 *Ibid.*

14 *Ibid.*

15 Mackenzie and Mackenzie, *Dickens*, p. 303.

16 William Makepeace Thackeray, Letter to Mrs Carmichael-Smyth, May 1858, *The Letters and Private Papers of William Makepeace Thackeray*, ed. Gordon N. Ray, 4 vols. (Oxford University Press, 1946), vol. IV, p. 86.

17 Kaplan, *Dickens*, p. 391.

18 See Jenni Calder, *Women and Marriage in Victorian Fiction* (London: Thames and Hudson, 1976), p. 88; see also Nancy F. Cott, 'Passionlessness: An Interpretation of Victorian Sexual Ideology, 1790–1850', *Signs* 4 (1978), 219–36.

19 W. R. Greg, 'Prostitution', *Westminster Review* 53 (1850). Reprinted in *Strong-Minded Women and Other Lost Voices from Nineteenth-Century England*, ed. Janet Horowitz Murray (Harmondsworth: Penguin, 1984), p. 410.

20 Quoted in Mary Lyndon Shanley, *Feminism, Marriage, and the Law in Victorian England, 1850–1895* (Princeton University Press, 1989), p. 40.

21 Peter Ackroyd, *Dickens* (London: Sinclair-Stevenson, 1990), p. 813.

22 Charles Dickens, Letter to Frederick Ouvry, 26 May 1858, reprinted in K. J. Fielding, 'Dickens and the Hogarth Scandal', *Nineteenth-Century Fiction* 10 (1955), 67.

23 'London, Sat June 12', *Court Circular*, 12 June 1858, 8.

24 H. Buchanan MacPhail, Letter to Charles Dickens, 14 October 1858, reprinted in K. J. Fielding, 'Charles Dickens and Colin Rae Brown', *Nineteenth-Century Fiction* 7 (1952), 104.

25 See Nancy F. Anderson, 'The "Marriage with a Deceased Wife's Sister Bill" Controversy: Incest Anxiety and the Defence of Family Purity in Victorian England', *Journal of British Studies* 21 (1982), 67–86.

26 Quoted in Cynthia Behrman, 'The Annual Blister: A Sidelight on Victorian Social and Parliamentary History', *Victorian Studies* 11 (1968), 491.

27 Accompanying note to the 'Violated Letter', reprinted in Michael Slater, *Dickens and Women* (London: Dent, 1983), p. 373.

28 Charles Dickens, Letter to Frederick Ouvry, 5 September 1858, reprinted in *Mr and Mrs Charles Dickens: His Letters to Her*, ed. Walter Dexter (London: Constable and Co., 1935), p. 258.

29 Charles Dickens, 'Violated Letter', reprinted as Appendix A in Slater, *Dickens and Women*, pp. 373–5.

30 Charles Dickens, *Letters from Charles Dickens to Angela Burdett Coutts 1841–1865*, ed. Edgar Johnson (London: Jonathan Cape, 1953), pp. 354–5.

31 Slater, *Dickens and Women*, p. 146.

32 Forster, *Life*, vol. 11, p. 199.

33 Elizabeth Barrett Browning, Letter to Miss Bayley, nd 1858, quoted in Kaplan, *Dickens*, p. 394.

34 Charles Dickens, Letter to Frederick Ouvry, 5 September 1858, in Dexter, ed., *Mr and Mrs Charles Dickens*, pp. 258–9.

35 Walter Dexter comments upon the direction to Arthur Smith: 'In view of this, one can hardly understand Dickens's anger when he found the letter had got into print', *Mr and Mrs Charles Dickens*, p. 276. Michael Slater observes that Dickens's 'continued regard and friendship for Smith give rise to the suspicion that he may have connived at its publication', *Dickens and Women*, p. 400 n. 2.

36 Quoted in Johnson, *Charles Dickens*, p. 463.

37 Quoted in Ackroyd, *Dickens*, p. 819.

38 'Mr C. Dickens', *Reynolds's Newspaper*, 13 June 1858, 3.
39 *Ibid.*
40 'Gossip of the Week', *Reynolds's Newspaper*, 20 June 1858, 6.
41 'Our Civilisation', *Saturday Review*, 28 June 1856, 195.
42 Forster, *Life*, vol. II, p. 200.
43 Lane, 'Dickens on the Hearth', pp. 170–1.
44 See Lawrence Stone, *The Family, Sex and Marriage in England 1500–1800* (London: Weidenfeld and Nicolson, 1977); Randolph Trumbach, *The Rise of the Egalitarian Family: Aristocratic Kinship and Domestic Relations in Eighteenth-Century England* (New York: Academic Press, 1978); Peter Laslett and Richard Wall, *Household and Family in Past Time* (Cambridge University Press, 1972); Alan Macfarlane, *Marriage and Love in England: Modes of Reproduction 1300–1840* (Oxford: Blackwell, 1986).
45 Jeffrey Weeks, *Sex, Politics and Society: The Regulation of Sexuality since 1800*, Themes in British Social History (London: Longman, 1981), p. 25.
46 Lawrence Stone argues that the form he identifies as the Closed Domesticated Nuclear Family existed from 1640, and by the late eighteenth century the growth of 'affective individualism' had helped to produce the four key features of the modern family in the middle and upper sections of English society: 'intensified affective bonding of the nuclear core at the expense of neighbours and kin; a strong sense of individual autonomy and the right to personal freedom in the pursuit of happiness; a weakening of the association of sexual pleasure with sin and guilt; and a growing desire for physical privacy', Stone, *Family, Sex and Marriage*, p. 8.
47 Jean-Louis Flandrin, *Families in Former Times: Kinship, Household and Sexuality*, trans. Richard Southern, Themes in Social Sciences (Cambridge University Press, 1979), p. 4.
48 Raymond Williams, *Keywords: A Vocabulary of Culture and Society* (Oxford University Press, 1977), pp. 131–4.
49 *Ibid.*, p. 132.
50 *Ibid.*, p. 133.
51 Census 1851: Report, pp. xxxiv and xli. *British Parliamentary Papers – Population* vol. VI.
52 *Ibid.*, p. xli.
53 Gramsci employs the term 'hegemony' to describe the 'moment' of collective political consciousness when a class brings about an 'intellectual and moral unity' in which its specific interests are 'universalised' so as to become 'right' for everyone. Hegemony is secured when the class-specific norms of the dominant group disappear into the 'common sense' of everyday life. See Antonio Gramsci, *Selections from the Prison Notebooks*, trans. and ed. Quintin Hoare and Geoffrey Nowell-Smith (London, 1971). Extracts reprinted in *Culture, Ideology and Social Process: A Reader*, ed. Tony Bennett, Graham Martin, Colin Mercer and Janet Woollacott (London: Batsford, 1981), p. 198.
54 Census 1851: Report, p. xxxvi.
55 *Ibid.*

56 'Charles Dickens and *David Copperfield*', *Fraser's Magazine*, December 1850, xlii, 698–710. Reprinted in *Dickens: The Critical Heritage*, ed. Philip Collins (London: Routledge, 1971), p. 244.

57 Margaret Oliphant, 'Charles Dickens', *Blackwood's Magazine* 77 (1855), 451–66. Reprinted in Collins, ed., *Critical Heritage*, pp. 328–9.

58 'The Death of Mr Dickens', *Saturday Review*, 11 June 1870, xxix, 760–1. Reprinted in Collins, ed., *Critical Heritage*, p. 511.

59 A. W. Ward, from *Charles Dickens: A Lecture*, 30 November 1870. Reprinted in Collins, ed., *Critical Heritage*, p. 539.

60 Lane, 'Dickens on the Hearth', p. 154.

61 Anny Sadrin, *Parentage and Inheritance in the Novels of Charles Dickens*, European Studies in English Literature (Cambridge University Press, 1994).

62 My critical approach owes much to the work of Mary Poovey and Nancy Armstrong, among others, in analysing the mutual articulation of class and gender difference in a range of nineteenth-century discourses. See Mary Poovey, *Uneven Developments: The Ideological Work of Gender in Mid-Victorian England* (London: Virago, 1989) and Nancy Armstrong, *Desire and Domestic Fiction: A Political History of the Novel* (Oxford University Press, 1987).

63 Joanne Shattock and Michael Wolff, eds., *The Victorian Periodical Press: Samplings and Soundings* (Leicester University Press, 1982), p. xv.

64 See Sally Mitchell, 'The Forgotten Woman of the Period: Penny Weekly Family Magazines of the 1840's and 1850's', in *A Widening Sphere: Changing Roles of Victorian Women*, ed. Martha Vicinus (Bloomington: Indiana University Press, 1977), pp. 29–51.

65 Circulation figures are taken from Richard D. Altick, *The English Common Reader: A Social History of the Mass Reading Public 1800–1900* (University of Chicago Press, 1957).

66 'Popular Literature – the Periodical Press', *Blackwood's Edinburgh Magazine* 85 (1859), 188.

67 'To Correspondents', *Family Herald* 1 (1844), 72.

68 'Preface', *Magazine of Domestic Economy* 1 (1836), iii–iv. The *Magazine of Domestic Economy* was a monthly journal of instructive reading devoted to all branches of 'domestic economy', including articles on household duties and operations, cookery and confectionery, dietetics, gardening, medical advice, public institutions, exhibitions and amusements, trips and lists of conveyances, tide tables and local fairs. The *Waterloo Directory* lists no price information, but the contents suggest it was designed for a middle-class audience (sample monthly household accounts in the first number, for example, are based upon an average monthly income of £18).

69 'Preface', *Johnstone's Penny Fireside Journal: a Magazine of Amusing and Instructive Literature* 1 (1843), iii.

70 'Preface', *Family Friend* 1 (1849), iv.

71 'Little Dorrit Advertiser', *Little Dorrit* by Charles Dickens, December 1855, no. 1, p. 19.

72 'A Word to My Readers', *Eliza Cook's Journal* 1 (1849), 1.

73 'Letters from Aunt Peggy to her Niece', *Family Herald* 1 (1844), 12.
74 John Ruskin, 'Of Queens' Gardens', in *Sesame and Lilies, Unto This Last and The Political Economy of Art* (1865; London: Cassell, 1909), p. 73.
75 'Home Power', *Eliza Cook's Journal* 2 (1849), 129.
76 'Woman in Domestic Life', *Magazine of Domestic Economy* 1 (1836), 65–6.
77 *Ibid.*, 66.
78 *Ibid.*
79 Quoted in Jenni Calder, *The Victorian Home* (London: Batsford, 1977), p. 115.
80 'Home', *Magazine of Domestic Economy* 1 (1836), 36. My italics.
81 'Cheap Reading', *Eliza Cook's Journal* 1 (1849), 2.
82 'To Correspondents', *Family Herald* 1 (1844), 200.
83 'The Unknown Public', *Household Words*, 21 August 1858, 219.
84 'To Correspondents', *Family Herald* 1 (1844), 488.
85 *Ibid.*, 168.
86 'Our Novels. The Sensational School', *Temple Bar* 29 (1870), 422. Quoted in Winifred Hughes, *The Maniac in the Cellar: Sensation Novels of the 1860s* (Princeton University Press, 1980), p. 44.
87 'Our Civilisation', 195.
88 *Ibid.* My italics.
89 John Sutherland, 'Wilkie Collins and the Origins of the Sensation Novel', in *Dickens Studies Annual*, ed. Michael Timko, Fred Kaplan and Edward Guiliano, vol. xx (New York: AMS Press, 1991), p. 246.
90 'A Preliminary Word', *Household Words*, 30 March 1850, 1.
91 [Mrs George Gretton,] 'The Blind Man's Wreath', *Household Words*, 4 March 1854, 55.
92 [Hannah Lawrence,] 'Flying Coaches', *Household Words*, 12 August 1854, 610.
93 'A Preliminary Word', 1.
94 'Gossip of the Week', *Reynolds's Newspaper*, 20 June 1858, 6.
95 Michael Mason, *The Making of Victorian Sexuality* (Oxford University Press, 1994); *The Making of Victorian Sexual Attitudes* (Oxford University Press, 1994); Patricia Branca, *Silent Sisterhood: Middle-Class Women in the Victorian Home* (London: Croom Helm, 1975); Leonore Davidoff and Catherine Hall, *Family Fortunes: Men and Women of the English Middle Class, 1780–1850* (London: Hutchinson, 1987).
96 Jacques Donzelot, *The Policing of Families*, trans. Robert Hurley (1977; London: Hutchinson, 1979).
97 *Ibid.*, p. 6.
98 *Ibid.*, pp. 93–4.

2 FRACTURED FAMILIES IN THE EARLY NOVELS
OLIVER TWIST AND *DOMBEY AND SON*

1 Gillian Beer's work on the narratives of evolutionism has demonstrated this desire to reach 'the comforting limits of initiation', *Darwin's Plots* (London: Ark Paperbacks, 1985), p. 128.
2 Auerbach, 'Incarnations of the Orphan', *ELH* 42 (1975), 410.

3 Ginsburg, 'Truth and Persuasion: the Language of Realism and of Ideology in *Oliver Twist*', *Novel* 20 (1987), 220–36.

4 See Rosemarie Bodenheimer, *The Politics of Story in Victorian Social Fiction* (Ithaca: Cornell University Press, 1988).

5 See Lauriat Lane, 'The Devil in *Oliver Twist*', *Dickensian* 52 (1956), 133.

6 D. A. Miller discusses the role of the police in *The Novel and the Police* (Berkeley: University of California Press, 1988), pp. 1–32.

7 Letter to Walter Thornbury, 18 April 1862, in *The Letters of Charles Dickens*, ed. His Sister-in-Law and His Eldest Daughter, 2 vols. (London: Chapman and Hall, 1880), vol. ii, pp. 178–9.

8 Charles Dickens, *Martin Chuzzlewit*, ed. Margaret Cardwell, The World's Classics (1843–4; Oxford University Press, 1984), frontispiece.

9 Kathleen Wales makes this point in 'The Claims of Kinship: The Opening Chapter of *Martin Chuzzlewit*', *Dickensian* 83 (1987), 173.

10 See, for example, Helene Moglen, 'Theorizing Fiction/Fictionalizing Theory: The Case of *Dombey and Son*', *Victorian Studies* 35 (1992), 159–84.

11 Auerbach, 'Dickens and Dombey: A Daughter After All', in *Dickens Studies Annual*, ed. Robert B. Partlow, Jr, vol. v (Carbondale and Edwardsville: Southern Illinois University Press, 1976), p. 95.

12 *Remarks on the Law of Partnership Liability* (London, 1853), quoted in 'Partnership with Limited Liability', *Westminster Review* ns 4 (1853), 400.

13 'The Limited Liability Act of 1855', *Westminster Review* ns 9 (1856), 51.

14 Clark, 'Riddling the Family Firm: the Sexual Economy in *Dombey and Son*', *ELH* 51 (1984), 80.

15 See, for example, Lynda Zwinger, 'The Fear of the Father: Dombey and Daughter', in *Daughters, Fathers, and the Novel: The Sentimental Romance of Heterosexuality* (Madison: University of Wisconsin Press, 1991), pp. 30–45 and 144–6.

16 H. A. Shannon, 'The Coming of General Limited Liability', in *Essays in Economic History*, ed. E. M. Carus-Wilson, vol. iii (London: Edward Arnold, 1954), p. 361.

17 Davidoff and Hall, *Family Fortunes*, p. 200.

18 Miller, 'Subjectivity Ltd: The Discourse of Liability in the Joint Stock Companies Act of 1856 and Gaskell's *Cranford*', *ELH* 61 (1994), 139–57.

19 Davidoff and Hall, *Family Fortunes*, p. 200.

20 *Daily News*, No. 1, p. 4. Quoted in Gerald G. Grubb, 'Dickens and the *Daily News*: The Early Issues', *Nineteenth-Century Fiction* 6 (1951–2), 242.

21 Perera, 'Wholesale, Retail and For Exportation: Empire and the Family Business in *Dombey and Son*', *Victorian Studies* 33 (1990), 607–8.

22 'Partnership with Limited Liability', 402.

23 Clark, 'Riddling the Family Firm', 73.

24 Barbara Weiss discusses the auction in *The Hell of the English: Bankruptcy and the Victorian Novel* (London: Associated University Press, 1986).

25 Lyn Pykett discusses the importance of childhood in the novel in '*Dombey and Son*: A Sentimental Family Romance', *Studies in the Novel* 19 (1987), 16–30.

3 DICKENS, CHRISTMAS AND THE FAMILY

1 Margaret Oliphant, 'Charles Dickens', reprinted in Collins, ed., *Critical Heritage*, p. 559.
2 Charles Dickens, 'A Christmas Dinner', *Sketches by Boz*, New Oxford Illustrated Dickens (1833–6; London: Oxford University Press, 1957), p. 221.
3 'Dickens and Father Christmas', *Nineteenth Century* (1907), quoted in Davis, *The Lives and Times of Ebenezer Scrooge* (New Haven: Yale University Press, 1990), p. 53.
4 *Ibid.*
5 Ley, 'The Apostle of Christmas', *Dickensian* 2 (1906), 324.
6 Forster, *Life*, vol. I, p. 301.
7 George Stott, 'Charles Dickens', *Contemporary Review*, January 1869, in Collins ed., *Critical Heritage*, p. 500.
8 Charles Gavan Duffy, *Conversations with Carlyle* (1892) in Collins, ed., *Critical Heritage*, p. 204.
9 Forster, *Life*, vol. I, p. 371.
10 Louis Cazamian, *The Social Novel in England*, trans. Martin Fido (London: Routledge and Kegan Paul, 1973), p. 126.
11 Quoted by Philip Collins, '*Carol* Philosophy, Cheerful Views', *Etudes Anglaises* 23 (1970), 158.
12 John Ruskin, Letter to Charles Eliot Norton, 19 June 1870, in Collins, ed., *Critical Heritage*, p. 444.
13 Leigh Hunt, *Political and Occasional Essays*, ed. Lawrence H. Houtchens and Carolyn W. Houtchens (New York: Columbia University Press, 1962), pp. 162–3.
14 *Ibid.*, pp. 163–4.
15 *Ibid.*, pp. 162–3.
16 *Ibid.*, pp. 168–9.
17 Sir Walter Scott, *Marmion*, Intro. to Canto Sixth, *The Poetical Works of Sir Walter Scott*, ed. J. Logie Robertson (Oxford University Press, 1921), pp. 152–4.
18 Southey, *Letters from England*, ed. Jack Simmons (London: Cresset Press, 1951), p. 362.
19 'The Epic', *Alfred Tennyson: Selected Poetry*, ed. Douglas Bush (New York: Modern Library, 1952), p. 105.
20 Washington Irving, *Old Christmas: from the Sketch Book of Washington Irving*, illus. by Randolph Caldecott, 5th edn (London: Macmillan, 1886), pp. 9–10.
21 'Christmas Gambols, and Twelfth Night's Amusements', exhibit included in *Jackdaw No. 75: Christmas*, compiled by Howard Loxton (London: Jackdaw Publications, 1970).
22 Davis, *Lives and Times*, p. 19.
23 Charles Dickens, Letter to Washington Irving, 21 April 1841, *The Letters of Charles Dickens*, ed. Madeline House and Graham Storey, vol. II, Pilgrim Edition (Oxford: Clarendon Press, 1969), p. 267.

24 Unsigned review of *Pickwick*, nos. I–XVII, and *Sketches by Boz*, *Quarterly Review* October 1837, in Collins, ed., *Critical Heritage*, p. 60.

25 Daniel Maclise, *Merry Christmas in the Baron's Hall*, National Gallery of Ireland, in Davis, *Lives and Times*, figure 6, p. 21.

26 J. A. R. Pimlott, *The Englishman's Christmas: A Social History* (Brighton: Harvester, 1978), p. 86.

27 Charles Dickens, 'A Christmas Tree', in *Christmas Stories*, with an introduction by G. K. Chesterton, Everyman's Library (1850; London: Dent, 1982), pp. 11–12.

28 Nina Auerbach, *Private Theatricals: The Lives of the Victorians* (Cambridge, Mass.: Harvard University Press, 1990), p. 14.

29 Gavin Weightman and Steve Humphries, *Christmas Past* (London: Sidgwick and Jackson, 1987), p. 126.

30 Quoted *ibid*, p. 30.

31 *Ibid.*, pp. 50–1.

32 Jane Carlyle, Letter to Jeanne Welsh, 23 December 1843, *Jane Welsh Carlyle: A Selection of Her Letters*, ed. Trudy Bliss (London: Arrow Books, 1959), pp. 139–41.

33 Davis, *Lives and Times*, p. 4.

34 John Butt, 'Dickens's Christmas Books', in *Pope, Dickens and Others* (Edinburgh University Press, 1969), p. 133.

35 Forster, *Life*, vol. I, p. 283.

36 Ruth Glancy, Introduction, *Christmas Books*, by Charles Dickens, The World's Classics (Oxford University Press, 1988), p. x.

37 *Ibid.*, p. xi.

38 Davis, *Lives and Times*, p. 9.

39 W. M. Thackeray, 'A Box of Novels', *Fraser's Magazine*, February 1844, in Collins, ed., *Critical Heritage*, p. 149.

40 Lord Jeffrey, Letter to Charles Dickens, 26 December 1843, in Collins, ed., *Critical Heritage*, p. 148.

41 Forster, *Life*, vol. I, p. 300.

42 Jane Carlyle, *Jane Welsh Carlyle*, p. 138.

43 Davis, *Lives and Times*, p. 215.

44 Quoted by Collins, '*Carol* Philosophy', 159.

45 *Ibid.*

46 *Ibid.*

47 Forster, *Life*, vol. I, p. 302.

48 Collins, '*Carol* Philosophy', 160. A good-humoured corrective is provided by J. Hillis Miller in his contribution to the special issue of the *Dickensian* celebrating the *Carol*'s sesquicentenary, where he acknowledges Collins's observation with the facetious remark, 'I hope I shall not be guilty of irreverence in permitting myself to do a little of the latter [i.e. rhetorical analysis]', J. Hillis Miller, 'The Genres of *A Christmas Carol*', *Dickensian* 89 (1993), 193.

49 Michael Slater, 'The Christmas Books', *Dickensian* 65 (1969), 20.

50 Quoted by Deborah Thomas, *Dickens and the Short Story* (London: Batsford, 1982), p. 38.

51 Forster, *Life*, vol. I, p. 301.
52 Davis, *Lives and Times*, p. 76.
53 Review of *The Battle of Life*, by Charles Dickens, *Morning Chronicle* 24 December 1846. Quoted by Margaret Lane, 'Dickens on the Hearth', p. 171.
54 Deborah Gorham, *The Victorian Girl and the Feminine Ideal* (Bloomington: Indiana University Press, 1982), p. 6.
55 Nina Auerbach, *Woman and the Demon: The Life of a Victorian Myth* (Cambridge, Mass.: Harvard University Press, 1982), p. 143.
56 Forster, *Life*, vol. II, pp. 14–15.
57 Collins, '*Carol* Philosophy', 162.
58 *Ibid.*, 166.
59 See the discussion in chapter 6.
60 Unsigned review of *The Haunted Man*, *Macphail's Edinburgh Ecclesiastical Journal* January 1849, in Collins, ed., *Critical Heritage*, p. 179.

4 LITTLE DORRIT

1 Chris R. Vanden Bossche, 'Cookery, not Rookery: Family and Class in *David Copperfield*', *Dickens Studies Annual*, ed. Michael Timko, Fred Kaplan and Edward Guiliano, vol. XV (New York: AMS Press, 1986), pp. 87–109. Mary Poovey also discusses the symbolic significance of sphere ideology in *David Copperfield* in *Uneven Developments*, pp. 89–125.
2 Miller, *Novel and the Police*, pp. 58–106. Monica Feinberg, 'Family Plot: The Bleak House of Victorian Romance', *Victorian Newsletter* 76 (1989), 5–17.
3 Catherine Gallagher, *The Industrial Reformation of English Fiction: Social Discourse and Narrative Form 1832–1867* (University of Chicago Press, 1985).
4 Maine, *Ancient Law* (1861; Dorset Press, 1986), p. 141.
5 *Ibid.*, p. 106.
6 As Carol Pateman has pointed out, in the classic texts of the contract theorists only men can be 'individuals', *The Sexual Contract* (Cambridge: Polity Press, 1988), p. 6.
7 Michel Foucault, *The History of Sexuality: Volume I, An Introduction*, trans. Robert Hurley (Harmondsworth: Penguin, 1981), p. 147.
8 Dorothy Van Ghent, 'The Dickens World: A View from Todgers's', *Sewanee Review* 58 (1950), 419–38, reprinted in *Dickens: A Collection of Critical Essays*, ed. Martin Price, Twentieth Century Views (Englewood Cliffs, NJ: Prentice-Hall, 1967), p. 24.
9 Quoted by Forster, *Life*, vol. II, p. 183.
10 As Michael Ragussis has argued, the act of naming in baptism is meant to signify Christ's ownership of the one who is baptised 'in the name' of Christ, *Acts of Naming: The Family Plot in Fiction* (New York: Oxford University Press, 1986), p. 7.
11 Jeff Nunokawa discusses the crisis of ownership that occurs when property is seen to be acquired in *Little Dorrit* in *The Afterlife of Property: Domestic Security and the Victorian Novel* (Princeton University Press, 1994), pp. 19–39.

12 M. Jeanne Peterson, 'The Victorian Governess: Status Incongruence in Family and Society', in *Suffer and Be Still: Women in the Victorian Age*, ed. Martha Vicinus (Bloomington: Indiana University Press, 1972), pp. 3–19 and 207–11.

13 Quoted *ibid.*, pp. 9–10.

14 Charles Dickens, 'The Ghost of Art', *Household Words*, 20 July 1850, 386.

15 David Roberts, *Paternalism in Early Victorian England* (London: Croom Helm, 1979), p. 6.

16 Davidoff and Hall, *Family Fortunes*, p. 200.

17 Maine, *Ancient Law*, p. 110.

18 Max Weber, 'The Author Defines His Purpose', from Max Weber, *The Protestant Ethic and the Spirit of Capitalism*, trans. Talcott Parsons (New York: Scribner's, 1958), reprinted in *Protestantism, Capitalism, and Social Science: The Weber Thesis Controversy*, ed. Robert W. Green, 2nd edn (Lexington, Mass.: D.C. Heath and Co., 1973), pp. 1–8.

19 Davidoff and Hall, *Family Fortunes*, p. 198.

20 Weiss, *Hell of the English*, p. 43. Imprisonment for debt was formally abolished in 1869.

21 Davidoff and Hall, *Family Fortunes*, pp. 201–2.

22 Armstrong, *Desire and Domestic Fiction*, p. 75.

23 *Ibid.*, p. 80.

5 *A TALE OF TWO CITIES*

1 Quoted by Forster, *Life*, vol. II, p. 281.

2 *Ibid.*, p. 282.

3 Albert D. Hutter, 'Nation and Generation in *A Tale of Two Cities*', *PMLA* 93 (1978), 448.

4 Georg Lukács, *The Historical Novel*, trans. Hannah and Stanley Mitchell (London: Merlin, 1962), p. 243.

5 *A Tale of Two Cities* was serialised without illustrations in *All The Year Round* from April to November 1859, but appeared simultaneously in monthly numbers from June to December 1859, illustrated by Browne.

6 *A Tale of Two Cities*, ed. Andrew Sanders, The World's Classics (Oxford University Press, 1988), p. 481 n. 37.

7 For a discussion of Dickens's use of doubles to define the innocence of his own omniscient activity, see Catherine Gallagher's essay, 'The Duplicity of Doubling in *A Tale of Two Cities*', in *Dickens Studies Annual*, ed. Michael Timko, Fred Kaplan and Edward Guiliano, vol. XII (New York: AMS Press, 1983), pp. 125–145.

8 LADY MACBETH:

> I would while it was smiling in my face
> Have plucked my nipple from his boneless gums
> And dashed the brains out, had I so sworn as you
> Have done to this. (I. vii. 56–8)

9 For a discussion of the imagery of natural catastrophe in the novel, see Kurt Tetzeli Von Rosador, 'Metaphorical Representations of the French Revolution in Victorian Fiction', *Nineteenth-Century Literature* 43 (1988), 1–23.

10 For a classic study of the maleness of reason in philosophy, see Genevieve Lloyd, *The Man of Reason: 'Male' and 'Female' in Western Philosophy*, 2nd edn (London: Routledge, 1993).

11 Jane Rendall, *The Origins of Modern Feminism: Women in Britain, France and the United States 1780–1860*, Themes in Comparative History (London: Macmillan, 1985), p. 47.

12 Sir Henry Dickens, *The Recollections of Sir Henry Dickens, K.C.* (London, 1934), p. 54. Quoted in Martin Meisel, 'Miss Havisham Brought to Book', *PMLA* 81 (June 1966), 281.

13 Lee Sterrenburg, 'Psychoanalysis and the Iconography of Revolution', *Victorian Studies* 19 (1975), 241–64.

14 Sanders, ed., *A Tale of Two Cities*, p. 511 n. 321.

15 As John Carey has observed, 'Dickens, who saw himself as the great prophet of cosy, domestic virtue, purveyor of improving literature to the middle classes, never seems to have quite reconciled himself to the fact that violence and destruction were the most powerful stimulants to his imagination', *The Violent Effigy: A Study of Dickens' Imagination* (1973; London: Faber, 1979), p. 16.

16 For a psychoanalytic account of the links between erotic and political attitudes in the representation of the 1848 Revolution and the Commune, see Neil Hertz, 'Medusa's Head: Male Hysteria under Political Pressure', *Representations* 4 (1983), 27–54.

17 Thomas Carlyle, *The French Revolution: A History*, ed. J. Holland Rose, 3 vols. (1837; London: G. Bell and Sons, 1913), vol. I, p. 160.

18 Harriet Ritvo, *The Animal Estate: The English and Other Creatures in the Victorian Age* (1987; Harmondsworth: Penguin, 1990), p. 28. The fascination of the British public with tiger attacks led the East India Company to put a mechanical model of a tiger eating an Englishman on display at its London offices in 1800, where it drew large crowds for several generations.

19 See Rendall's description of the activities of these eighteenth-century French feminists. Rendall, *Origins of Modern Feminism*, p. 49.

20 Hutter, 'Nation and Generation', 457.

21 George Woodcock, Introduction, *A Tale of Two Cities*, by Charles Dickens, Penguin English Library (1859; Harmondsworth: Penguin, 1970), p. 21.

22 Slater, *Dickens and Women*, pp. 210–11.

23 Ruskin, 'Of Queens' Gardens', p. 74.

24 Davidoff and Hall note that 'Male domestic servants were the last category of men to be enfranchised and were banished from organizations such as the Freemasons who were concerned to establish bases for independence as alternatives to paternalistic hierarchies.' Davidoff and Hall, *Family Fortunes*, p. 199.

25 Donzelot, *Policing of Families*, pp. 49–50.

26 *Ibid.*, p. 51.
27 See also Hutter, 'Nation and Generation'. Hutter has analysed the relationship between the rival lovers in *A Tale of Two Cities* in psychoanalytic terms, showing how Sydney Carton functions as a double for Charles Darnay by enacting one side of his character.
28 Armstrong, *Desire and Domestic Fiction*, p. 66.

6 *GREAT EXPECTATIONS*

1 [E.S. Dallas] *The Times*, 17 October 1861, 6, in Collins, ed., *Critical Heritage*, pp. 430–1.
2 Peter Brooks, 'Repetition, Repression, and Return: The Plotting of *Great Expectations*', in *Reading for the Plot: Desire and Intention in Narrative* (New York: Knopf, 1984), pp. 116–17.
3 Steven Connor, *Charles Dickens*, Rereading Literature (Oxford: Basil Blackwell, 1985), p. 111.
4 Anny Sadrin, *Great Expectations*, Unwin Critical Library (London: Unwin Hyman, 1988), p. 122.
5 Forster, *Life*, vol. II, p. 285.
6 John Carey's comment about Dickens's imaginative interest in violence is again relevant here. See chapter 5, note 15.
7 Barbara Hardy discusses the use of food in the novel in *The Moral Art of Dickens* (London: Athlone Press, 1970), p. 140.
8 Charles Dickens, 'The Tuggses at Ramsgate', *Sketches by Boz*, New Oxford Illustrated Dickens (1833–6; London: Oxford University Press, 1957), p. 346.
9 Sally Shuttleworth, 'Female Circulation: Medical Discourse and Popular Advertising in the Mid-Victorian Era', in *Body/Politics: Women and the Discourses of Science*, ed. Mary Jacobus, Evelyn Fox Keller and Sally Shuttleworth (New York: Routledge, 1990), p. 62.
10 Sala, *Twice Round the Clock; or the Hours of the Day and Night in London*, The Victorian Library (1859; Leicester University Press, 1971), p. 211.
11 *Ibid.*, p. 209.
12 Lady Maria Clutterbuck [Catherine Dickens], *What Shall We Have For Dinner? Satisfactorily Answered by Numerous Bills of Fare For From Two to Eighteen Persons*, new edn (London: Bradbury and Evans, 1852), Introduction. While attributed to Catherine, the Introduction to this book is thought to have been written by Dickens himself.
13 See Robin Gilmour, *The Idea of the Gentleman in the Victorian Novel* (London: Allen and Unwin, 1981).
14 Foucault, *History of Sexuality*, p. 60.
15 *Ibid.*
16 See Poovey, *Uneven Developments*, chapter 4, for a more detailed discussion of this ideological work.

7 OUR MUTUAL FRIEND

1 J. Hillis Miller, Afterword, *Our Mutual Friend*, by Charles Dickens, Signet Classics (New York: New American Library, 1964), reprinted as '*Our Mutual Friend*' in *Dickens: A Collection of Critical Essays*, ed. Martin Price, Twentieth Century Views (Englewood Cliffs, NJ: Prentice-Hall, 1967), p. 169.

2 Frederick Engels, *The Origin of the Family, Private Property and the State*, ed. Eleanor Burke Leacock (1884; New York: International Publishers, 1972), pp. 71–2.

3 Jennifer Wicke discusses Dickens's relationship to advertising in *Advertising Fictions: Literature, Advertisement and Social Reading* (New York: Columbia University Press, 1988).

4 Leonore Davidoff, 'The Separation of Home and Work? Landladies and Lodgers in Nineteenth- and Twentieth-Century England', in *Fit Work for Women*, ed. Sandra Burman, Oxford Women's Series (London: Croom Helm, 1979), pp. 64–97.

5 *Ibid.*, p. 68.

6 *Ibid.*, p. 69.

7 *Ibid.*, pp. 76–7.

8 Census 1851: Report, p. xxxiv.

9 The most influential account of male specularity is Luce Irigaray's in *Speculum of the Other Woman*, trans. Gillian C. Gill (Ithaca: Cornell University Press, 1985). Laurie Langbauer discusses this critical debate in *Woman and Romance: The Consolations of Gender in the English Novel*, Reading Women Writing (Ithaca: Cornell University Press, 1990), chapter 5.

10 Lizzie's position by the hearth recalls the plight of another fire-gazer – Louisa Gradgrind – whose family circumstances also place her 'at risk' – from James Harthouse.

11 Audrey Jaffe, *Vanishing Points: Dickens, Narrative, and the Subject of Omniscience* (Berkeley: University of California Press, 1991), p. 6.

12 *Ibid.*, p. 12.

13 *Ibid.*, p. 159.

14 Kate Flint, *Dickens*, New Readings (Brighton: Harvester, 1986), p. 128.

15 See, for example, Jonathan Arac, *Commissioned Spirits: The Shaping of Social Motion in Dickens, Carlyle, Melville, and Hawthorne* (New Brunswick, NJ: Rutgers University Press, 1979).

16 Donzelot, *Policing of Families*, pp. 91–2.

17 Miller, *Novel and the Police*, p. 103.

18 Donzelot, *Policing of Families*, p. 92.

19 Deirdre David, *Fictions of Resolution in Three Victorian Novels: 'North and South,' 'Our Mutual Friend,' and 'Daniel Deronda'* (London: Macmillan, 1981), p. 70.

POSTSCRIPT

1 Kaplan, *Dickens*, pp. 458–61.

2 See Steven Connor, '"They're All in One Story": Public and Private

Narratives in *Oliver Twist*', *Dickensian* 85 (1989), 3.

3 Charles Dickens, preface to the original edition of 1839, *Nicholas Nickleby*, by Charles Dickens, ed. Paul Schlicke, The World's Classics (1838–9; Oxford University Press, 1990), p. xli.

4 See the discussion in chapter 1, pp. 23–4.

5 Charles Dickens, *Sketches of Young Couples*, in *Sketches by Boz* with an introduction by Thea Holme, New Oxford Illustrated Dickens (1840; London: Oxford University Press, 1957), p. 602.

6 Oliphant, 'Charles Dickens', *Blackwood's Magazine* 77 (1855), 465.

7 *Great Expectations*, ed. Margaret Cardwell, The World's Classics (Oxford University Press, 1994), p. 503 n. 479.

8 Census 1851 – Report, p. xxxvi.

Select bibliography

PRIMARY SOURCES

DICKENS, CHARLES

Barnaby Rudge: A Tale of the Riots of 'Eighty, with an introduction by Kathleen Tillotson, 1841, New Oxford Illustrated Dickens, London: Oxford University Press, 1954.

Bleak House, ed. George Ford and Sylvère Monod, 1852–3, Norton Critical Edition, New York: Norton and Co., 1977.

Christmas Books, ed. Ruth Glancy, 1843–8, The World's Classics, Oxford University Press, 1988.

Christmas Stories, with an introduction by G. K. Chesterton, 1850–67, Everyman's Library, London: Dent, 1910.

David Copperfield, ed. Nina Burgis, 1849–50, The World's Classics, Oxford University Press, 1983.

Dombey and Son, ed. Alan Horsman, 1846–8, The World's Classics, Oxford University Press, 1982.

Great Expectations, ed. Margaret Cardwell, 1860–1, The World's Classics, Oxford University Press, 1994.

Letters from Charles Dickens to Angela Burdett Coutts 1841–1865, ed. Edgar Johnson, London: Jonathan Cape, 1953.

The Letters of Charles Dickens, ed. His Sister-in-Law and His Eldest Daughter, 2 vols., London: Chapman and Hall, 1880.

The Letters of Charles Dickens, ed. Madeline House and Graham Storey, vol. II, Pilgrim Edition, Oxford: Clarendon Press, 1969, 8 vols. to date, 1965– .

Little Dorrit, ed. Harvey Peter Sucksmith, 1855–7, The World's Classics, Oxford University Press, 1982.

Martin Chuzzlewit, ed. Margaret Cardwell, 1843–4, The World's Classics, Oxford University Press, 1984.

Mr and Mrs Charles Dickens: His Letters to Her, ed. Walter Dexter, London: Constable and Co., 1935.

The Mystery of Edwin Drood, ed. Margaret Cardwell, 1870, The World's Classics, Oxford University Press, 1982.

Nicholas Nickleby, ed. Paul Schlicke, 1838–9, The World's Classics, Oxford University Press, 1990.

Oliver Twist, ed. Kathleen Tillotson, 1837–8, The World's Classics, Oxford University Press, 1982.

Our Mutual Friend, ed. Michael Cotsell, 1864–5, The World's Classics, Oxford University Press, 1989.

The Pickwick Papers, ed. James Kinsley, 1836–7, The World's Classics, Oxford University Press, 1988.

Sketches by Boz: Illustrative of Every-Day Life and Every-Day People, 1833–6, New Oxford Illustrated Dickens, London: Oxford University Press, 1957.

A Tale of Two Cities, ed. Andrew Sanders, 1859, The World's Classics, Oxford University Press, 1988.

NINETEENTH-CENTURY JOURNALS

Blackwood's Edinburgh Magazine, 1817–1980.
Eliza Cook's Journal, 1849–1854.
Family Economist, 1848–1860.
Family Friend, 1849–1921.
Family Herald, 1842–?
Household Words, 1850–59.
Johnstone's Penny Fireside Journal, 1843–1845.
Magazine of Domestic Economy, 1836–1844.
Reynolds's Newspaper, 1850–1967.
Saturday Review, 1855–1938.
Westminster Review, New Series 1852–1914.

SECONDARY SOURCES

Ackroyd, Peter, *Dickens*, London: Sinclair-Stevenson, 1990.

Altick, Richard D., *The English Common Reader: A Social History of the Mass Reading Public 1800–1900*, University of Chicago Press, 1957.

Anderson, Nancy F., 'The "Marriage with a Deceased Wife's Sister Bill" Controversy: Incest Anxiety and the Defense of Family Purity in Victorian England', *Journal of British Studies* 21 (1982), 67–86.

Arac, Jonathan, *Commissioned Spirits: The Shaping of Social Motion in Dickens, Carlyle, Melville, and Hawthorne*, Brunswick, NJ: Rutgers University Press, 1979.

Armstrong, Nancy, *Desire and Domestic Fiction: A Political History of the Novel*, New York: Oxford University Press, 1987.

Auerbach, Nina, *Woman and the Demon: The Life of a Victorian Myth*, Cambridge, Mass.: Harvard University Press, 1982.

  Private Theatricals: The Lives of the Victorians, Cambridge, Mass.: Harvard University Press, 1990.

'Dickens and Dombey: A Daughter After All', in *Dickens Studies Annual*, ed. Robert B. Partlow, Jr, vol. v, Carbondale and Edwardsville: Southern Illinois University Press, 1976, pp. 95–114.

'Incarnations of the Orphan', *English Literary History* 42 (1975), 395–419.

Beer, Gillian, *Darwin's Plots: Evolutionary Narrative in Darwin, George Eliot and Nineteenth-Century Fiction*, London: Ark Paperbacks, 1985.

Behrman, Cynthia, 'The Annual Blister: A Sidelight on Victorian Social and Parliamentary History', *Victorian Studies* 11 (1968), 483–502.

Bennett, Tony, Graham Martin, Colin Mercer and Janet Woollacott, eds., *Culture, Ideology and Social Process: A Reader*, London: Batsford, 1981.

Bodenheimer, Rosemarie, *The Politics of Story in Victorian Social Fiction*, Ithaca: Cornell University Press, 1988.

Branca, Patricia, *Silent Sisterhood: Middle-Class Women in the Victorian Home*, London: Croom Helm, 1975.

Brantlinger, Patrick, 'What is "Sensational" about the "Sensation Novel"?' *Nineteenth-Century Fiction* 37 (1982), 1–28.

Brooks, Peter, 'Repetition, Repression, and Return: The Plotting of *Great Expectations*', *Reading for the Plot: Desire and Intention in Narrative*, New York: Knopf, 1984, pp. 113–42 and 339–41.

Butt, John, 'Dickens' Christmas Books', *Pope, Dickens and Others*, Edinburgh University Press, 1969, pp. 127–48.

Calder, Jenni, *Women and Marriage in Victorian Fiction*, London: Thames and Hudson, 1976.

The Victorian Home, London: Batsford, 1977.

Carey, John, *The Violent Effigy: A Study of Dickens' Imagination*, 1973, London: Faber, 1979.

Carlyle, Jane Welsh, *Jane Welsh Carlyle: A Selection of Her Letters*, ed. Trudy Bliss, London: Arrow Books, 1959.

Carlyle, Thomas, *The French Revolution: A History*, 1837, ed. J. Holland Rose, 3 vols., London: G. Bell and Sons, 1913, vol. I.

Cazamian, Louis, *The Social Novel in England*, trans. Martin Fido, London: Routledge and Kegan Paul, 1973.

Census 1851: Report, *British Parliamentary Papers, Population*, vol. VI.

Clark, Robert, 'Riddling the Family Firm: The Sexual Economy in *Dombey and Son*', *English Literary History* 51 (1984), 69–84.

Clutterbuck, Lady Maria [Catherine Dickens], *What Shall We Have For Dinner? Satisfactorily Answered by Numerous Bills of Fare For From Two to Eighteen Persons*, new edn, London: Bradbury and Evans, 1852.

Collins, Philip, '*Carol* Philosophy, Cheerful Views', *Etudes Anglaises* 23 (1970), 158–61.

'The Popularity of Dickens', *Dickensian* 70 (1974), 5–20.

Collins, Philip, ed., *Dickens: The Critical Heritage*, London: Routledge, 1971.

Connor, Steven, *Charles Dickens*, Oxford: Basil Blackwell, 1985.

'They're All in One Story: Public and Private Narratives in *Oliver Twist*', *Dickensian* 85 (1989), 3–16.

Cott, Nancy F., 'Passionlessness: An Interpretation of Victorian Sexual Ideology, 1790–1850', *Signs* 4 (1978), 219–36.

David, Deirdre, *Fictions of Resolution in Three Victorian Novels: 'North and South', 'Our Mutual Friend', 'Daniel Deronda'*, London: Macmillan, 1981.

Davidoff, Leonore, 'The Separation of Home and Work? Landladies and Lodgers in Nineteenth- and Twentieth-Century England', in *Fit Work for Women*, ed. Sandra Burman, Oxford Women's Series, London: Croom Helm, 1979, pp. 64–97.

Davidoff, Leonore, and Catherine Hall, *Family Fortunes: Men and Women of the English Middle Class, 1780–1850*, London: Hutchinson, 1987.

Davis, Paul, *The Lives and Times of Ebenezer Scrooge*, New Haven: Yale University Press, 1990.

Donzelot, Jacques, *The Policing of Families*, trans. Robert Hurley, London: Hutchinson, 1979. Trans. of *La Police des Familles*, Les Editions de Minuit, 1977.

Edmond, Rod, *Affairs of the Hearth: Victorian Poetry and Domestic Narrative*, London: Routledge, 1988.

Engels, Frederick, *The Origin of the Family, Private Property and the State: In the Light of the Researches of Lewis H. Morgan*, ed. Eleanor Burke Leacock, 1884, New York: International Publishers, 1972.

Ettlinger, L. D., and R. G. Holloway, *Compliments of the Season*, London: Penguin, 1947.

Feinberg, Monica, 'Family Plot: The Bleak House of Victorian Romance', *Victorian Newsletter* 76 (1989), 5–17.

Feltes, Norman, '1789/1859: Revolution, Ideology and Entrepreneurship', in *1789: Reading, Writing, Revolution*, Essex Conference on the Sociology of Literature, July 1981, Colchester: University of Essex, 1982, pp. 170–9.

Fielding, K. J., 'Charles Dickens and Colin Rae Brown', *Nineteenth-Century Fiction* 7 (1952), 103–10.

'Charles Dickens and his Wife – Fact or Forgery?' *Etudes Anglaises* 8 (1955), 212–22.

'Dickens and the Hogarth Scandal', *Nineteenth-Century Fiction* 10 (1955), 64–74.

'The Recent Reviews: Dickens in 1858', *Dickensian* 52 (1955), 25–32.

Fitzgerald, Percy, *Memories of Charles Dickens*, Bristol: J. W. Arrowsmith, 1913.

Flandrin, Jean-Louis, *Families in Former Times: Kinship, Household and Sexuality*, trans. Richard Southern, Themes in Social Sciences, Cambridge University Press, 1979. Trans. of *Familles: parenté, maison, sexualité dans l'ancienne société*, Librairie Hachette, 1976.

Flint, Kate, *Dickens*, New Readings Series, Brighton: Harvester Press, 1986.

Forster, John, *The Life of Charles Dickens*, 1872–4, ed. A.J. Hoppé, Everyman's Library, 2 vols., London: Dent, 1969.

Foucault, Michel, *Discipline and Punish: The Birth of the Prison*, trans. Alan Sheridan, Harmondsworth: Penguin, 1979. Trans. of *Surveiller et Punir: Naissance de la Prison*, Editions Gallimard, 1975.

The History of Sexuality: Volume I, An Introduction, trans. Robert Hurley,

Harmondsworth: Penguin, 1981. Trans of *La Volonté de Savoir*, Editions Gallimard, 1976.

Gallagher, Catherine, *The Industrial Reformation of English Fiction: Social Discourse and Narrative Form 1832–1867*, University of Chicago Press, 1985.

'The Duplicity of Doubling in *A Tale of Two Cities*', in *Dickens Studies Annual*, ed. Michael Timko, Fred Kaplan and Edward Guiliano, vol. XII, New York: AMS Press, 1983, pp. 125–45.

Ghent, Dorothy Van, 'The Dickens World: A View from Todgers's', *Sewanee Review* 58 (1950), 419–38. Reprinted in *Dickens: A Collection of Critical Essays*, ed. Martin Price, Twentieth Century Views, Englewood Cliffs, NJ: Prentice-Hall, 1967, pp. 24–38.

Gilmour, Robin, *The Idea of the Gentleman in the Victorian Novel*, London: Allen and Unwin, 1981.

Ginsberg, Michel Peled, 'Truth and Persuasion: The Language of Realism and of Ideology in *Oliver Twist*', *Novel: A Forum on Fiction* 20 (1987), 220–36.

Gorham, Deborah, *The Victorian Girl and the Feminine Ideal*, Bloomington: Indiana University Press, 1982.

Gramsci, Antonio, *Selections from the Prison Notebooks*, trans. and ed. Quintin Hoare and Geoffrey Nowell-Smith, London, 1971. Extracts reprinted in *Culture, Ideology and Social Process: A Reader*, ed. Tony Bennett *et al.*, London: Batsford, 1981.

Grubb, Gerald G., 'Dickens and the *Daily News*: The Early Issues', *Nineteenth-Century Fiction* 6 (1951–2), 234–46.

Hardy, Barbara, *The Moral Art of Dickens*, London: Athlone Press, 1970.

Hertz, Neil, 'Medusa's Head: Male Hysteria under Political Pressure', *Representations* 4 (1983), 27–54.

Hobsbawm, E.J., *The Age of Capital 1848–1875*, London: Weidenfeld and Nicolson, 1975.

Hughes, Winifred, *The Maniac in the Cellar: Sensation Novels of the 1860s*, Princeton University Press, 1980.

Hunt, Leigh, *Political and Occasional Essays*, ed. Lawrence H. Houtchens and Carolyn W. Houtchens, New York: Columbia University Press, 1962.

Hutter, Albert D., 'Nation and Generation in *A Tale of Two Cities*', *PMLA* 93 (1978), 448–62.

Irving, Washington, *Old Christmas: From the Sketch Book of Washington Irving*, illus. by Randolph Caldecott, 5th edn, London: Macmillan, 1886.

Jaffe, Audrey, *Vanishing Points: Dickens, Narrative and the Subject of Omniscience*, Berkeley: University of California Press, 1991.

Jann, Rosemary, *The Art and Science of Victorian History*, Columbus: Ohio State University Press, 1985.

Johnson, Edgar, *Charles Dickens: His Tragedy and Triumph*, 1953, rev. and abr. edn, London: Allen Lane, 1977.

Kaplan, Cora, *Sea Changes: Essays on Culture and Feminism*, London: Verso, 1986.

Kaplan, Fred, *Dickens: A Biography*, London: Hodder and Stoughton, 1988.

Lane, Lauriat, 'The Devil in *Oliver Twist*', *Dickensian* 52 (1956), 132–6.

Lane, Margaret, 'Dickens on the Hearth', in *Dickens 1970: Centenary Essays*, ed. Michael Slater, New York: Stein and Day, 1970, pp. 153–71.

Langbauer, Laurie, *Women and Romance: The Consolations of Gender in the English Novel*, Reading Women Writing, Ithaca: Cornell University Press, 1990.

Laslett, Peter, and Richard Wall, *Household and Family in Past Time*, Cambridge University Press, 1972.

Leavis, F. R., and Q. D., *Dickens the Novelist*, Harmondsworth: Penguin, 1972.

Levy, Anita, *Other Women: The Writing of Class, Race, and Gender, 1832–1898*, Princeton University Press, 1991.

Ley, J. W. T., 'The Apostle of Christmas', *Dickensian* 2 (1906), 324–6.

Lloyd, Genevieve, *The Man of Reason: 'Male' and 'Female' in Western Philosophy*, 2nd edn, London: Routledge, 1993.

Loxton, Howard, compiler, *Juckdaw No. 75: Christmas*, London: Jackdaw Publications, 1970.

Lukács, Georg, *The Historical Novel*, trans. Hannah and Stanley Mitchell, London: Merlin, 1962.

Macfarlane, Alan, *Marriage and Love in England: Modes of Reproduction 1300–1840*, Oxford: Blackwell, 1986.

Mackenzie, Norman and Jeanne, *Dickens: A Life*, Oxford University Press, 1979.

Maine, Sir Henry Sumner, *Ancient Law: Its Connection with the Early History of Society and its Relation to Modern Ideas*, 1861, Dorset Press, 1986.

Manning, Sylvia, 'Families in Dickens', in *Changing Images of the Family*, ed. Virginia Tufte and Barbara Myerhoff, New Haven: Yale University Press, 1979, pp. 141–53.

'Dickens, January, and May', *Dickensian* 71 (1975), 67–75.

Mason, Michael, *The Making of Victorian Sexuality*, Oxford University Press, 1994.

The Making of Victorian Sexual Attitudes, Oxford University Press, 1994.

Meisel, Martin, 'Miss Havisham Brought to Book', *PMLA* 81 (June 1966), 278–85.

Miller, Andrew H., 'Subjectivity Ltd: The Discourse of Liability in the Joint Stock Companies Act of 1856 and Gaskell's *Cranford*', *English Literary History* 61 (1994), 139–57.

Miller, D. A., *The Novel and the Police*, Berkeley: University of California Press, 1988.

Miller, J. Hillis, Afterword, *Our Mutual Friend*, By Charles Dickens, 1864–5, Signet Classics, New York: New American Library, 1964. Reprinted as '*Our Mutual Friend*', in *Dickens: A Collection of Critical Essays*, ed. Martin Price, Twentieth Century Views, Englewood Cliffs, NJ: Prentice-Hall, 1967, pp. 169–77.

'Narrative and History', *English Literary History* 41 (1974), 455–73.

'The Genres of *A Christmas Carol*', *Dickensian* 89 (1993), 193–206.

Mintz, Stephen, *A Prison of Expectations: The Family in Victorian Culture*, New York University Press, 1983.

Moglen, Helene, 'Theorizing Fiction/Fictionalizing Theory: The Case of *Dombey and Son*', *Victorian Studies* 35 (1992), 159–84.

Mott, Graham, 'Was There a Stain Upon Little Dorrit?' *Dickensian* 76 (1980), 31–6.

Moynahan, Julian, 'The Hero's Guilt: The Case of *Great Expectations*', in *Victorian*

Literature: Selected Essays, ed. Robert O. Preyer, New York: Harper and Row, 1967, pp. 126–45.

Murray, Janet Horowitz, *Strong-Minded Women and Other Lost Voices from Nineteenth-Century England*, Harmondsworth: Penguin, 1984.

Myers, William, 'The Radicalism of *Little Dorrit*', in *Literature and Politics in the Nineteenth Century*, ed. John Lucas, London: Methuen, 1971, pp. 77–104.

Nead, Lynda, *Myths of Sexuality: Representations of Women in Victorian Britain*, Oxford: Basil Blackwell, 1988.

Nunokawa, Jeff, *The Afterlife of Property: Domestic Security and the Victorian Novel*, Princeton University Press, 1994.

Oddie, William, *Dickens and Carlyle: The Question of Influence*, London: Centenary Press, 1972.

Olsen, Frances E., 'The Family and the Market: A Study of Ideology and Legal Reform', *Harvard Law Review* 96 (1983), 1497–578.

Pateman, Carol, *The Sexual Contract*, Cambridge: Polity Press, 1988.

Patten, Robert L., '"A Surprising Transformation": Dickens and the Hearth', in *Nature and the Victorian Imagination*, ed. U. C. Knoepflmacher and G. B. Tennyson, Berkeley: University of California Press, 1977, pp. 153–70.

Perera, Suvendrini, 'Wholesale, Retail and For Exportation: Empire and the Family Business in *Dombey and Son*', *Victorian Studies* 33 (1990), 603–20.

Perkin, Harold, *The Origins of Modern English Society 1780–1880*, London: Routledge and Kegan Paul, 1969.

Peterson, M. Jeanne, 'The Victorian Governess: Status Incongruence in Family and Society', in *Suffer and Be Still: Women in the Victorian Age*, ed. Martha Vicinus, Bloomington: Indiana University Press, 1972, pp. 3–19 and 207–11.

Pimlott, J. A. R., *The Englishman's Christmas: A Social History*, Brighton: Harvester, 1978.

Poovey, Mary, *Uneven Developments: The Ideological Work of Gender in Mid-Victorian England*, London: Virago, 1989.

Poster, Mark, *Critical Theory of the Family*, New York: Seabury Press, 1978.

Pykett, Lyn, '*Dombey and Son*: A Sentimental Family Romance', *Studies in the Novel* 19 (1987), 16–30.

Ragussis, Michael, *Acts of Naming: The Family Plot in Fiction*, New York: Oxford University Press, 1986.

Rendall, Jane, *The Origins of Modern Feminism: Women in Britain, France and the United States 1780–1860*, Themes in Comparative History, London: Macmillan, 1985.

Ritvo, Harriet, *The Animal Estate: The English and Other Creatures in the Victorian Age*, Harmondsworth: Penguin, 1990.

Roberts, David, *Paternalism in Early Victorian England*, London: Croom Helm, 1979.

Rosador, Kurt Tetzeli Von, 'Metaphorical Representations of the French Revolution in Victorian Fiction', *Nineteenth-Century Literature* 43 (1988), 1–23.

Ruskin, John, *Sesame and Lilies, Unto This Last and The Political Economy of Art*, 1865, London: Cassell, 1909.

Sadrin, Anny, *Great Expectations*, Unwin Critical Library, London: Unwin-Hyman, 1988.

    Parentage and Inheritance in the Novels of Charles Dickens, European Studies in English Literature, Cambridge University Press, 1994.

Sala, George Augustus, *Twice Round the Clock; or the Hours of the Day and Night in London*, 1859, The Victorian Library, Leicester University Press, 1971.

Sanders, Andrew, *The Victorian Historical Novel 1840–1880*, London: Macmillan, 1978.

Scott, Sir Walter, *Marmion*, *The Poetical Works of Sir Walter Scott*, ed. J. Logie Robertson, Oxford University Press, 1921.

Shanley, Mary Lyndon, *Feminism, Marriage, and the Law in Victorian England, 1850–1895*, Princeton University Press, 1989.

Shannon, H. A., 'The Coming of General Limited Liability', in *Essays in Economic History*, ed. E. M. Carus-Wilson, vol. III, London: Edward Arnold, 1954, pp. 358–79.

Shattock, Joanne and Michael Wolff, ed., *The Victorian Periodical Press: Samplings and Soundings*, Leicester University Press, 1982.

Shuttleworth, Sally, 'Female Circulation: Medical Discourse and Popular Advertising in the Mid-Victorian Era', in *Body/Politics: Women and the Discourses of Science*, ed. Mary Jacobus, Evelyn Fox Keller and Sally Shuttleworth, New York: Routledge, 1990, pp. 47–68.

Slater, Michael, *Dickens and Women*, London: J. M. Dent and Sons, 1983.

    'The Christmas Books', *Dickensian* 65 (1969), 17–24.

Southey, Robert, *Letters from England*, ed. Jack Simmons, London: Cresset Press, 1951.

Spence, Gordon, 'Dickens as a Historical Novelist', *Dickensian* 72 (1976), 21–9.

Steig, Michael, 'Dickens's Excremental Vision', *Victorian Studies* 13 (1970), 339–54.

Sterrenberg, Lee, 'Psychoanalysis and the Iconography of Revolution', *Victorian Studies* 19 (1975), 241–64.

Stone, Harry, *Dickens and the Invisible World: Fairy Tales, Fantasy and Novel-Making*, London: Macmillan, 1979.

Stone, Lawrence, *The Family, Sex and Marriage in England 1500–1800*, London: Weidenfeld and Nicolson, 1977.

Sutherland, John, *Victorian Novelists and Publishers*, London: Athlone Press, 1976.

    'Wilkie Collins and the Origins of the Sensation Novel', in *Dickens Studies Annual*, ed. Michael Timko, Fred Kaplan and Edward Guiliano, vol. XX, New York: AMS Press, 1991, pp. 243–58.

Tambling, Jeremy, 'Prison-bound: Dickens and Foucault', *Essays in Criticism* 36 (1986), 11–30.

Tennyson, Alfred, *Alfred Tennyson: Selected Poetry*, ed. Douglas Bush, New York: Modern Library, 1951.

Thackeray, William Makepeace, *The History of Henry Esmond*, 1852, London: Dent, 1940.

The Letters and Private Papers of William Makepeace Thackeray, 4 vols., ed. Gordon N. Ray, vol. IV, London: Oxford University Press, 1946.

Thackeray's Contributions to the 'Morning Chronicle', ed. Gordon Ray, Urbana: University of Illinois Press, 1966.

Thomas, Deborah A., *Dickens and the Short Story*, London: Batsford, 1982.

Trodd, Anthea, *Domestic Crime in the Victorian Novel*, London: Macmillan, 1989.

Trollope, Anthony, *The Way We Live Now*, 1874–5, The World's Classics, London: Oxford University Press, 1941.

Trumbach, Randolph, *The Rise of the Egalitarian Family: Aristocratic Kinship and Domestic Relations in Eighteenth-Century England*, New York: Academic Press, 1978.

Veeser, H. Aram, ed., *The New Historicism*, New York: Routledge, 1989.

Vicinus, Martha, ed., *Suffer and Be Still: Women in the Victorian Age*, Bloomington: Indiana University Press, 1972.

ed., *A Widening Sphere: Changing Roles of Victorian Women*, Bloomington: Indiana University Press, 1977.

Wales, Kathleen, 'The Claims of Kinship: The Opening Chapter of *Martin Chuzzlewit*', *Dickensian* 83 (1987), 167–79.

Watt, Ian, 'Oral Dickens', in *Dickens Studies Annual*, ed. Robert B. Partlow, Jr, Carbondale and Edwardsville: Southern Illinois University Press, 1974, pp. 164–81.

Weber, Max, 'The Author Defines His Purpose', from *The Protestant Ethic and the Spirit of Capitalism*, trans. Talcott Parsons, New York: Scribner's, 1958. Reprinted in *Protestantism, Capitalism, and Social Science: The Weber Thesis Controversy*, ed. Robert W. Green, 2nd edn, Lexington, Mass.: D. C. Heath and Co., 1973, pp. 1–8.

Weeks, Jeffrey, *Sex, Politics and Society: The Regulation of Sexuality Since 1800*, Themes in British Social History, London: Longman, 1981.

Weightman, Gavin, and Steve Humphries, *Christmas Past*, London: Sidgwick and Jackson, 1987.

Weiss, Barbara, *The Hell of the English: Bankruptcy and the Victorian Novel*, London: Associated University Press, 1986.

Welsh, Alexander, *The City of Dickens*, Oxford: Clarendon Press, 1971.

Wicke, Jennifer, *Advertising Fictions: Literature, Advertisement and Social Reading*, New York: Columbia Univeristy Press, 1988.

Williams, Raymond, *Keywords: A Vocabulary of Culture and Society*, Oxford University Press, 1977.

Wohl, Anthony, ed., *The Victorian Family: Structure and Stresses*, London: Croom Helm, 1978.

Wollstonecraft, Mary, *An Historical and Moral View of the Origin and Progress of the French Revolution and the Effect It Has Produced in Europe*, 1794, Facsimile re-edition, Delmar: Scholars' Facsimiles, 1975.

Woodcock, George, Introduction, *A Tale of Two Cities*, By Charles Dickens, 1859, Penguin English Library, Harmondsworth: Penguin, 1970, pp. 9–25.

Yates, Edmund, *Edmund Yates: His Recollections and Experiences*, 4th edn, London: Bentley, 1885.

Yeazell, Ruth Bernard, 'Podsnappery, Sexuality, and the English Novel', *Critical Inquiry* 9 (1982), 339–57.

Zwinger, Lynda, *Daughters, Fathers, and the Novel: The Sentimental Romance of Heterosexuality*, Madison: University of Wisconsin Press, 1991.

Index